DICK TIGER

Adeyinka Makinde trained as a barrister and has worked as a law lecturer at a number of colleges and universities in the United Kingdom. A long time student of boxing, his writings have appeared in a number of boxing sites on the World Wide Web. This is his first book.

DICK TIGER

THE LIFE AND TIMES OF A BOXING IMMORTAL

ADEYINKA MAKINDE

ISBN 10: 1-59571-042-6
ISBN 13: 978-1-59571-042-0
Library of Congress Control Number: 2004113190

Word Association Publishers
205 5th Avenue
Tarentum, PA 15084
www.wordassociation.com

Dedicated to the memory of my father, Emmanuel Oladipo Adeshiyan Makinde, once a boxer.

CONTENTS

AUTHOR'S ACKNOWLEDGEMENTS

I would like to thank the following persons who kindly consented to be interviewed.

The widow of Dick Tiger, Madam Abigail Ihetu; his sons Richard, Charles and Joseph Ihetu.

His opponents; Patrick McAteer, Terry Downes, Gene Fullmer, Joey Giardello, Emile Griffith, Jose Torres and Bob Foster.

Those who observed snippets and other portions of the man during his career; Gil Clancy, Lou Duva, Reg Gutteridge, Sam Toperoff, Jonathan Carroll, Arthur Mercante and Victor Zimet.

Special thanks are due to Larry Merchant, Dave Anderson and Tommy Kenville.

Thanks to the 'Mersey connection' of Martin Banasko and Michael Valerio as well as to Maurice Foran who to my regret felt compelled to keep most of his recollections to himself.

Thank you to Dr. Paddy Davies and Paul Eze Onwuachi also known as 'White Horse.' A mention also to Jupo Ifediora-Ezike and Mike DePaula.

Thanks are due to those who helped put me in touch with interviewees; Steve Farhood, former editor-in-chief of the Ring; John Morris, former Secretary to the British Boxing Board of Control; Burt Sugar, former executive editor of Fight Game; Ed Brophy of the International Boxing Hall of Fame; Bob Duffy and staff at the New York State Athletic Commission; Tom Hoover, Secretary to Ring 8 New York Veteran Boxers Association; Al Certo, Kirby Bradley of HBO Sports; Bernard Hart, Managing Director of the Lonsdale Organization; Chukwudum Ikeazor; Stephen Gordon, Editor-In-Chief of cyberboxingzone.com and Mike Delisa, Founder of cyberboxingzone.com.

My thanks to the respective members of staff at the British Newspaper Library in London and at the National Archives and Records Administration at College Park, State of Maryland, United States.

Thank you for your help and encouragement Harold Alderman.

I am indebted to Ron Lipton for his help and assistance. Finally, I would like to pay homage to my uncle, my father's elder brother and the family patriarch, Chief Moses Ajibade Makinde for the great interest he has taken in the project as well as his help and support in facilitating its coming to fruition.

FOREWORD

'Spirit of Aba'

All those who have had the slightest association with the story of Dick Tiger, will be filled with a sense of nostalgia after reading this book.

My association with it begins with his life in Aba, Eastern Nigeria, (as it was known then.) Aba has always been, and still is, one of the most vibrant cities in West Africa. It was within this teeming vibrancy that Dick Tiger grew up. His rugged determination to optimize glimpses of opportunities, and excel in his aspirational endeavours, bears testament to his principled and disciplined childhood background on the one hand, and a response to the concept of 'cognitive universals' within the Aba rugged cultural terrain, on the other.

The 'Life and Times of a Boxing Immortal' paints a copious picture of Dick Tiger's fascinating origins, his transportation through life, ambitions, achievement, and principles. Thus, it elucidates new horizons to those who hitherto would have claimed knowledge of the story of Dick Tiger; whilst giving a neophyte into the story a relentless historical calendar of learning, not only about the man, but also of his craft of boxing.

'Not a Visiting Apprentice,' the title of Chapter Six, graphically demonstrates the prevalent boxing atmosphere in Dick Tiger's era, his adeptness at adaptation, and his capacity for conversion of nascent opportunities into beneficial successes. This culture is exhibited again in the aptly titled 'Twilight: 'As Long as There's Money'.'

Those already familiar with Dick Tiger's story may have had cause to question the wisdom of his motive for supporting Biafra, and for returning his MBE: they may even have assumed (albeit) wrongly that the one was concomitant with the other. For the reader, a juxtaposition of 'Rebel With a Cause' with 'Twilight' resolves the mystery.

Adeyinka Makinde, in writing this book, has excavated the knowledge and story of a hero, Dick Tiger; made his life a historical indelibility, and set a course for others to travel. The author's patient tenacity in researching facts is patently evident in every page of the book. It is a must read!

Dr. Paddy Davies
Oxford

INTRODUCTION

'Ode to the Tiger in Boxing Valhalla'

Over the thirty-three years since his passing, I have never been fully satisfied by anything I have read on Dick Tiger because none have truly reflected the magnitude of his greatness. But for those many fans of boxing who feel the same way as I, 'The Life and Times of a Boxing Immortal' redresses this injustice. This book, painstakingly researched by Ade, will keep his memory alive and delight anyone who appreciates hard work and dedication.

I believe there are few people left who knew him like I did. I was his fan, his sparring partner and later, a close friend. I knew how to make him laugh — even at himself. His laugh and his gentle way was what made his company so easy to be in. You would immediately like him. He was very shy, respectful and a decent man.

One of the things I got a kick out of was observing a most amusing and revealing habit of his which occurred at the end of his bouts. He would find his way over to his opponent and gently pat them on the shoulder or on the waist saying, "Good fight, good work." That gentle gesture defined his underlying respect for people.

The flipside of that coin was his deadly focus and determination to win. No one and I mean no one, had grim determination etched in their face quite like Dick Tiger. That look is the epitome of boxing focus, ranking alongside Joe Louis' deadpan stare and Sonny Liston's fearsome scowl. It was frightening in its message: 'I ask no quarter and will give none.'

Dick Tiger always came to fight. He was the 'King of the Shoot-Outs' and if you elected to fight him toe-to-toe, he would always win. Gene Fullmer, Rubin Carter and Henry Hank found out the hard way. I personally cannot see any middleweight ever hurting Dick Tiger, make him quit or fight him all out without having to back pedal at least once. He didn't so you would have to or be crunched.

I have been teaching an accredited boxing class at Marist

College in New York State for over three years now and I find the generational gap between the students and myself overwhelming when I discover that some of them do not know who 'Smoking' Joe Frazier is or who Joe Louis was. I always present Dick Tiger to them as one of my favorite middleweight champions and show them all the films of his fights.

I can assure him that he is alive in my memory and that I keep him alive through the stories I tell of him to my family, friends and students as well as by practicing the training routines he taught me to this very day.

I wish I could give him one last hug, see his handsome, smiling face and tell him he was my favorite fighter of all time. I wish I could tell him that he is not forgotten and that he lives on in our collective memories.

It is so sad and tragic for a great warrior to meet his end like Dick Tiger did, bear the agony of his stand for Biafra, endure the loss of his health and finances and suffer his ultimate demise at so young an age to the ravages of dreaded cancer.

Gone though he may be, he lives on through the telling of his deeds and the singing of his praises. Richard Ihetu deserves a golden legacy and with this book, a labour of love by Adeyinka Makinde, a fitting tribute is now with us.

Ron Lipton
Hyde Park, New York

PREFACE TO THE LIFE AND TIMES OF A BOXING IMMORTAL

There have perhaps been only a few in the modern epoch of boxing who have represented the themes of blue collar fighter and ageless ring warrior as compellingly as did Richard Ihetu better known by the ring pseudonym of Dick Tiger.

It was once written of him that that he "was the type of fighter who rolled up his sleeves, spat on his hands and went to work, giving an honest labouring mans effort. Each time. Every time." An aptly succinct and unglamorous portrayal of a modest and uncomplicated man who despite his many achievements remained steadfastly uncorrupted by the excesses and ego manifestations that wealth and success can bring in their wake.

By the time he hung up his gloves after an 18-year career, he had already fashioned an exemplary image and fighting record that accorded him the status of a ring legend.

But it was never an easy passage in both the life and the career of the Tiger who along the way battled against what must have appeared to him to be an unceasing stream of obstacles and setbacks. Yet, when viewed in hindsight, they only serve to magnify the triumphs that he was able to muster.

He emerged from an environment devoid of any substantive traditions in boxing but would ascend nonetheless to the dizzying heights of his profession. In between, however, there was very much to contend with: the disastrous line of defeats in his first English bouts, there were the fighters who dodged him and the champions who evaded his challenges. So too were the perverse decisions and the promises cynically reneged upon by fight promoters. Yet with remarkable stoicism, he eschewed it all finding in each instance what he termed "a new courage" to continue.

When the Nigerian-Biafran conflict erupted in all its brutality and ugliness, Dick Tiger showed that his physical courage did not end in the ring and that personal conscience and social responsibility are attributes not alien to the make up of the pugilist.

Even though he had laid the foundations of what by any standards would be a very successful career, his formative years in Nigeria were not the straightforward tale of achievement given, for one, that he was never officially recognised as the national champion. Nor would he win the nation's prestigious Collister Belt Tourney (named for Douglas Collister, a patriarchal figure in the Nigerian fight game). And contrary to his official fight record, he was unable to defeat a local rival by the name of 'Tommy West' in any of their three meetings.

Nevertheless, it became apparent in time that he was superior to the local opposition. Not for the last time, he outgrew his surroundings and would move on. Besides, there were in his words "too many boxers and too few fights." So in 1955, he joined the transatlantic migration of West African fighters.

In an unbearably cold and strange English environment, he lost his first four contests and it looked, ostensibly to be a grossly miscalculated career move. But in refusing to "give in to despair," persistence would yield great dividends and by the time he left British shores for America in the spring of 1959, he was the middleweight champion of the Empire.

In going on to surpass the achievements of another Nigerian world champion, Hogan Bassey, Tiger paved the way for future African stars like Ghana's Azumah Nelson and Uganda's John Mugabi, showing that despite the difficulties sportsmen face in that continent—the endemic problems of organisation and infrastructure—it is possible to dedicatedly nurture dormant ability and go on to compete and win at the highest levels of world sport.

Blue collar pugilist, ageless ring-man, commercial venturer, conscientious soldier, patriot and then rebel, devoted family man; Tiger had many dimensions, but underpinning them all was a sincerity and a rich vein of integrity.

His story is one of succeeding against the odds, in Afro-American parlance, he ascended from the 'guttermost to the uttermost,' living a kind of 'American dream' life voyage: from empty bottle trader to wealthy businessman, from Nigerian boxing booths to Madison Square Garden, from journeyman fighter to world championship fighter.

Alas the ending was not a happy one, dying in tragic circumstances at the age of only 42; the extent of his post civil war wealth uncertain and his legacy among his countrymen overshadowed by his role in that war.

The purpose of this book is to provide the long overdue appraisal which his life and career merit.

Adeyinka Makinde
London

One
ORIGINS

He began his life journey where it ended; in Eluowere Ubu Amaigbo. Amaigbo is a village situated close to the approaches of the River Niger. The Amaigbos, literally meaning 'compound of Igbos,' form one of numerous settlements of ethnic Igbos dotted around the dense rainforest belt in the vast hinterland of what was formerly referred to as the 'Bight of Biafra.' They are the largest among the groups of traditionally stateless peoples who in preferring to operate along individualistic and egalitarian precepts were never to develop the monarchical based systems typical of many other forest groups like the Edo and the Yoruba. Although not entirely acephalous communities, the economic and political relationships were largely underpinned by an amalgam of family and kinship ties; the villages being autonomous enclaves headed by councils of elders and self-made men who served as the arbiters of social policy and cohesion.

The chain of Igbo civilisation, lasting for well over a millennia, is a rich one that finds much glory in the copper and bronze discoveries of Igbo-Ukwu, a site located close to the modern city of Onitsha. Dating from around the ninth century A.D. these artefacts of religious paraphernalia are the grandiose remains of the elaborate cemeteries of an ancient ruling class of diviners and titled priests. As is the case with many of the peoples of Black Africa, the method of transmitting group myths and customs was a largely unwritten one; but a unique form of written language known as the N'sibidi Script would develop among the initiates of the secret societies that flourished among the Delta peoples.

A culture of enterprise, one of the more salient attributes of the Igbo people in the modern age, developed through the ages creating in the process a network of trade routes which criss-crossed the heavily forested and occasionally swampy landscape, converging at intervals at large market venues where the practice

1

of bartering produce and goods simultaneously existed with a system of metal currencies. Another commodity, human beings, was added to this commercial smorgasbord around the beginning of the 16th century. Consisting in the main of captive warriors, they were marched southwards to the Atlantic coast to be sold to Portuguese and British slavers enroute to slave markets in the Americas. By the end of the 18th century it is estimated that about 20,000 human beings were being sold by the litany of Igbo controlled slave rackets emplaced around the Eastern Niger Delta.

In 1807 the British Parliament abolished slavery and Royal Navy warships patrolled the West African coast with the aim of enforcing the law. But while the transatlantic trade in humans was largely ended, the institution of slavery continued among the Igbo who sold their kith and kin southwards to the Ijo and Efik city-states situated along the coast. These city-states were dominated by what was known as the 'House System,' in essence, trading associations which were comprised of freemen and slaves. The Houses grew wealthy in their role as middlemen between African traders in the hinterland and the European and American trading groups who bought huge quantities of commodities and raw materials which they transported home through their 'Super Cargoes.'

In the early 1830s, an adolescent boy who had been born in Amaigbo was sold and taken to Bonny, one of the prominent city-states. Jubo Jubogha was indentured to the House of Annie Pepple but the workings of the House system did not preclude the possibility of upward mobility and Jubo (abbreviated to 'Jojo' and popularised in British historical literature as 'Jaja') would rise to head the House. An extremely intelligent and astute man, he turned around the fortunes of the debt ridden House before civil strife in 1869 forced him north eastwards the following year to form the kingdom of Opobo.

King Jaja enjoyed good relations with the British and in 1875 was awarded the Sword of Honour by Queen Victoria. The relationship however would soon sour as the British, anxious to gain direct access to goods from the hinterland as well as being fearful of what they perceived to be an encroaching German sphere of influence, crudely engineered his downfall. Jaja was exiled first to Ghana and then to the West Indian Island of St. Vincent before dying in 1891 in Tenerife never again seeing his homeland.

Following the 'Scramble for Africa,' completed at the Berlin Conference of the European powers in the 1880s, the imperial red of the British empire held sway in a chunk of territory that extended from the swampy regions bordering the Atlantic to the savannah homelands of the Hausa-Fulani emirates; the Igbo groups falling into what the British named the Oil Rivers Protectorate in 1891. The name was derived not from richness in oil deposits (this would remain undiscovered until the 1950s), but from an abundance of palm trees, the source of the raw materials used in the manufacture of soaps and detergents. Later, it would be joined to the territories consisting of the conquered Yoruba city-states and the defeated empire of Benin to form the southern protectorate of Nigeria (an acronym of 'Niger area').

In 1915, the Northern and Southern protectorates of Nigeria were merged under the administration of Lord Frederick Lugard, the Govenor-General. It was Lugard's wife, once a reporter for the London *Times*, who coined the name 'Nigeria.'

For the Igbo people, the problems caused by Nigeria's conglomerate society would be far reaching, manifesting first in the system of rule adopted by the British. The programme of governing indirectly through traditional rulers, while successful in the feudal strictures of the Northern emirates, was not successful in the South and particularly among the Igbos who were culturally unfamiliar with the concept of inherited rulers. Rioting, striking and other forms of civil disobedience would be commonplace expressions of dissent from a people whom a British soldier, speaking to a London audience in 1909, would describe as being the most "troublesome" in Nigeria despite being a "small portion" of the country. Later in the century, it would culminate in a war which the Igbos claim was against

Britain's postcolonial interests.

The dawning of the colonial era brought with it the Church Missionary Societies who from the nineteenth century embarked upon a crusade that facilitated the rapid Christianisation of Igboland. By 1921, almost 300,000 Igbos out of a total of four million claimed to be Christians. Among them were Ubuagu and Rebecca Ihetu, the parents of Dick Tiger. Ubuagu's surname had originally been Nnamajogu. The background to the change of name is a tale in itself. After some years of a marriage that had produced only one daughter, Ubuagu's father nursed a great fear that his family line would be extinguished. Happily for him, fate intervened and finally his wife bore him the yearned for son. Assured then, that his family line would now be perpetuated, he held the infant up to the heavens and expressed his gratitude with the words 'I-he-tu' which means, "I received what I wanted."

Ubuagu's ancestors, the forbears of Richard, were steeped in the tradition of wrestling. For many young men searching for prestige and social elevation in the meritocracy of traditional Igbo society, wrestling provided a means to achieving wealth and status. Wrestling contests were at one time used as a medium for settling disputes concerning inter village rights and even as a means for legitimising the transfer of clan leadership. It could bring not only honour and fame, but also political influence and the right to take the hand of the most beautiful maidens. Indeed, it was a fellow wrestler, Ononiwu who had offered him the hand of his daughter, Rebecca.

Ubuagu's father had been known as 'Ugbugbo je eju re okuku,' meaning literally: 'If the bark of a tree imitates a broken pot that is being used as a receptacle for fire, it will be burnt.' His grandfather was called 'Ike agwugh agagh ezu ike': 'A person who is not tired will not rest,' while his great-grandfather was 'Omehihe,':'a man who exhibits his (physical) power in public.' It is from these range of personalities that we can perhaps deduce the traits that would characterise and shape the destiny of their famous decendant 'Dick Tiger': a man possessing great physical acumen, an extraordinary work ethic and as a boxer gaining a level of fame that none of his long departed progenitors would have been able to comprehend.

Ubuagu did what most men did in his village: He was a farmer and his life centred round the seasonal shifts of planting and harvesting a plot of land where the soil sprouted a staple of yams and sweet potatoes. It was a subsistence kind of existence, one that was not far removed from the manner in which his people had lived through the ages. But farming did not form the sum total of the typical Amaigbo man's working life. Whereas the Igbos of Nri were noted for their priests and diviners, the Akwa for their herbal doctors, metalsmiths and carvers and the Abiribas for their mercenary soldiers, the Amaigbos, who were part of the Nkwerris, were disposed to indulging in commercial ventures and today, they are still noted for their skills in trading. Ubuagu was a trader and provided the atypical model of the hardworking and enterprising Amaigbo man. During the 1920s and 1930s, when public transport was a largely unevolved concept, he would trek 70 miles through passages cleared through the jungle and the red clay dusty roads to the market town of Aba. It was a journey fraught with many risks but which to the relief of Rebecca, he always completed safely.

In Aba, one of the most important of the four and eight day markets spread over Igboland, he sold his farm produce together with the chickens he raised. The money he received was used to buy goods for the household and the farm; items like pots, kerosene fuel, salt, soap and matches. The rest of the money he used to purchase clothes which he took back to re-sell in Orlu and Amaigbo.

The son, who would be christened Richard, arrived in August 1929, the month in which the womenfolk of Aba rioted in protest against the poll tax, which the colonial authorities were rumoured to be on the verge of levying on them. Such turbulence was a world away when Rebecca held her third born child in her arms. Richard, the 'lion hearted,' was a fitting name for the son whom she believed to be the reincarnation of Ononiwu, her fearless, warrior father. Far from being eradicated, the uncomplicated

5

tenets of Igbo traditional beliefs endured contemporaneously with the acquired Christian faith and Richard's 'Chi' (personal God of destiny) would be guided by Ofoi, his ancestor, the traditional symbol of authority for the Ihetus. Although Richard in his lifetime would adhere to the strictures of the Anglican faith, traditional rites played a part at various stages in his life. The hieroglyphic like blueish markings etched onto his chest and back by a very sharp and very hot knife were not the result of an initiation ceremony as he told many enquiring British and American journalists, but were actually the results of a course of 'treatment' administered by traditional doctors seeking to cure him of an arthritic like ailment when he was 20 years old.

When barely past the stage of a toddler, Richard like other village kids joined his older brothers, Chinaka and Nelson on the farm. He drew water to nourish the crops and fetched firewood from the outlying forest. He was quick to develop an insatiable habit for the hard work later to characterise his approach both to his fights and his business endeavours. Always, he persisted in matching and surpassing the workload given to his elder brothers. "While working on my father's farm," he recalled, "I was always keen to build up my body and most of the heavy work came my way because I sought it."

He went to the village school. The Holy Trinity School was built like many other village schools in Igboland by the combined resources of missionary societies, in this case the Anglican Church Missionary Society, and the locals. A small hall sized affair, Richard's curriculum was transmitted via the Igbo language and he would not learn to speak English for some more years.

It was in his adolescent years when Richard's life was suddenly plunged into a crisis caused by Ubuagu's early death. The cause and his age are uncertain, but it meant that Richard would grow up without a father. Rebecca took up the running of the farm, aided by male relatives and her growing sons. Life, however, became that much harder without a male breadwinner and Richard was forced to abandon his school education.

Rebecca decided to foster Richard and his siblings to the households of her husband's male relatives where she hoped that they would learn a trade. Chinaka was sent to Orlu town where he worked for the Oil Mill Company while Nelson resided first in Aba Township where he lived with an uncle, Josiah Nwosu before moving to Elele in Port Harcourt. Richard travelled to Enugu where he stayed with an uncle, Jonathan Iwueke, at the local Police barracks. In 1943, when he was fourteen, he moved to Aba where he stayed with Josiah's brother Abel.

Little more than a village at the dawn of the 20th century, Aba owed its growth to a number of factors. For one, its importance of being the major market venue of southern Igboland was one reason why the British earmarked it as a centre for administration. Its geographical location enabled it to become the conduit to a wide network of towns and villages among them Port Harcourt, Ekot Epene and Opobo. The building of the Nigerian railway system in the second decade of the 1900s further enhanced this position.

Young Richard's arrival coincided with the increasing drift from the villages to the burgeoning urban centres. The abandonment of his schooling following the sudden death of his father only hastened what in all likelihood would have been inevitable even if his father had lived. It reflected a trend among the rural poor, many of whose children were forced to give up their studies after a year or two because they were needed on the farms or to earn remuneration from labouring jobs. And of course the place to earn money was not in a village but in the townships which were swelling from the arrivals of rural dwellers leaving their communities in order to escape increasing poverty and hopeful of broadening their horizons.

Richard, although sad about the circumstances that had necessitated his departure nonetheless was glad to be away from the stifling circumstances of his own village. "I knew that I could make little money on the farm," he recalled. The soil, he explained, did not lend itself to planting a great range of crops and the scope for other facets of agriculture such as raising cattle were non-existent.

In the larger scheme of things, the lack of opportunities caused by a generally harsh and unproductive soil type as well as a bourgeoning population –Igboland remains one of the most densely populated areas in sub-tropical Africa- would help create a highly mobile people. From the dawn of the 20th century, many Igbos migrated not only to the towns within their native Eastern Region, but also to other corners of Nigeria, particularly to the North, where they traded and put their often miniscule education to use as clerks, administrators and railwaymen. Initially appraised by the British colonists to be comparatively among the most backward of the conquered ethnic groups, the Igbo with a natural inclination to trading and a seemingly overwhelming thirst for education, turned out to be the most willing of the indigenous peoples to adapt to the process of Westernisation. As the Igbo born novelist Chinua Achebe put it, "Unlike the Hausa-Fulani, the Igboman was unhindered by a weary (Moslem) religion and unlike the Yoruba, (he was) unhampered by traditional hierarchies….This kind of creature, fearing neither God nor man was custom made to grasp the opportunities….of the white man's dispensation."

Nigerian census records dated from 1920 to 1925 show that of the 15 barristers and 12 physicians practicing in the country, 20 came from the Yoruba ethnic group while the remainder were so-called 'Native Foreigners' from Sierra Leone and Ghana. Thirty years later, the progress of the Igbos was glaring: Among the 300 practising lawyers and physicians, 49 were Igbo as against 76 Yoruba and one Hausa. Again, prior to the outbreak of the Second World War, a poll of Nigerians studying in the United States recorded only one Igbo, Nnamdi Azikiwe, the country's first President. In the post-war period, however, Igbo representation would consistently account for more than half the students. It was this astoundingly rapid rate of progress that prompted Azikiwe in 1949 to arrogate that it "would appear that the God of Africa has specifically created the Igbo nation to lead the children of Africa from the bondage of the ages."

Richard settled down to work as a delivery boy, trudging

barefoot along the township's mostly unpaved roads while pushing a handcart laden with goods to businesses on Asa Road and Park Road. The handcart would also provide a devise that he adapted to his own business venture; that of collecting empty bottles, which he sold back to manufacturers. He also joined his brothers on shopping expeditions to the Delta town of Ogoni where they bought monkeys, parrots and cats, which they trained and sold at a stall at Aba's Eke Oha market.

The importance of Aba in the construction of the values and life philosophy of Richard Ihetu cannot be underestimated. A teeming, sleepless urban sprawl of commercial, administrative and spiritual activity, Aba forged in Richard a sense of a communal camaraderie and a belief that any level of success was achievable by following the path of sobriety and hard work. For most Igbos, including those possessed with what may be termed the 'Aba Spirit,' the era between the end of the Second World War and the beginning of the Nigerian Civil War were times of an almost unbridled optimism; an infectious spirit of social and economic 'can-doism.' These values, readily imbibed by a burgeoning proletariat, were reflected in the markings on the buses and lorries that went past him bearing inscriptions like 'Glory Be To God' and 'Let the Good times Roll' and also were perpetuated by the phenomenon that came to be known as 'Onitsha Market Literature.'

Conceptually originating in the northern Igbo market town of Onitsha, 'chapbooks,' cheaply produced popular form pamphlets provided advice on how to achieve success in life. Written in English and Igbo for the benefit of young Igbos in their homelands and the diaspora, titles churned out including 'Determination is the Key to Success,' 'How to become Rich,' and 'How to Stay Rich' propagated a value system underpinned by a juxtaposition of Christian, traditional and entrepreneurial precepts.

The hustling, bustling 'world is your oyster' culture that Richard found himself in also served to underline the necessity for him to resume his education. The modicum of schooling that

9

he had received in Amaigbo had not been sufficient enough to enable him to speak and read in English. He enrolled at the Christ the Kings Church School (later CMS) Orlu, where he attended night classes after a hard days slugging on the streets.

The streets of Aba were an education not only in regard to commerce but provided the means through which he discovered and developed a prowess at fighting. Like any other growing urban centre, Aba provided fertile ground for the nurturing of tensions and frustrations that were liable to be unleashed in a variety of situations. The centre point for many fights came at the township's communal water pumps. Constant water shortages meant queuing at water pumps morning, noon and evening; rain or shine. Richard arrived bucket in hand but unwilling to spend what he considered to be an inordinate period of time waiting his turn. His chunky physique, his natural strength and stamina were vital assets in fighting off or otherwise intimidating what he termed the "opposition." His philosophy was that "success went to the strong," and although admitting that it was "unfair," "it had to be a case of (taking care of) number one if you were not to be left high and dry." His brother Godwin remembers a group of trouble making friends who always ran to Richard for protection when their pranks got out of hand. These incidents represented the beginnings of the fighter in Richard Ihetu who became feared and respected on Aba's occasionally mean streets.

Young men like Richard sought respite from the stress and drudgery brought on by the high pace of urban dwelling in the form of sports and games. Football was the mainstay of most young Nigerians and the Aba team was among the best in the land providing, many of the players who lined up for the Igbo elevens that often battled with their perennial opponents, the Yorubas in the highly popular inter-tribal competitions. Richard's first love was football, and although he did not progress to the top echelon of Aba's soccer stars, he became a very useful forward line player.

It was in boxing, however, that Richard would find his metier, joining the Emy Boxing Club. The club was run by a Gold

10

Coast born former boxer named A.K. Gikonou. His interest in the sport, he often claimed, had been sparked from the reports of the successes of migrant Nigerian fighters based in England. The newspaper sports pages were also filled with stories about fighters from the games citadel, America. "I started to read about such great Negroes like Henry Armstrong, Joe Louis and Ray Robinson," he remembered. "I thought I'd like to try my luck as a fighter."

His decision to begin pursuing the sport in a serious vein met with protests and signals of disapproval in his family. While Chinaka felt that his passions would get in the way of work, Rebecca naturally felt concerned about the lumps and bruising that occasioned his features. Despite the family tradition of wrestlers, she felt that the "age of physical power" was over. Richard would acknowledge that "My mother wanted me to stop" but he ignored her.

Although the Emy gymnasium was woefully lacking in boxing equipment, Richard's enthusiasm for the sport was not dampened. He shared the few overstitched gloves that were available with the other boys, developing an understanding of the mechanics of the sport from browsing through boxing manuals and by watching short films on amateur boxing provided by the British Council. He also attended cinema presentations featuring American fights; intently observing the stances of the boxers and the manner in which they threw their punches. The American 'style' impressed him over the British and he was partial to the skills of Archie Moore, Henry Armstrong and Sugar Ray Robinson.

A British Army barracks stationed on Aba's outskirts also became a focal point in his development. "It was just after the war," he recalled, "and some of the British soldiers in the camp would coach us. We were able to get fights maybe twice a month." He did not, however, attach any particular significance to this aspect of his tutelage, considering himself in essence to have been self-taught. He fought boldly in his contests and although still limited, had set in place a style and an ethos that

11

would remain constant, even as he began developing a more comprehensive array of skills.

"From the beginning," he would recall in 1962, "I knew nothing except moving in." His aggression and his short stature together contributed to the name he would find fame with. "I must have been a funny looking fighter," he admitted, "I didn't know anything about boxing, and all I had was my strength and my toughness. I would crouch low and, then jump at my opponent. An Englishman saw me one night and said that I reminded him of a tiger. I liked the sound of it, so I became Dick Tiger."

Dick Tiger had by the beginning of the 1950s compiled a more than decent record, or more appropriately perhaps, a great reputation, since the lack of availability of organised records make it virtually impossible to produce anything representing a comprehensive list of his amateur bouts. What we have is Tiger's comment to a Canadian journalist that over the two year period he fought as an amateur, he had fought a total of thirty-two fights of which two were lost.

Like other Nigerian boxing clubs of the era, Gikonou's club catered for boys fighting in the amateur and professional ranks, resulting unfortunately in the delineation of these distinctions (The formation of a national board of control in 1949 and the strengthening of its regional outposts would gradually stamp this out.) As a result, the bout often referred to as his professional debut, against Simon Eme, may not in fact have been the first time that he fought for a purse, or at least, fought a professional boxer. One such fight may have been a drawn bout with one Sonny Boy, reported as having taken place on March 18, 1951. The *Daily Times* referred to Tiger as being a "leading welterweight" and his opponent as a "lightweight." What is certain, however, is that by 1952, Tiger had come around the decision to make a career out of the fight business. There were promising signs that boxing, in the long run, could bring him greater rewards than he was sowing as a bottle trader.

Two

NIGERIAN BOXING AND THE GREAT MIGRATION

The broad spectrum of sports and games were introduced into Nigerian society by British colonists: Administrators, missionaries and military officers. Organised competitions, which were sanctioned by the authorities, had at their root the idea of promoting social cohesion, that is, to aid in the fostering of the sense of national identity, which was critical to harmonising the disparate ethnic and religious communities that had been brought together in nationhood. National identity aside, the primary aim of British sponsored activities was geared towards the perpetuation of their rule and the introduction in 1893 of 'Empire Day' which was marked, amongst many activities, by sports and games, presented an ideal forum for colonial citizens to renew their allegiance to the British crown.

Sporting events were an important facet in the social lives of the colonists and around the centres of administration and commerce, they formed a number of tennis, cricket, rifle and polo clubs, memberships of which were restricted to Europeans. These clubs served as a forum for event gatherings, inter-town competitions as well as the so called 'intercolonial duels' with fellow expatriates based in the Gold Coast, Britain's other major West African colony. The clubs also matched themselves against makeshift teams composed of visiting businessmen and civil servants or those that could be culled from visiting Royal Navy warships.

Members of the small but growing indigenous middle classes in time adapted the structures of these clubs but in the larger frame, sports would develop through a range of media. One was through the system of education. The British, it should be mentioned, placed a greater deal of emphasis on sporting participation within school curricula than the French or Portuguese did in their African colonies. This has had wide reaching ramifications in perhaps accounting for the disparity in sporting achievements continuing even today, between athletes from the Anglophone and Francophone nations of the African continent. Thus the preponderance of African boxing champions represented by the likes of Dick Tiger, Azumah Nelson, John Mugabi and Cornelius Boza-Edwards are from the English speaking nation states.

Another was through the numerous 'Challenge Cup' competitions held annually and covering a wide breath of sports, most notably in football, where teams from government and commercial sponsored agencies vied for the honour of winning trophies that were named in honour of some or other colonial figure.

Individual interest and initiative also played a part. One such character was Jack Farnsworth, who incidentally, would play a pivotal role in the initial careers of Hogan Bassey and Dick Tiger. Referred to by a local journalist as a "zealous sports enthusiast," Farnsworth was born in 1912 in the northeastern English town of Grantham. He developed a marked interest in sports from an early age, winning several school and county level competitions in athletics and in the process attaining his 'colours.' He took up table tennis after emigrating to South Africa in the 1930s, once representing the Transvaal against a visiting Hungarian team. After Word War Two and demobilisation from the British Merchant Navy, he arrived in Nigeria to take up a post as an insurance manager for the British West African Company (B.E.W.A.C.). Blessed with superb organising skills, he would go on to establish a reputation as a sort of sporting Godfather. For instance, the mentoring role, which he played in regard to a host of sporting clubs and societies, earned him the moniker 'father of youth clubs.' Farnsworth played a part in the formation of the Nigerian Boxing Board of Control, an organisation that for many years he served as General Secretary. He was also a longstanding chairman of the Nigerian Amateur Boxing Association and as General Secretary respectively of the country's Olympic and Empire Games Associations.

A system of youth clubs, modelled on the British type and which would serve as the starting point for sportsmen like Dick Tiger, provided a forum for extra-curricular activities centred mainly on the provision of sports like football, table tennis, swimming, athletics, softball and boxing. Amateur boxing contests were a mainstay of these clubs and by the mid-1950s, every major city and town, had its own Amateur Boxing Association.

Boxing had operated for at least two decades before the institution of a national body of control in the late 1940s, the game being perpetuated through a collection of independent clubs that were owned and controlled by Nigerians. Styled along the lines of American Athletic and Sporting Clubs, one of the first such clubs was the International Boxing and Sporting Club founded in 1930 by one 'Kid Davis.' A self-described 'ex-pro,' Davis often claimed to have fought in Europe and America over a 20-year period during which time he made the acquaintance of the likes of Battling Siki, Tiger Flowers and Harry Wills. He claimed also to have won the 'featherweight championship of Europe.' Whatever the truth of these, and they are highly suspect, his club was responsible for churning out an array of local stars like Bomb Dawodu, Al Okonkwo and Domingo Bailey. Among the foreign membership were a West Indian, Jack O'Brun and a Sierra Leonian called Wellington Coker.

By the mid-1930s, the popularity of the sport was enough to warrant contests on a monthly basis at several regular venues around Lagos such as the Hotel Metropole, the Capitol Cinema and Glover Memorial Hall. Promotions decreased during the war years. Young Nigerian men played a part in the British effort by contributing a significant contingent to the Royal West African Fighting Forces (R.W.A.F.F.) and continued to box during postings with units serving in places as far flung as India and Burma. Among those who fought against European, Asian and American opposition was Roy Ankrah, a sergeant serving in Burma as part of the R.W.A.F.F. contingent from the Gold Coast, who would become West Africa's first Empire boxing champion.

15

As tends to be the case, the end of wars bring forth an upsurge in the spirits of the populace; a hunger for the pleasures and entertainments of which they have been deprived and sport played a great part in this process of 'social gratification.' The number of boxing clubs increased significantly, notable amongst them being the Broadway Boxing Club which would develop Israel Boyle and Napoleon Preregrino's Nigerian Boxing Club (later known respectively as the Imperial and Paramount Boxing Club) from among their ranks would come Hogan Bassey, Sandy Manuel and Roy Jacobs.

The club owners tended to function as both managers and promoters, while the trainers came from the ranks of retired fighters and the senior, more established boxers. Although the majority of these clubs were located in Lagos, a number came to be established in other parts of the country. For instance, Dick Tiger's Emy Club of Aba often vied with the Corinthian Boxing Club of Onitsha for supremacy in the country's Eastern Region. The most prominent club in the Western Region was the Olympic Boxing Club of Ibadan and even in the Northern Region, a character called Super Human Paul (or Super Human Power) formed the Northern Boxing Club in Kano while he was still an active fighter. In Paul's case, a pseudo-evangelical like sense of purpose prevailed as he travelled the length and breath of Nigerian cities with his own boxing booth, staging exhibitions and co-sponsoring fights with local promoters.

Few fighters fought under their real names, most preferring the most ostentatious of nomme de guerres. They entered the ring with a cacophony of names designed in part to facilitate a type of self-exultation and partly to outdo the opposition. There were the colourful sounding ones like 'Johnny Fears No Fall,' 'Hollywood Terror,' 'Lefty Satan,' 'Bad Medicine,' 'Slow Poison,' and 'Buzz Saw.' Some like 'Jimmy Zale' and 'Homicide' Ilori were derivative of popular British and American stars while others like 'Little Chocolate', 'Sammy Langford' and 'Dick Turpin' were outright replications. In choosing names like 'Slow Poison,' the fighters were in a way harking back to the bygone era of

16

traditional wrestlers who went by the grandiose sounding parables alluded to in the previous chapter. "We take those names to sound big," Tiger would tell an American journalist, but not everyone was impressed, indeed one influential Nigerian sportswriter found them "embarrassing" and "absurd." Many would be changed when these fighters travelled to earn their livings in the British Isles.

Big sounding though the names may have been, the pay packets received by boxers was decidedly miniscule. They were forced to put up with an exploitative cabal of promoters who appeared to care little for their financial and medical wellbeing. Little existed in the way of pre or post-fight medical examination and little of the profits garnered from promotions went back into developing the game. It led one fighter to write to the premier national daily to complain of the "disgusting" treatment that was the lot of the average fighter. It was obvious to all interested parties that some semblance of organisation would need to be brought to the game if it was to prosper. Many contributed toward this goal but the man who was universally credited with bringing standards up to a more or less acceptable level was an Englishman named Douglas Collister. A number of expatriate figures had at various points in time being credited with playing critical roles in the developing of the sport. A certain O.T. Jones of the Posts and Telegraphs Service was a prominent referee around Lagos venues in the 1930s and 1940s while Henry Fowler, a doctor, was reputed to be one of the first to actively attempt to get British promoters interested in the local talent. But it is Collister whose name was to become synonymous with beginnings of something of a golden age in Nigerian boxing. An employee of the United Africa Company, Douglas J.C. Collister came to Nigeria in 1925. While based in Port Harcourt, where he was serving as the manager of the Nigerian Cold Storage Company, he set up a boys boxing club in which he served as chief organiser and instructor. In time the club became a converging point for many of the local fighters, a number of whom would go on to attain national prominence and in the case

17

of Dan Collie, a pioneer migrant boxer to Britain.

In 1943, Collister was transferred to Lagos where he established another club, the U.A.C. Boxing Club. While in Lagos, the story goes, he watched an evening's promotion of bouts put on by the Nigerian Boxing Club and was not at all impressed with the proceedings, so much that he offered the club and its rival clubs his free services. Acting in concert with Nap Preregrino and Jack Giwan, the first tentative steps were taken towards achieving a measure of the centralised authority which the undisciplined and ill organised boxing promotions needed so desperately. The resulting body, the West African Sports Syndicate, offered fight fans a regular programme of bouts, many of which were promoted at the Glover Memorial Hall. From a base at 102 Broad Street, in the commercial heartland of Lagos Island, Collister co-ordinated matters, taking care of fight scheduling and bookings. At the fights too, he undertook a wide range of roles functioning alternately as a ringside judge, a referee, timekeeper and steward.

The creation of the syndicate quickly led to a vastly improved state of affairs. The promoters went some way towards improving the pay structure of the long suffering fighters resulting in a significant reduction in the unpunctuality and absences of boxers. The fans also benefited from the new regime. The co-operation among the major clubs provided more competitive matches since there were more inter-club duels as opposed to the previously common intra-club fights. Picking up on these positive developments, the press began devoting substantial amounts of space to boxing news and views in the sports pages.

Despite the obvious successes of the syndicate, the game continued to be plagued by a host of problems. For all its virtues, the syndicate was not the same thing as a Board of Control. It did not operate under any stipulated rules or articles laying down express and enforceable standards of practice. Thus there were no controls existing in regard to the grant of licences, manager/boxer contracts, safety measures and the like. Another problem related to the promotions themselves, which continued to happen within the exclusive confines of Lagos. Few links existed with promoters in the provinces. Meanwhile, pressure for the formation of a national boxing board of control that would work towards promoting cohesion among the provinces and which would of course be obliged to set stringent standards and be empowered to act to maintain them, remained the central focus of debate in boxing columns.

It came to pass on Tuesday, August the 9th 1949. In a conference room of a Lagos Island hotel, 11 persons were appointed to the Nigerian Boxing Board of Control. Strictly following the British model, it was, rather tellingly, composed of eight Britons and three Nigerians. Collister was elected to serve as its first chairman.

The formation of the Board reflected the needs of the times, for the late 1940s saw the beginnings of the widespread migration of African fighters who were mainly Nigerian, to the British Isles. Many like Sammy Wilde, Roy Thomas, Reggie Williams and Dan Collie had become name fighters, boxing regularly on fight bills and making a great deal more money than their contemporaries back home could ever hope to make in Nigeria.

There had been earlier migrants, among them MacJordan Tarone, a self-proclaimed bantamweight champion of Nigeria. Tarone, who left Nigeria for England in 1937, had made a good impression fighting British lightweights, while Reggie Williams, a middleweight, arrived in 1943 but war conditions did not permit him to box more than a handful of matches during what should have being his prime years. (He would later become a boxing coach at Kings College, Oxford.)

The surge in the numbers of migrant fighters was attributable in great measure to the relaxation in travel restrictions to Britain from its colonies. The British Nationality Act of 1948 granted citizenship to all members of the colonies, enabling travellers from the colonies to stay for an indefinite period of time. Government policies designed to attract labour desperately needed for the purpose of national reconstruction, tackled the manpower shortage in the post war period. Recruitment drives were staged to encourage blacks from the Caribbean Islands to staff the bourgeoning National Health Service as well as the newly nationalised transportation system. They were also needed in the hotel and catering industries.

They arrived from all corners of the Empire; from the West Indies to the antipodes, Black, White, Asian and Polynesian boxers partook in contests held on bills in London and the provinces. Gradually, networks and cross-Atlantic alliances were formed between Nigerian promoters and English based managers like Peter Banasko and Buddy Martins. Both were based on Merseyside and had firm links with the premier promoter of the English North West, Johnny Best, the owner of Liverpool Stadium. The shifting of fighters, occurring as they did at regular intervals, would be prompted for instance by a manager such as Martins writing a letter to a Nigerian promoter like G.O. Olowu requesting that he send "six good young, well behaved boxers ranging from bantamweight to middleweight."

The man who was central to giving Nigeria's future world champions their initial breaks was Peter Banasko. The product of a union between an African immigrant from the Gold Coast (later Ghana) and a local bred girl with Irish antecedents, Banasko became an English schoolboy champion and a minor celebrity of sorts, which allowed him the accolade of being included in a fundraising boxing exhibition held in the presence of Edward, the Prince of Wales, Prince George and Lord Lonsdale. At the end of his exertions, the young Banasko was presented with an inscribed gold watch by the later to abdicate Royal heir.

At 17, after much press build up, he turned professional and built up a decent record after suffering the initial humiliation of being knocked out cold in the first round of his first fight. It was a career that was blighted by racism and the interruption of war. He decided against resuming his career after being demobbed from the Army, and instead, opted to become a fight manager finding his niche in importing boxers from British West Africa.

His Nigerian agent was Jack Farnsworth who handed over both Tiger and Hogan Bassey to his care. Although his association with both men was destined to end in bitter circumstances, Banasko considered his role as being one that transcended the confines of a manager and trainer. Many times he paid for the fighters passage, lodgings, clothing and initial upkeep. He offered them his friendship and made them part of a sort of extended family in which his wife played an active part. According to his family, he never signed formal contractual agreements with the fighters.

Banasko, like other Liverpool managers, arranged for their fighters to appear on bills at venues like Liverpool Stadium, the Blackpool Tower Circus and the Engineers Club in West Hartlepool. But while they may have been heavily concentrated in Liverpool and North West England, they appeared all over Britain. The presence of black fighters in the British Isles was not a new thing. Bill Richmond, the son of American slaves who was adopted by the Duke of Northumberland, in the 18th century became the first black fighter of record. He was followed early in the next century by an ex-Virginia slave named Tom Molyneaux who like his predecessor would lose to Tom Cribb, the British heavyweight champion.

Only a few from the African continent had managed to make their marks in the world of Anglo-Saxon fisticuffs, the most significant having occurred in 1907 when Andrew Jeptha, a black South African won the British welterweight title. Although a black presence had existed for a considerable length of time, their numbers had never approached anything near to the levels active in the late 1940s, a situation that would provide a set of problems over the years. The matter of the acceptance of these fighters by local fans would have preoccupied many a British promoter worried about the impact on their coffers and in the supervening years some would refuse the services of what were popularly termed 'coloured fighters.'

The times however were changing and the ending of the notorious 'colour bar,' set the tone of tolerance. The boxing

21

'colour bar' referred to a policy instituted in the 1920s by the National Sporting Club, then the premier institution of control, which debarred British born blacks from contesting for British titles. It was a policy that was continued by the N.S.C.'s successor, the British Boxing Board of Control. In justification, its General-Secretary, Charles Donmall would say, "It is only right that a small country such as ours should have championships restricted to boxers of white parents –otherwise we might be faced with a situation where all our British titles are held by coloured Empire boxers." Echoing the post-Jack Johnson era policy in the United States of barring black heavyweights from fighting for the world championship, the board had always claimed that the Home Office had tacitly supported their view that black versus white championship matches carried with them the threat of civil disorder breaking out in parts of the Empire.

The triumphs in the 1940s of the mixed race Turpin brothers, Randolph and Dick, the latter having won Amateur Boxing Association (A.B.A.) titles at welterweight and middleweight respectively in 1945 and 1946 put pressure on the Board. Both embarked on successful careers in the professional ranks and were faced with the absurd position of not being eligible to fight for the British title. A campaign aimed at demolishing this state of affairs found favour in Parliament where the Colonial Secretary, Greech Jones responded to a tabled question by announcing that he regarded the Board's position as being "quite unjustified." The B.B.B.C. formally abrogated its position in 1947.

The lifting of the 'colour bar' did not mean that black fighters from the colonies, although invested with citizenship rights, would be able to fight for the British title. But the boxing authorities did recognise that they needed to be able to fight for major honours and this was provided by the Empire titles. Inaugurated in 1908, the Empire titles, though open in principle to boxers living in any part of the realm, had been contested in the main by combatants from a narrow range of countries, namely those from the British Isles and the 'white' nations of

Australia, Canada and South Africa. The Empire boxing system was reformatted. In 1950, the British Empire Championships Committee was established and structured to ensure that each country, including those from Black Africa, would, through a representative steward, have an input in determining rankings and championship fights. Thus, the committee was designed to break the monopoly of the 'old' dominion countries and to pave the way for deserving title challenges from the ranks of fighters from the 'new' commonwealth. It would not be long before the West Africans made their first title acquisition. In April 1951, Roy Ankrah dethroned the Empire featherweight champion, Ronnie Clayton and the success of the man dubbed the 'Black Flash,' served to galvanise African fighters in Britain and back home. Among the fighters of Nigerian origin, it was the welterweight Israel Boyle who initially made the best impact, winning praise for his skill and gentlemanly deportment. Born in the Niger Delta town of Abonnema, he grew up on Lagos Island where he worked as a motor mechanic. His passion was redirected from soccer to boxing when a local star of the time, Red Raymond, persuaded him to lace up the gloves and spar at the Broadway Boxing Club. His progress was rapid, culminating in a West African lightweight title fight with Roy Ankrah to whom he lost narrowly on points. Britain beckoned. "I had been hearing about our boys doing well in England. Boxers like Sammy Wilde and Reggie Williams and I said 'one day, I'll go'." In November 1949, he departed for Liverpool to be managed by Peter Banasko. Although Boyle came close to fighting for the Empire Welterweight title, eye problems forced him to abandon his career. Nevertheless, he remained an influential figure, becoming a licensed corner man and serving as a mentor of sorts to a succession of migrant fighters, including Hogan Bassey.

Born Okon Bassey Asuquo in Creek Town, Calabar on the southeastern tip of Nigeria, like Boyle, he was brought up on Lagos Island where he joined Nap Preregrino's Imperial Boxing Club. In 1949, while still a student in secondary school, he won the Nigerian flyweight title. By the time he added the West African title, many where convinced that he would be able to hold his own against British fighters. A group led by Jack Farnsworth raised money to pay his passage to England.

He was still only nineteen when he arrived in Liverpool in November 1951 and only a few weeks later, after a hastily arranged fitness test held before a B.B.B.C. Inspector in order to confirm the issue of his license, he stopped Simon Hillyard in four rounds at the Liverpool Stadium. Bassey would go on to become a hero among many Liverpudlians. "If you could hear the reception Hogan Bassey gets from the crowd in (Liverpool) Stadium," said Johnny Best Junior in 1954, "you would think that he was a white boy. The whole crowd just rises to him. He is a thorough gentleman inside and outside the ring. In my opinion, boxing has deteriorated since before the war, but Hogan Bassey as a fighter is as good, if not better, than pre-war English boxers." He would in time surpass the achievements of Roy Ankrah and set the standards for ambitious Nigerian fighters like Dick Tiger.

Three
THE FIREMAN

Dick Tiger, like the multitude of Nigerian fighters, was inspired by the inroads that were being made by the expatriate West African fighters. He could see a pathway but was prudent enough to recognise that he would first have to establish his credentials at home before joining the ongoing exodus. Fighting in the regions however placed him in a disadvantageous position: It was in faraway Lagos that the major promotions were held. The national media largely ignored provincial bouts, concentrating its coverage in the capital city. Lagos was also the place to find the agents who had contacts with British managers and promoters. Tiger would have been aware of the perception that provincial fighters were usually of inferior quality and were a frequent drain on the financial resources of the undiscerning promoter. An article in the *West African Pilot* titled 'Advice to Boxers in the Provinces' went:

"A boxer travelling from afar requires his fare and accommodation in addition to his purse money. Of the few provincial boxers who have come to Lagos, most have talked a lot before they...met an early defeat."

In the Eastern Province, the boxing game thrived under the helm of a few promoters the most prominent being N.A. Okorie with whom Tiger became associated. Okorie was an ex-fighter who plied his trade under the pseudonym Black Panther and had been associated in the early part of his career with Douglas Collister's Port Harcourt Boxing Club. Moving to Lagos in 1948, he joined the Royal Boxing Club and later won the Nigerian welterweight title before retiring undefeated in 1950. Continuing his association with the club as a trainer and co-promoter, he found the time to undertake his own promotions in his native province. Among these were Dick Tiger's first pro-bouts and his connections with the capital would prove critical to Tiger's progress.

Fights in the east were concentrated in select towns like Aba, Enugu, Umuahia, Calabar and Port Harcourt, places where Tiger would experience his first measure of fame. He won the first of his recorded bouts in Aba against one Simon Eme and proceeded to polish his fists against a slew of opponents, one of whom, the spectacularly named 'Easy Dynamite,' was knocked out in the third of a scheduled six round contest. As 1952 approached its end, he had notched up a record of seven wins and no losses.

Okorie now felt that he had a fighter to be reckoned with and decided that the time was apt for Tiger to step up a gear in the calibre of opposition. A match was arranged for December 13th with an up and coming Lagosian middleweight fighting under the name 'Tommy West.'

West had started his career as an amateur welterweight in 1949, representing the Faji Boys Club of Lagos' Onikan district. After what a *Daily Times* writer described as an "outstanding career," West turned professional, amid much media hype and fanfare in May of 1952.

Tiger versus West was the main event of a four-bout programme billed as the first time clash between Aba and Lagos. The venue was the Rex Cinema Hall, where two days previously, Tiger had staged an exhibition session with 'Super Human Paul' then on one of his crusades around the Eastern Region. (Nothing went above Tiger's head. Cinema ownership provided one of the few means for an indigene to amass a relative fortune during the colonial era and would continue over the years to represent a sound investment. In the 1960s he would construct his own cinema complex.)

Both men were a study of contrasts, Tiger's stocky physique and brawling manner the complete opposite to West's tallness, slimness and textbook stance. The *Daily Times* report described Tiger as utilising "a semi-crouching style with left shoulder slightly raised" against the Lagosian who in turn had him "puzzled through out the contest" with his southpaw stance. Tiger boxed with his chin tucked firmly into his glove, and with West willing only to box from a safe distance, exchanges were fairly limited. There was little between them in the scoring when the bout ended and Tiger's home support filled the hall with a crescendo of boos and catcalls when the referee raised West's hand in victory.

Far from being a calamity, the loss to Tommy West did not unduly affect Tiger's rising star. The Lagos media after all had begun to take notice of his talent and many were convinced that an ensuing rivalry with West would give the game a much needed boost at a time when it was feeling the effects of the exodus of fighters to Britain. The benefits were quick to come his way. Seated ringside at the Rex Cinema Hall was Jack Farnsworth who saw signs of promise in Tiger. He impressed his views on the N.B.B.C. stewards who proceeded to invite Tiger to Lagos to participate in the most prestigious event in the Nigerian boxing calendar, the Collister Belt Tournament.

In 1950, a little short of a year after his appointment at the N.B.B.C., Douglas Collister was retired by the U.A.C. Before leaving for Liverpool in July, the fight fraternity honoured him with the staging of a series of events. The affection and high esteem in which he was held was obvious from the tribute paid by fight aficionado and future Nigerian President, Dr. Nnamdi Azikiwe. Said 'Zik,' "When the history of Nigerian boxing is written, a large part will be devoted to the man who has laboured so laudably in bringing the game up to its present standard." It was announced afterwards that an annually held invitation tournament bearing his name would be created.

While the object of the tournament was to select the 'Boxer of the Year,' it was also designed to provide the N.B.B.C. with a major source of revenue. Scheduled to be held on the final Friday of every January, the tourney provided the forum for the country's best fighters to face each other in a series of same weight contests, all taking place on a single evening bill. At the end of the bouts, a panel would select the boxer who had put up the most impressive performance to wear the diamond-encrusted belt.

The first tournament was held in 1951. From 1953, it was decided to award two belts; one for the 'heavier' fighters, that is, from lightweight upwards while the other would go to a fighter from the 'lighter' category that encompassed the featherweights and all the divisions below. Four bouts showcased the first tournament but no official decisions were rendered. So in order to elevate the level of competitiveness to one above a series of glorified exhibitions, a points system was introduced and fighters were encouraged to put national titles on the line.

Tiger was now billed to face Blackie Power, the Nigerian Middleweight champion. But the N.B.B.C.'s decision to select him over Tommy West was controversial. The stewards were expected to consider a fighter's record as well as current form and many felt that West, by virtue of his victory of Tiger was the more deserving of the spot. Support for Tiger, nevertheless, came from some quarters, the *West African Pilot* opining that the "Board's decision is an excellent one (since) it serves as an encouragement to provincial boxers." Indeed, West had already made an unsuccessful attempt at wresting Blackie Powers's title. Despite his success in knocking over the champion for an eight count, his inexperience cost him the decision.

The champion had won the title in 1951 by beating Battling Roberts. Despite the fearsome assumption raised by his moniker, Blackie was nothing near the fighter that his name suggested. The press attacked him for being 'lazy' and of having a cavalier attitude. His style, which depended on 'tying up' opponents and fighting 'inside' (holding his opponent close while pawing at him) was considered dull and unimaginative. Many hoped that the emergence of Tiger and West would bring his days as the champion to an end.

The Glover Memorial Hall, the venue of the fight, was a handsome edifice dedicated to the first colonial governor of the Lagos protectorate. A centre for political and cultural events, Glover Hall while being the country's premier boxing site, remained a far cry from the television age splendour of Madison Square Garden that Tiger would later acquaint himself with. A national daily satirist noted that its ring was "awful" and that the "boxers cannot mix it in the centre of the ring for fear of knocking down the light," adding that when the fighters tussled in the corners, to the viewer, "it is like watching…through a dark veil." Tiger could hardly wait for the introductory speeches and parade of fighters through the ring to be ended before acquainting his fists with Blackie's ribcage. He continued building up the pace in the second when he followed up a succession of poking jabs to Blackie's face with a damaging uppercut. The champion held on to Tiger for dear life. Badly out of condition, the best he could do was to smother Tiger in clinches and hit him around the kidneys. Tiger's swings, wild in instances, left gaping holes that Blackie was unable to exploit until a blow put him on the canvas in the fifth. But, wrote the *Daily Times* correspondent, "he was down for a second and up like a flash to resume the fight." The referee administered no count. It was the only blemish in an otherwise dominating performance and Tiger won easily.

The next morning's headlines in the *Daily Times*'s sports pages read: "TIGER BEATS THE CHAMPION." Although he had been far from the reckoning as a belt winner, the reporter had him winning almost every round, "if for no other reason than his aggression" adding that Tiger "was obviously the stronger man. In (him) Nigeria has a potential champion. He lacks skilled technique and general ring craft –but he punches with his weight and keeps on attacking. With proper handling and a lot more fights, he has a chance of going far."

Tiger had beaten the champion but was not the champion, the fight with Blackie Power having been a non-title bout. Two months later, Tommy West became the champion after forcing Blackie to retire at the end of the eighth round. He quickly defended the title against one Cyclone Duru in early May after which Tiger decided to issue a challenge. May the 27th was quickly pencilled in with the Victoria Gardens of Glover Hall the selected venue.

Tiger arrived in Lagos on the 25th of May, a toiling, sweaty Monday morning. As befitted the mounting war of words between he and West, Tiger's appearance at Ikeja Airport, dressed in combat fatigues and pilot shades, struck the right tone of out and out belligerence. Accompanied by Gikounou and

Okorie, Tiger smiled at the incessant questions that were being fired at him from the pressmen and with hand thumping his broad chest bellowed that he would not "allow Tommy to retain the title." On hearing about the performance, West, training across town at the Royal Hotel asserted that Tiger would not last the 12 round duration.

Tiger's preparation had been meticulous; The *West African Pilot* reported the presence of his unnamed European trainer (actually an Englishman from the Isle of Wight) who had travelled from Aba, to observe the West-Duru bout. While most observers were keeping an open mind as to who the victor was likely to be, others remained steadfastly unconvinced about his chances, feeling he "lacked polish" and the experience that West had garnered from fighting better quality Lagos-based opposition.

A heavy downpour caused the bout's postponement and relocation two days later to the Ikoyi Tennis Club. The delay may have contributed to the fights frenetic start as both men unleashed their frustrations on each other. Tiger scored with successive crashing hooks, which took their toll as West's legs gave way, collapsing on to the canvas for a five count. West was careful to back away from Tiger after this, utilising his longer reach as he boxed from the outside. Then the fight changed: West scored well with his jabs, which he rounded off with straight right hands or hooks. In the fourth round Tiger was on the receiving end of a left hook described as the "heaviest blow of the fight." Yet, he did not flinch and doggedly worked himself back into the fight to the point where West's replies trailed his by two blows to one. In the following round, he pinned West to a corner, dazing him with full-blooded whacks on the temple. The intervention of the bell probably saved West from being stopped. That, it turned out was unfortunate because Tiger returned to his corner nursing a sprained thumb.

West, Tiger was discovering, was a resourceful opponent whom he could not dominate at will. In the seventh, both traded punches toe-to-toe and remained on equal terms until Tiger, the pain from his injury steadily increased, began to back up until. Then with a sudden, jerky movement, he threw his hands up, to signal that he could not continue. Astounded, officials and a group of fans bounded into the ring and made straight for his corner where they carefully inspected the bruises.

The ending was an anti-climax and one which given Tiger's reputation for unflappability in the face of extreme physical pressures many later fans would possibly have a hard time believing. Comforting words of support came from the Lagos based members of the Amaigbo Youth Association, who held a fete in his honour. During the toast, he was advised to "accept defeat calmly and honourably."

He did not fight in Lagos for the rest of 1953. This development was unexpected and caused one sports journalist to express surprise at the fact that the promoters seemed to be passing up the big gate that Tiger, known to Lagosian fans as the 'Fireman,' was capable of drawing. He did however renew the rivalry with West in the New Year at the Collister Belt Tournament. It almost did not happen because the invitation sent by the N.B.B.C. stewards reached him at short notice. He requested that it be a non-title bout because he had not been in active training for sometime and appeared to be making his excuses beforehand by telling pressmen that he would not be fighting at full fitness. Tiger clearly felt obligated to the Board who were effectively acknowledging that he and West were the only middleweights of note in the country. Yet many still felt that Tiger was West's pugilistic inferior. A preview in the *West African Pilot* assessed his skills with the comment that "Tiger must learn to defend himself effectively." While he was a "strong puncher," his precision of punch was often poor. But while West was declared a points winner, one report maintained that many of the present observers felt that Tiger would have been capable of winning the bout had it not been limited to its six round duration.

So Tommy West, who won the senior category belt, defeated Tiger for a third time. Tiger would never beat West and for reasons best known to him, he would never acknowledge the feat, conceding only the points loss of the first contest but untruthfully maintaining that he defeated West in the return match for the Nigerian middleweight championship. (As per interviews that he held with the *Liverpool Echo* in 1958 and with the *Daily Times* in 1970.) The official records of Tiger recorded after moving to England were inaccurate and although a few updated versions have recorded West's technical knock out win, they still wrongly affix Tiger's supposed return title win.

Nevertheless, it is Tiger and not Tommy West who is remembered today. West, a doomed figure, would die mysteriously less than two months after their third meeting. His sudden passing on March 14th 1954 was the culmination of a bizarre set of sequences. The front page story run the following morning reported that a grief stricken West had been inconsolable in the aftermath of the unexpected death of his elder brother, refusing all offers of food and entreaties from family members to communicate. Two days after his brother's death, he collapsed in a feverish state and later died at the physician's practice where his family had taken him. Still only 22 years old, West had been due to leave for Liverpool the following month, hoping like many of his countrymen to make his mark in England.

Boxing professionally in Nigeria, for many, amounted to an itinerant occupation and this proved to be the case for Tiger. Fighting did not provide his primary source of income. He and his brothers continued their commercial activities, making a successful trade out of the sale of second hand goods. Together, they travelled around the towns and cities of southern Nigeria like Port Harcourt, Lagos, Enugu, Benin and Onitsha looking for car tyres, bicycles and items of household and industrial appliance which they went on to sell at the family stall in Aba market.

When in Aba, he continued taking whatever fights came his way. His bouts against Mighty Joe in June and Super Human Paul the following month ended in convincing points victories. He also acted as a mentor to various up and coming fighters one of whom, Silas Boko, he would later assist in migrating to

Liverpool. Life for him had become an altogether peripatetic experience, for when not a travelling trader he was a travelling fighter, partaking in boxing booth contests organised by the Alpha Carnaval which he joined at some point in 1954.

The Alpha Carnaval was an all purpose entertainment company run by Lebanese entrepreneurs that travelled the length and breath of the land, staging seasonal gala events, dances, beauty pageants and wrestling shows. Tiger, who occasionally frequented an Aba club owned by the group, was at one time persuaded to travel to Kano where he acted as a bouncer at Carnaval events. The Carnaval, in partnership with G.O. Olowu, also promoted boxing bouts in Lagos and various parts of the Western region. Tommy West in fact had made his professional debut in a match sponsored by the Carnaval. For Tiger, the rationale for joining the carnaval was simple, "I left Aba," he later explained, "because I wanted to keep on boxing –all the boys in the East (ern region) had been beaten."

The concept of boxing booths was standard fare at traditional English fairs; a troupe of boxers would be paraded 'outfront' as members of the audience were invited to lace up the gloves and try to go three or four rounds with any of the fighters. A cash prize awaited the contestant who was able to remain standing at the end of the allotted period.

At the funfairs, Tiger would stand to the fore of the booth, dressed up in the outfit of a cowboy in order to attract the attention of a crowd. When the crowd became sizeable enough and the spieling finished, he would disrobe to his boxing trunks and commence battle with a pre-selected local fighter. It was not quite what he had initially perceived as being "the boxer's life" but it did prove financially rewarding. From a career standpoint, the booths did not represent progress as such although he would admit that the experience did provide its learning points, such as being forced to adapt constantly to cope with the most awkward of foes. Altogether, his travels would take him to practically every major city in Nigeria including Jos, Kaduna, Zaria, Onitsha and Ibadan. His final engagement took place in July 1955 in

Abeokuta. These commitments together with his commercial activities were perhaps the reason why the N.B.B.C. in December of 1954, were unable to ascertain his whereabouts. They wanted to send him an invitation to contest the forthcoming Collister Belt Tournament and had just about given up hope when they received a letter from him informing them that he was still active and interested in participating.

At the start of 1955, Tiger was the number one ranked contender for the middleweight title still vacant after Tommy West's untimely demise. The N.B.B.C. matched him against their number two rated fighter, Raheem Fagbemi in a non-title bout. Fagbemi proved to be no soft touch; a left hook of his would send Tiger to the canvas in the second round while a looping left in the later rounds left him "staggering into the ropes." Both however were rare instances of success and Tiger's work rate made him the convincing points winner.

As was the case the previous year, there were no offers to Tiger from Lagos promoters. He continued his travels with the Alpha Carnaval, going to the Western Province where he was reportedly "successful in all his engagements." While it was clear that West's death had left him the nation's best middleweight, he was becoming increasingly frustrated by the lack of promotions, which effectively made him inactive.

This state of affairs was symptomatic of the times. There was an obvious dearth of middleweight challengers but also the fighter exodus to Britain that had continued unabated was stripping promoters of many marketable fighters who were not being replaced at a quick enough rate. Although amateur boxing continued to thrive in the numerous boys clubs, few seriously considered boxing professionally.

The promoters had remained as shrewd as ever when it came to paying their fighters, continuing to underpay fighters who by now were demanding higher purses. Flyweights, who once were content to fight for a rate of five shillings per round, by 1954, would accept nothing less than a pound per round. Once, promoters could have got the combatants in a championship bout

34

to share ten pounds with 60 per cent going to the winner and the remainder to the loser but by the middle 1950s, they were demanding the promoters make an outlay of 30 to 40 pounds. The result was stalemate because many promoters simply refused to give into the fighters. Although Tiger received news of a fight scheduled to take place on July 15th with a Lagos middleweight called Sunday Dudu, it was first postponed after a torrential downpour and later cancelled when the headliner, Gold Coast middleweight, Atu Clottey decided not come to Nigeria. The following week Tiger informed the press that arrangements for him to depart for Liverpool into the care of Peter Banasko had been completed. Not satisfied with his range as a fighter, Tiger knew that there were no more routes of progress if he continued plying his trade at home. It was now time to move on.

He had one more fight, in August, against Bolaji Johnson, a Lagos middleweight who had boxed successfully in the amateur ranks for Costains Boys Club. He knocked Johnson down, twice in the third and once in the fifth, on the way to a six round unanimous victory. He rejected the persistent demands of Cornell Ufibro who was keen to meet him before his left.

The Amaigbo Union held a party in Tiger's honour. Speeches were made and counsel given in the sort of farewell commonplace among the so called 'improvement unions' that sponsored young men and women going abroad to further their studies. A photograph at the time shows Tiger, as plump as he would ever get, sitting in front of a large group and looking quite dapper in suit and bow tie. On October 25th, he boarded the M.V. Aureol at Lagos's Apapa Wharf and departed for Liverpool.

Four
LIVERPOOL AND THE TAX

More than a fair proportion of African boxers –the overwhelming majority, perhaps, entered Britain through the northwestern port city of Liverpool. Liverpool was a city of immigrants, becoming the repository of the multitudinous egress from Ireland of men and women escaping the devastating effects of the potato famine of the mid-18th century. For the many who would settle in the 'New World', the city served as the first port of transit. The city was also the longstanding home to a large black and mixed race community. Like its west of England counterpart Bristol, it had been transformed from rural origins to a hustle and bustle beehive of commerce through profits reaped from the transatlantic trade in African slaves. The city's black population dates to Elizabethan times and was composed in the main of runaway servants and seamen; predominantly males, whose intermarriage with local girls produced a substantial mixed race populace; in itself a defining aspect of the city. Liverpool thus was confirmed as a major settling point for West Africans long before the wave of post World War immigration to the British Isles.

"I knew that if I could get to Liverpool I would be among friends," Tiger once reminisced. Allied to the sizeable number of settled African fighters who offered each other mutual support was a network of English persons helping to advance their interests. The resettled Douglas Collister, now living in semi-retirement in Blundellsands, a district situated on the outskirts of the city, was now a B.B.B.C. area steward and had been appointed in 1953 to serve as Nigeria's representative steward on the Empire Championships Committee. His efforts on behalf of West African boxers was recognised by the British fight fraternity who in 1954 awarded him the Arthur Tracey Sportsman of the Year Award in the non-boxer category.

Tiger would also become acquainted with Harry Ormesher, a betting commissioner from nearby St. Helen's who he later credited with providing him with much valued advice and encouragement in what he would find almost immediately to be among the most trying and discouraging times of his career. Bessie Braddock, the city's formidable Member of Parliament and for a time, the President of the Mersey Professional Boxers Association would take an interest in his career much in the manner that she had done with Hogan Bassey's.

It was a cold December's morning when the shivering, unprepossessing figure clad in t-shirt, slacks and pumps emerged from the darkness of the ship's gangway to clasp the outstretched hand of Peter Banasko. It was a rude introduction to the British climate and he would never shake off a deep aversion to the cold weather. As with other fighters, Banasko informed Collister of his arrival and after confirming his Nigerian issued licence, referred him to Arthur Ballard, then the Chief Inspector of the B.B.B.C. The Board then subjected Tiger to a series of medical tests which he passed. After this, his application was forwarded to the local B.B.B.C. Area Council for a 'meeting of enquiry,' that is, a meeting to assess a fighter's suitability. Satisfied, his papers were forwarded to the B.B.B.C. headquarters in London from where his British licence was issued.

Tiger of course was one of the many boxers who continued to come to England, but the volume of West Africans in the British fight game did not meet with universal approval. Four years previously, an article had appeared in the *Sunday Dispatch* asserting that British boxing was "going black" and that what was termed "the black element" needed "cleaning up." Its author, one Tony Horstead followed up with wild and unsubstantiated claims about a propensity for the fighters to becoming enmeshed with racketeers and rather bizarrely, that they engaged in the use of narcotics which he claimed afforded them the 'Dutch Courage' to engage in bouts. (Inspired by false rumours that the non-stop attacking style employed by Roy Ankrah could only have been facilitated by the intake of stimulants).

Such views, however, were by no means representative of the

majority of people in the boxing industry. Freddie Mills, the former world light heavyweight champion, for instance welcomed the influx of African fighters whom he said brought "an added dimension" that could only serve to improve the British game. Indeed, while Horstead and his ilk were frowning at what they considered an invading rabble, many would come to credit the West Africans for playing a major role in keeping the English game afloat during what may be termed as the era of the 'double tax.' Prior to 1952, a standard 15 per cent tax had been levied on the gross receipts of major sports like football, rugby and boxing. However, the supervening legislation that came into effect in September of that year increased this to 30 per cent (hence its tag). The effects were profoundly unsettling, within a few months over half of the promoting outlets for boxing were closed, most of them small and medium scale operators. The larger, established ones like the London based Jack Solomons and the Best family in Liverpool, survived only by cutting back massively on their events.

The extent of the ensuing turmoil is apparent from statistics that showed a marked diminution in the numbers of active fighters. While in 1949 over 5,000 boxers held B.B.B.C. licences and the number of promotions averaged 1,000 a month, by the time of Tiger's arrival, the number of licensed boxers had plummeted to just over a thousand with perhaps 150 monthly promotions.

For Dick Tiger, it was a new life. Directed by Banasko, he commenced training in the damp and drafty Professional Boxing Association Gymnasium located at Stanley House in the downtown area of Liverpool. The P.B.A. gym was patronised by many of the expatriate Nigerian fighters to whom he not unnaturally gravitated towards. He braced himself for the sterner calibre of opposition he would certainly be facing. "There are some good fighters at home," he would mention recalling his thoughts at this time, "but the scope was greatly limited." Tiger entered this new world firmly believing in his capabilities as a fighter. To have thought otherwise would, he noted, have been

38

"nonsensical."

A fight was soon arranged for December the 8th at Liverpool Stadium. This legendary establishment had been under the stewardship of the Best family since 1929, the year that Best senior sited the stadium's second incarnation at the location adjoining the city's St. Paul's Station. It was built like the equally legendary Blackfriars Stadium in London, to cater specifically for boxing promotions. With not a pillar or post in sight, spectators could view the action unimpeded from any vantage point. In the following decade, local heroes like Nel Tarleton and Ginger Foran entertained the boxing mad English northwest to a series of stirring contests against local and international opposition. Its weekly bills, staged on Thursday evenings provided a release for the drudgery of working class life. "It was always full of dockers," recalls Pat McAteer, for years a popular performer at the stadium. "If it was a local match or a local fighter involved in the main event, all the dockers would come. They were always noisy, shouting and screaming for the local guy –which Dick was incidentally. He was considered local."

It was on a chilly winter's evening that Tiger climbed through the ropes to face his first European opponent, Alan Dean. Dean hailed from Birkenhead, the district separated from Liverpool by the River Mersey, and was a regular on the stadium undercards. Described as "stiff legged and unexciting," he was the sort of journeyman opponent that Banasko hoped Tiger would overcome before progressing to the 'big boys.' The fight was a rude awakening for Tiger. He tried utilising his strong points, coming in close with jabbing motions that were followed by hooks to the body. But according to the fight report in *Boxing News* he was "often wild and short with his punches," while Dean "dominated the exchanges." Sitting in the stadium audience was Douglas Collister who later told him that he had made the mistake of not going forward enough and allowing Dean to settle down. The only significant success he enjoyed came in the fifth round when he backed Dean into a neutral corner and landed a solid right hand blow to the head of his opponent. At the end of six rounds, it was Dean's hand that the referee unhesitatingly held aloft.

Tiger's next engagement was held in the New Year at the seaside resort town of Blackpool. Here the Tower Circus provided an alternative to Liverpool Stadium. Against Gerry McNally, a Liverpool based middleweight, he performed a lot better than he had against Dean, scoring with snappy left leads and following with short right crosses. But while he succeeded in opening a cut above McNally's left eye, his opponent took advantage of his wild swinging, catching him with a steady stream of counter punches. Even so, the decision granted in McNally's favour did not accord well with the crowd who booed and catcalled.

Hoping for a change in his luck, he returned to the Tower Circus at the beginning of March to face Jimmy Lynas. Many observers felt that he had done enough to win, but again, the referee saw it differently from the crowd who were more vociferous in registering their disapproval than they had after the McNally bout.

He returned to Liverpool Stadium three weeks later to face George Roe, a middleweight from the midland town of Wolverhampton. Tiger's success came in the early rounds when his aggression continually forced Roe to back off, but as the bout wore on, Roe began showing flashes of skill; forestalling his rushes with evasive lateral moves and accurate jabbing. Time after time, Roe beat him to the punch and according to the report by *Boxing News*, was twice staggered by "heavy rights." Yet again, he swallowed the sight of the match official lifting the arms of his opponent.

With the darkness of a winter's evening around him, Tiger headed back to his bedsit a forlorn figure, his dreams of glory seemingly at an end. If, he thought to himself, he could not crack it fighting second and third raters, what hope was there for fighting for Empire and world title honours? Confidence utterly deflated, his instinctual feeling was he recalled, "to pack my bags and clear off home."

Words of encouragement, however, were forthcoming. Banasko, inwardly mortified, remained outwardly supportive. This was crucial, for had Banasko decided to drop him, a course of action that he was entitled to pursue, Tiger would have been finished. "Fortunately," he would later tell the *Liverpool Echo*, "Banasko never lost his belief in me. That would have been the last straw." In view of what transpired later, these comments were something of an overstatement.

Others added their voices. Many of his Nigerian friends urged him to give it another try and even the brain trust at Liverpool Stadium made a plea for him to continue. He came around to the idea of staying and toughing things out. But for all the ministrations of others, it was personal pride that proved to be the deciding factor. The thought of returning home a "failure" irked him no end. "To some extent," he recalled, "I had burnt my boats. I would have hated to have sneaked back home and admit I had failed my sponsors (and) I had to stay (to) justify their confidence in me."

A reporter had noted after his fight with Alan Dean, that while he was "a game and determined fighter," possessing "many bright ideas," Tiger needed time to "accustom himself to English standards." Yet while true enough, problems of acclimatisation encompassed a great deal more than a reorientation of boxing stratagems. The British weather, for one was a formidable obstacle in itself and Tiger, who was prone to perching himself in front any source of heat, abhorred the cold. He would never become reconciled with the wintry chimes of England and North America. Later, when he resided in New York, many would recall him attired in a large winter coat and hat during what were apparently summer months.

A great many of those of his compatriots who had come before him had faced difficulties in adapting to the climate. Israel Boyle had himself arrived during the bleak mid-winter and succumbed to successive defeats in his opening contests. Hogan Bassey, whom Tiger would refer to as having offered him advice on coping with the cold, would in his autobiography humorously recall his 'baptism in the cold.' Standing on the deck of the liner en route to Liverpool, he noticed what appeared to him to be 'smoke' coming out of his mouth and nostrils. He lost his nerve and bolted back to the cabins where a passenger acquaintance laid his fears to rest.

Added to these were difficulties related to readapting his culinary habits. Tiger, as was the case with other newly arrived West Africans, had been brought up on a diet of yam and cassava derived meals that were topped off with richly peppered vegetable stews. It took time to accustom oneself to what appeared to African tongues to be tasteless British food. He admitted that he was unable to "eat the food at the start" and may even have boxed while suffering from a mild form of inanition.

A humorous deviation from this generally morose episode is provided by Godwin Ihetu who insists that his brother appeared to worry not so much about his losing streak, which he was confident of reversing, as he was about the shipment of native foodstuffs like gari, egusi and stockfish, the task with which he entrusted his younger sibling. In time Godwin became so efficient at his chores that Tiger felt compelled to inform him at one point that he was over laden with supplies. Although he was resolved to continuing his career, Tiger would not be able to do this without the consent of the B.B.B.C., its rules clearly stating that a fighter losing four consecutive bouts was liable to be subjected to proceedings that could lead to the suspension or the revocation of his licence. A specially constituted panel of the local area council was set up to review his case and by the end of the session he had succeeded in convincing the stewards, among them Douglas Collister, of the viability of resuming his career. After renewing his licence, Tiger and Banasko set about the task of resurrection. There were many aspects of his game that were in need of refining, poor habits that were developed during his formative years in the Eastern Region. On visits to Lagos, sportswriters often made reference to his 'peculiar' stance as well as the 'take-no-prisoners' style that often left him vulnerable to counters. The undisciplined lunges and the careless swinging would have to be curtailed, or better still, be eradicated. While he strengthened his natural assets of power, aggression and endurance, he would also become aware of the defensive strategies rewarded by English judges. The 'make or brake' fight was arranged for May the third as part of the undercard bouts of Hogan Bassey's contest with Aldo Pravisani at the Liverpool Stadium. His opponent, Dennis Rowley, a Welsh fighter from Pontypridd did not last long: Tiger confused him with feints and jabs before landing a venomous left hook flush on his chin. Rowley was counted out after seventy-nine seconds of the opening round. One week after this demolition, he returned to the stadium. With only a few hours to go before the start of an under card slot of the British and Empire middleweight title bout between Pat McAteer and Jimmy Elliot, Banasko informed him that his nemesis Alan Dean was short of an opponent. Tiger needed little prompting. The contest made for cumbersome viewing so much as to compel the restive audience into two sessions of slow handclapping. Still, Tiger was adjudged the clear winner after eight rounds.

He made his first appearance at West Hartlepool's Engineers Club before the month was through. This was the venue where in Douglas Collister's words Nigerian boxers were "more popular than any other venue in England." Tiger was dominant throughout the contest; his punches carried authority and were more precise. He floored Wally Scott in the first round and for a second time in the fourth. Although Scott, blood streaming down an eyebrow, roused himself just as the count reached nine, his manager knew that he was on the verge of being knocked out and promptly threw in the towel. The fight was described by *Boxing News* as "probably (Tiger's) best performance to date in this country." He returned to West Hartlepool in July to exact a 'revenge' defeat on Jimmy Lynas.

Summer finally came and Tiger felt more comfortable with life. He was selected to play for the 'boxers' in their annual football match against the 'wrestlers.' Football was of course his original sporting passion, a trait that was not uncommon among

Nigerian born fighters, many of whom played in successive 'boxers' outfits. On this occasion Hogan Bassey (in a central attacking role), Sandy Manuel and goalkeeper Sammy Langford were fielded. Although the boxers succumbed to a 3-2 defeat, Tiger, in his role as an attacking right-winger, won the accolade of 'best player.' He was, noted Collister in his *Daily Times* column, "fast off the mark and time after time sent over centres that just begged to be converted."

But while Tiger was succeeding in resurrecting his career, there seemed to be little prospect of doing the same for the flagging boxing industry. The effects of the 'double tax' were biting as hard as ever, each succeeding week bringing news of the closure of one or more of the small boxing halls –the traditional nurturing ground of the future stars of the game. Fewer fighters were coming through the ranks and attendances continued to dwindle.

In the four years that had passed since the Act came into force, Best Junior, whose father had braved the threat of Luftwaffe air raids during the war years to stage a few promotions, and who thus far had contrived to maintain a regular schedule of bouts, was speaking of finding it "impossible" to carry on with the well established weekly shows at the Liverpool Stadium. Almost all the promotions held since 1954 had, he claimed, "lost money."

In desperation, promoters began canvassing a range of strategies geared to alleviating their burdens and surviving the financial stranglehold. One suggestion had them staging promotions as charitable events so as to qualify them for tax free status. Another idea had the boxers receiving their remuneration from the taxed box office receipts but neither came to pass.

Collister continually referred to the conditions in his articles for the Nigerian press, advising boxers over there not to venture to England unless they had made plans to obtain some form of employment: "Promotions are getting fewer and fewer," he wrote in a July edition of the *Daily Times*, "and while West Africans over here do get a share, there just isn't enough work for everyone."

Tiger, who arrived at the height of the 'double tax', realised that Banasko was having an awfully terrible time finding work for him. In the seven months between December 1955 and July 1956, he had a total of eight bouts – regular enough under normal circumstances but in the straitened circumstances of the era, remuneration was relatively little. So little that Hogan Bassey, a reigning Empire champion was forced to take on a job as an apprentice electrical technician at the British Electrical Company's local plant.

Tiger would have to wait three and a half months after fighting Lynas before Banasko was able to arrange another bout. "How I would have loved more fights," he recalled. One fight every other week would have suited him nicely. He could not, he felt, develop his skills when fighting haphazardly and considered actual ring combat as opposed to sparring, as the only avenue through which he could improve on timing his punches, keeping an appropriate distance from his opponent as well as his hand-eye co-ordination.

He ended the year with two bouts against Alan Dean whom he decisioned in November, after having dropped an unpopular verdict the previous month. He felt more settled, thoughts of fighting for the Empire title, and not merely for survival and adaptation, began to cross his mind. He was however pragmatic enough to realise that he was way below in the pecking order and that the prospect of challenging the holder, Pat McAteer, remained in the distant future. His future hopes now rested on him continuing to churn out winning performances until the B.B.B.C. recognised him as a viable contender.

The policy operating at the Liverpool Stadium was based on a system of gradual development –a fighter had to be seen to improve before 'moving up' a rung. "Alf McAvoy was the matchmaker," recalls Pat McAteer, "and they drew all the Liverpool fighters very, very well. Never overmatched you. I have always said that they could have got me beaten anytime they wanted by overmatching me. The same thing with Dick, they were bringing him along slowly and it was up to the individual whether he learnt anything from the last fight. Well, Dick learnt something from every last fight. He made it his business to learn the game."

Yet, if Tiger was learning, it was not apparent to Peter Banasko, whose interest in the game had been fading since the defection of his leading fighter, Hogan Bassey. It began on the November's night in 1955 when a haymaker punch delivered by Bassey separated Billy 'Spider' Kelly from his senses and his Empire featherweight championship. Such was the power of Bassey's blow, that concern grew over Kelly's well being. A priest was summoned to the ring, in anticipation of the delivery of the last rites. Fearing that the Belfast crowd might subject him and his fighter to a lynching if Kelly failed to recover, Banasko fell to his knees and silently prayed for deliverance. When, finally, the Irishman was roused, Banasko breathed a huge sigh of relief. All it seemed was well again, or so he thought. Shortly afterwards in the dressing room Bassey turned to him and curtly informed him that he wanted a change of manager. Banasko was stunned. 34 years afterwards at the prompting of English boxing writer, Ron Olver, he wrote about the incident "unexpectedly the memory of which still hurts today."

"I couldn't believe it," Banasko wrote, "I had fed him, clothed him, got him lodgings, trained him through nearly fifty contests to become Empire champion; a world famed fighter, and he wanted a change of manager. Our next fight could well have been a world title eliminator, but Bassey was determined. Outside influences, realising Bassey's potential and the money that they could make, lured him away while the offer of big money had convinced him that he wouldn't get much further with a coloured manager. Bassey refused to fight for me, so I had no alternative but to let him go."

One year later, with Bassey departed and on the verge of gaining the world championship, Banasko decided to sell the contracts of his remaining fighters. After informing the B.B.B.C., he broke the news to Tiger whom he would recall as been "very upset." According to Banasko's son Martin, Tiger's reaction on receiving the news was to burst into a fit of weeping. "My dad decided to pack in boxing completely as the manager not just of Tiger, but of several other boxers. His main concern was for people like Dick Tiger who had a very close relationship with him, and he was able to place him with another manager. I remember my mum saying that when Dick found out, he just burst in to tears."

For Tiger, it was another low, dispiriting period. Banasko, he would relate a few years later, had explained that it was futile to continue because "he could not obtain fights for me." But his comments to the *Daily Times* that Banasko had handed him his contract "because he felt that I was not doing well" appeared closer to the mark, the gist being that Banasko had little faith in his ability to reach the top. Years later, Banasko would admit to this, recording that while Bassey had arrived into his care from Nigeria as "the complete article," Tiger, who in the beginning had been "losing more than he was winning," had "shown no real sign of potential."

More than a few Liverpool managers clearly felt this way and Tiger endured a number of refusals. While Banasko continued making enquiries on his behalf, Tiger also had to cope with unemployment, a situation he would describe as being "desperate." With no money coming in, he struggled to pay his rent and to put food on his table.

His luck changed in March 1957, when Tony Vairo, a prominent Liverpool manager, decided to take him onboard. Born Anthony Valerio, the son of Italian immigrants, he and his brother Dom were World War One veterans who drifted into the boxing business. Both coached a number of fighters, one of whom defeated Jack 'Kid' Berg for the British lightweight title.

He ran a gymnasium in the Islington district of downtown Liverpool. Situated on the ground floor of Transport House, a building owned by the Transport and General Workers Union, it boasted the facilities of a full sized ring, sauna and full range of training accoutrements. Among the fighters Tiger joined in the

Vairo stable were Martin Hansen, a middleweight and the South African featherweight, Alby Tissong. Vairo also found Tiger work as a paint mixer in a local factory.

Michael Valerio, Vairo's teenaged nephew, watched and timed many of the sparring sessions at Transport House. "I spent a lot of my youth down there in the gym. Dick was a lovely man, a gentle person and my uncle Tony loved him –he thought he was marvellous. Dick was always very nice to me. I remember one time I was timing his shadow boxing and he said, 'Get in with me Michael and give me a round.' Well of course, all that he did was parry my punching. But that's the sort of the chap that he was, very likeable and very jovial. A perfect gentleman."

It was around this time that he met the man who would train him for the rest of his English sojourn, Maurice Foran. The brother of Chris 'Ginger' Foran, Foran was himself an ex-fighter. Redheaded and inclined to be a loner, he ran coaching clinics at the Professional Boxers Gymnasium at Stanley House in the Toxteth area of the city, a place Tiger had frequented often ever since his arrival. In the film documentary *'Profile of Dick Tiger,'* Foran explained the time during which he entered Tiger's life: "He had the basic things of a great fighter but he didn't punch correctly, he didn't move very well but the strength was there, the material was there of a great fighter. I started to help him because he was very discouraged at this point and I remember saying to him that if he could organise himself more he would do well in boxing. But at that point he was very disheartened (because) he'd lost a few fights and living conditions were hard, he had a very hard job and he didn't seem to be getting anywhere and I think he was thinking about going back to Nigeria."

As events were subsequently to show, the introduction of Vairo and Foran gave Tiger a new lease of life. Banasko had failed to bring the best out of Tiger not only as a trainer, but also as a manager. Israel Boyle, whom he managed, argues that he tied himself too closely to the Liverpool Stadium powers to the detriment of his fighters who were prone to stagnate. Vairo would now attempt to take Tiger out of the almost 'incestuous' rounds of the north-western circuit in order to test his mettle against highly ranked opposition from the south of the country. He secured a bout at London's Café Royal, location of the National Sporting Club, which was scheduled to take place in April.

A recurring bout of influenza hampered Tiger's preparations for his bout with Johnny Read and he was forced to pay forfeit for weighing three pounds in excess of the contractually stipulated 11-8. He had heard about Read and expected to be extended but instead had a walk in the park. At about the half way mark of the first, a left hook thundered off Read's jaw, sending him to the canvas. Read got up by the count of six but was soon swept off his feet by the same punch. This time he got up at nine. Read was barely in a standing position when another left hook left him sprawled on the floor. The bell saved him. Tiger floored him two times in the following round after which the referee halted the match.

As he celebrated in his dressing room, Tiger received an offer that would dramatically alter his career.

Five

REBORN

Mickey Duff, an ex-fighter and now the rising matchmaker for Harry Levene promotions, had seen Tiger lose by a decision. To him, Tiger's six wins-to-five losses record spelt 'journeyman fighter' convenient fodder for Terry Downes, the great hope of British boxing. "I thought I had done my homework," Duff recalled in his autobiography. "I had seen Tiger lose to a nobody in Liverpool and thought he was a perfect opponent –one who would make a show but wouldn't be good enough to win."

A lot was expected of Downes. He had taken up boxing during a brief sojourn in the United States, fighting for the Marines as well as in Golden Gloves competitions. His record was solid enough to have him co-opted onto the American Olympic squad bound for the Melbourne games until it was discovered that he was not an American national.

Vairo hastily completed the details with Duff, the bout being scheduled for May 14th -barely two weeks after the Read match- at East London's Shoreditch Town Hall. Tiger, like Vairo, was anxious to take the bout. It did not perturb him that he would receive £60 ($170) of the total £185 purse fee: He had consistently earned less than this on the northwest circuit. This was an opportunity. What struck him most was the extent of Downes' popularity and the expectations that were being dumped on his young shoulders. The only thing bothering him about the fight was his weight, the matter that had caused him to pay forfeit to Johnny Read.

On the morning of the fight, he stood on the scales and was stunned to hear his weight declared as being one and a half pounds above the stipulated weight of eleven stone and nine pounds. The room, filled with pressmen and assorted spectators, broke out into a general titter. He surveyed the faces impassively but inwardly he burned with anger. The promoters agreed to give him one hour to shed the excess. He spurned an offer to use the facilities of a nearby Turkish bath because of the weakening effects on the body and instead scurried around borrowing garments, which he piled on his torso before embarking on a furious workout. It proved just enough to make the weight.

Looking on, Downes had reason to be confident: Tiger's record, for one, suggested that he was up against a 'trial horse.' He had seen Tiger demolish Johnny Read but he reckoned the result had been hugely influenced by Read's lack of motivation on account of his impending emigration to Canada. Although Tiger appeared to him to be a "well built fighter," Downes suspected that Tiger's weighing in exertions would likely have left him in a weakened state.

Later on that evening, the hall quickly filled to capacity. The demand for tickets had been so great that "hundreds" were reportedly locked outside. Inside, the smallness of the venue ensured a semi-claustrophobic atmosphere as spectators, many of them sitting and standing shoulder-to-shoulder, crowded around the ring. Above them were a number of balconies that hung steeply, seemingly above the ring, the occupants, according to Reg Gutteridge "practically breathing down the necks of the contestants."

At the din of the opening bell, Downes sprang out of his corner throwing leather from all angles –aiming, Tiger surmised, to secure a quick rout over what he expected to be a weight weakened, muscle bound duck. Tiger held his ground until Downes waded into a powerful left hook, which deposited him on to the canvas for a seven count. At this moment Tiger would claim later that he knew his man was beaten. With indecent haste, Downes scrambled up, dusting the resin from his scarlet trunks. He was still in the process of gathering his senses when the referee yelled for both men to "box on." Outweighed by six pounds, Downes was yet to shake off the effects of the blows when in the second round another of Tiger's left hooks sent him tumbling over. But this did not finish him off. He gathered himself again and both men traded punches with some of Downes' combinations ending under Tiger's heart. The damage, nevertheless had already been done and while Tiger waited for the sounding of the seventh round, Downes' handlers, mindful no doubt about the effects that a prolonged assault would have on their youthful charge, decided to withdraw him from the contest.

"That fight, he found himself," says Downes. "He'd become acclimatised. He'd been stuck in Liverpool probably not eating properly and God knows what. (Afterwards) he went from glory to glory. I don't put (losing) down to overconfidence; I put it down to Dick being a good fighter. He caught me with a good punch and that was it." He recalls Tiger fondly; "He was a wonderful gentleman. I saw him in New York a couple of times and another time in Boston at the time I fought Paul Pender. Dick was always friendly and hospitable. We had a repartee going on between us. He would call me 'Mr. Terry' and ask me how I was and I'd tell him, 'Not bloody well, thanks to you'!"

Back in his dressing room, Downes, the irrepressibly loquacious wit, bandied trademark quips in response to the question being asked by the journalists. When one asked him whether he thought Tiger might have being too big for him he responded, "Yeah, he did look a big middleweight to me too, then I realised I was lying down and he was standing up." Another then asked him which opponent he would like to face next and Downes shot back a gem: "I'd like it to be the bastard who suggested Dick Tiger."

The fight was the breakthrough Tiger had sought. The result confounded pre-fight expert opinion, turning on its head the expectation that, as *Boxing News* put it, "he was a lamb waiting to be led to the slaughter." Vairo, who was now inundated with offers to feature Tiger in promotions around the country, proceeded to milk whatever publicity he could get. Writing to one publication, he boasted that Tiger had "everything to be a champion" and concluded that he could beat "any middle or junior cruiser (light heavyweight) in Europe." Jack Solomons wasted little time in contacting Vairo after the bout to offer Tiger a part on his next bill scheduled for London's Haringey Arena. Vairo in turn, wasted little time in accepting this, the most prominent promotion in which any of his fighters had participated in recent years.

Marius Dori, a Frenchman, would be Tiger's first ever experience of European continental opposition. He was not a particularly good one, using up practically every inch of the ring in an effort to keep Tiger at bay. When cornered, he was apt to cover his entire torso before sliding into an unceremonious retreat. Tiger hated fighting 'runners' but the problem Dori set him was solved by the seventh round when the referee intervened to end the bout.

He was back in northern England the following month at West Hartlepool's Engineers Club taking on a Glaswegian light heavyweight called Willie Armstrong. It was an experience that he could well have done without. After knocking over his heavier opponent on three occasions and dealing out a punishment befitting the three separate stitches that had to be placed above Armstrong's right eyebrow, the referee still adjudged him to be the loser.

While it is true that he had on occasion lapsed into the wild swinging forays of old, the official apparently found Armstrong's southpaw angled counterpunches to be more impressive than Tigers aggression. The crowd roundly booed the decision and Tiger quickly challenged Armstrong to a return bout, adding a £100 sidestake as an inducement. The offer unsurprisingly was not taken up.

There was much for Tiger to ponder further than the natural disappointment he felt at losing the bout. The opportunities that he had envisaged would flow from his defeat of Terry Downes were simply not materialising. The top middleweight fighters of the British Isles were giving him a wide berth. It spoke volumes that the only fight Vairo could get him at this juncture was against a fully fledged light heavyweight. "The trouble," as Vairo informed *Boxing News,* "is that we can't get middleweight contenders, so Tiger is having to take on (light) heavyweights and as a result suffers from a weight disadvantage."

Tiger, it is pertinent to mention, was not alone in

experiencing this particular sort of predicament. Several other black fighters from the Empire who were endowed with above average talent or who in other ways were earmarked as being 'dangerous opposition' faced problems in advancing their careers. In the middle 1950s, the Nigerian light heavyweight Sammy Langford (Idowu Olaoye), got so tired of waiting for the many challenges that he had issued to be taken up, he felt obliged to return home for a period of time. At home, he seriously contemplated giving up the sport but returned to England hopeful that his fortunes would change. They did not and his manager continually struggled to find him work. Atu Clottey, a fighter from the Gold Coast and perhaps a better illustration of a talent than Langford was ignored by his welterweight contemporaries and had to resort to the options usually taken by fighters facing similar problems. These were taking overweight contests and embarking on fighting tours to destinations outside of Britain the most popular of which appeared to be Italy and Australia.

A *Daily Times* article in November would pose the following question: 'Are Commonwealth Boxers being Fairly Treated?' The writer wondered whether there was "room at the top" for the boys from Ghana and Nigeria. "Five years ago (during the desperate era of the double tax), they were in great demand and used as hand picked opponents for British up and coming boxers. Today, at the mention of any of the commonwealth ring performers, managers weave a blanket of words round their charges for protection. Why did Atu Clottey leave for Australia....? The answer is simple: he had to fight and he had to live. Two years ago at the mention of his name, the homegrown English welterweights ducked for cover and still do. Hogan Bassey hit the jackpot, but how long did he walk in the wilderness before getting the kind of bouts that directed his footsteps to the world title? Today, Dick Tiger is facing the same prospect (of fighter's avoiding him)." Tiger himself would later comment to the Nigerian press that the " white boys are afraid of the black boys stamina." But there were economic considerations at hand; many British promoters feeling that black fighters, even the best of their ranks, rarely translated into substantive box office attractions.

Tiger's sights were now focussed firmly in the direction of Pat McAteer's British Empire middleweight title. But the champion's handlers it appeared were keen on avoiding him: When McAteer's manager, Johnny Campbell, asked Johnny Best Junior to arrange 'one or two' warm up bouts in preparation for a British title defence against Tiger's stable mate, Martin Hansen, Best immediately suggested a non-title ten round contest with Tiger. Campbell, however, drew a blank and Tiger fought on the under bill of McAteer's tune-up against a familiar opponent, Alan Dean scoring a decisive points victory in the fifth and last of their duels.

In September Vairo wrote to the Empire Championships Committee requesting that Tiger be granted official recognition as the leading contender for McAteer's Empire title. He also dispatched a challenge to the McAteer camp, offering to stage a contest at Liverpool Stadium. The message even drew up a precise date: Thursday the 10th of October.

While Vairo continued campaigning on his behalf, Tiger busied himself taking on willing opposition. In September, he out pointed Phil Edwards, the Welsh middleweight champion at Cardiff's Sophia Gardens Pavilion before returning there a month later to face a French opponent, Jean Claude Poisson. Poisson represented seasoned opposition and Tiger found himself often befuddled by what a writer referred to as his "elegant style and superb ring craft." The Frenchman however, had a penchant for hitting him with an open glove; a transgression for which the referee gave repeated warnings. This together with the fact that Tiger was able to land clean, solid blows accounted for the referee's choice of Tiger as the winner. The crowd booed the decision and while Poisson was cheered out of the ring, Tiger reportedly received what was described as a "mixed reception."

This decision may have played a part in Johnny Campbell finally agreeing to stage a bout between McAteer and Tiger. The bout, quickly scheduled for November would not, however, involve the title. Tiger was disappointed to fight a titleless contest but was quick to realise the implications were he to defeat McAteer. He knew McAteer very well having sparred many hours with him at the Campbell owned Birkenhead Gymnasium. There he helped prepare McAteer for an impending opponent who fought a similar style to his. Aiding a potential opponent while a generally rare occurrence in the game was, according to McAteer, an established part of Mersey fight culture "The Liverpool fighters and the Birkenhead fighters that were in the same weight category usually mixed with each other at sometime in each others career. We always thought that people down south (boxers based in London and south east England) got the best deal and all that kind of stuff, and if anyone of us was training for a fight with a boxer from London, we'd help each other. Dick was no different from us, we all did the same thing."

The fight took place at the Sophia Gardens Pavilion. To Tiger's chagrin, McAteer did not appear to him to have come for a fight, preferring instead to stay at a safe distance from where he stuck out a long left jab. He stalked his man, throwing left hooks and looping right swings. McAteer however caught many on his gloves and his shoulders and his wild missing manoeuvres left him frequently off-balanced and open to a right hand counterpunch. In the fourth round he presented McAteer with the inevitable opening: A relatively powerless right hand delivered in a chopping motion caught the incoming Tiger who fell to his knees. Instinctively, he bounced up to resume the bout to no count.

It was a rare piece of drama and the crowd grew increasingly restless. In the ninth round, the referee called both men together and requested that they make a fight of it; advice that Tiger would have felt ought to have been solely directed at McAteer. In the event, he used the impasse as an opportunity to rush McAteer and pin him to the ropes where both exchanged punches. McAteer emerged with an inch long gash on his left cheekbone, blood trickling down his face. Tiger continued a relentless but ultimately vain pursuit.

The drawn result brought a chorus of boos. Most blamed McAteer for his spoiling tactics. *Boxing News* commented that McAteer had boxed "with a nonchalance that bordered at times on sheer laziness." Most newspaper commentary however thought that McAteer albeit uninspiring in his performance, had won the fight: *The Daily Herald* and the *Sketch* thought that McAteer had the narrow edge, while the *News Chronicle* thought that Tiger was lucky to have received a draw. The *Daily Mail*, decidedly in the minority, opined that Tiger had won the contest.

"McAteer only boxed me," Tiger would later comment, "he did not fight me."

The fight amounted to a moral victory of sorts; Tiger after all, had not lost to the champion and Vairo again wrote to the Empire Championships Committee urging them to nominate Tiger for a title fight. Shortly afterwards, he received public backing from Teddy Waltham, the General Secretary to the British Boxing Board of Control.

While he waited for developments to crystallise, Tiger busied himself with a succession of opponents. Freddie De Largy was stopped in Birmingham, Jean Roellet was decisioned in Hull while previous opponents, Jimmy Lynas and Johnny Read were unable to last the distance.

A date was finally set for a title fight with McAteer on March 27th. His employers at the paint factory granted him a month's leave of absence. For Tiger the moment of fulfilment was at hand and he was determined to seize it. For a man who instinctually trained for bouts with a zeal often bordering on the fanatical, Tiger surpassed himself this time and amazed those who witnessed his preparations. In all, he accumulated 100 rounds of sparring at the Professional Boxers Association gym and at Transport House.

The bout was scheduled to take place at the Liverpool Stadium, a venue with an unnerving reputation for being the 'graveyard of the champions.' Best Senior had actually built the stadium on the site of an old churchyard, an act that had brought storms of protest from sections in the Liverpool community.

Superstition aside, Tiger had other things to worry about. The ring selected by the Stadium for one measured in at 18 feet –four feet longer than the length of rings to which he was accustomed. Ring size can be an important consideration for fighters when set against the 'styles' they adopt. A boxer who relies on mobility to achieve distance from his opponent by applying lateral movement with retreating manoeuvres, is apt to prefer the inherent advantages of space which the larger ring brings while the fighter with a combative bent, geared towards the employing of close fighting techniques is logically disposed to prefer the smaller ring where his ability to successfully utilise the technique referred to as 'cutting off the ring,' (applying stepping motions that shorten the distance between himself and his opponent) is greatly enhanced. The tactics employed by McAteer in the previous meeting would have weighed heavily on his mind. But if he felt disadvantaged in this regard, there were other areas which his opponent's camp were confident would work against him. The championship duration for one would be in effect and while McAteer had successfully negotiated 15 rounds, Tiger had not.

His other source of worry was his weight, that is, of his ability to reduce himself down to the championship standard limit of 160 pounds. It was and is the custom for boxers to fight their non-title bouts outside the demarcated title weight limits and Tiger had rarely been called upon to fight within the middleweight limit in most of his Nigerian and British bouts. What would have preyed on his mind was the knowledge that the maturation of the body over time diminishes the boxer's capacity to reduce his weight while at the same time keeping his strength. Aware, no doubt, of Tiger's problems in reducing before his bouts with Johnny Read and Terry Downes, Johnny Campbell was obviously indulging in psychological mind games when he pointed out that Tiger had never engaged in a contest at less than three pounds over the middleweight limit. Indeed many observers, including Douglas Collister, were doubtful that his naturally stocky physique would make it practicable for him to continue to campaign as a middleweight for much longer.

It was a day of the changing of the guard. In the early hours of March 27th, Radio Moscow announced that Nikita Khrushchev had relieved Nikolai Bulganin of the Soviet premiership. Tiger, who had watched two of his compatriots, Sandy Manuel and Roy Jacobs, win their preliminary contests by knockout, stepped into the ring wearing a deep blue dressing gown. The cheers from the crowd brought a brief grin as he strode purposefully around the ring waiting for McAteer's entrance. His thoughts tracked back to their last encounter, their sparring sessions and to the strategy he had devised along with Foran and Vairo. All were convinced that his priority would be to prevent McAteer from settling down to his classical boxing posture. He knew of McAteer's flaws. The champion was for instance inclined to drop his left hand after throwing the jab. McAteer also had a habit of carelessly catapulting himself off the ropes.

The opening rounds were uneventful, seeming largely to be a continuation of the pattern developed in the first meeting. McAteer constantly stuck out a long left jab at him as he retreated, while Tiger plodded forward, hoping for an opportunity to breach the champions guard. Five rounds passed and Tiger lagged behind McAteer on the judges score sheets. Fate, however, now dealt an intervening hand. The fans in the stadium, undoubtedly aware of the dullness of the first encounter, were getting restless and chanted for both men to slug it out. McAteer responded by adopting a more stationary position the result of which enabled Tiger to get in close to his man. A series of intense exchanges ensued. The crowd rose to this, roaring their approval at each hook, cross and uppercut. In the midsts of this clanger, fans of the champion worried at the sight of McAteer receiving a beating, beseeched him to "Box! Box! Box!" and advised him to "Keep away Pat!" But to Tiger's relief, McAteer paid them no heed.

In round six, two swift left hooks landed squarely on McAteer's chin buckling his knees and forcing him to gasp for air. The effect of this according to the *Liverpool Echo*, was to send McAteer "plunging across the ring like a hop, skip and jump contestant." Although now largely bereft of his customary ring elegance and poise, McAteer was able to summon attacks of his own. But when he caught Tiger in the nose with a full-blooded swing, retribution came swiftly with a left hook that caused McAteer to stagger backwards against the ropes near to his corner.

The end came in the ninth. McAteer now bled from the nose, his mouth was permanently agape and the strain on his legs was becoming intolerable. At the two minute mark, Tiger shot out a left-right combination that froze the champion, setting him up for the coup de grace, a sweeping hook that deposited McAteer on the floor. Tiger watched as he attempted vainly to raise himself only to tumble over into a heap. Referee Tommy Little stepped in to wave the bout over.

After he was roused, McAteer went over to congratulate the new champion. He recalls: "(In the first fight), I took him too lightly. I was training but my heart wasn't in it. He took me by surprise and they gave us a draw. The next time we boxed, he'd improved. People said to me, 'What punch did he hit you with?' and I said, 'I didn't see it, I was asleep'."

Still on leave, Tiger spent the next day relaxing and contemplating his future. It was the sort of future that the bedraggled journeyman bound boxer of one year past could only have viewed as a virtually unattainable dream. The reviews in the morning papers would have pleased him, his performance having received praise from previously disbelieving quarters. The *Daily Mail*'s Harry Carpenter for one had in the past been unimpressed by what he termed Tiger's "wild swinging." Against McAteer however, he noted that Tiger "hit with deadly precision and a calculating grimness."

There were those who felt that Tiger had reached his finite level. Of course, they argued, there was no harm in facing the top middleweight contenders and trying his luck as it were –that was his prerogative, but they felt that he was in essence a limited fighter who appeared to rely more on strength than skill. One journalist wrote that he could "come close" to winning a title but no more. Others like Douglas Collister felt him capable but were doubtful of his chances of continuing to make the middleweight championship limit. Nevertheless, enough support and encouragement came from British fight fans, promoters and sportswriters; all sensing, perhaps, expecting that he would in the words of a *Boxing News* editorial, "Bridge the gap that has existed between rated American and British middleweights since Randolph Turpin."

It was a gap that would not be narrowed if he continued to fight the likes of Billy Ellaway whom he dismissed in two rounds at the Liverpool Stadium. He needed quality opposition of the sort that could only come from the United States. A match with Gene Fullmer was touted and was looking a distinct possibility before the American came down with a serious kidney ailment.

In Fullmer's stead came Ellsworth 'Spider' Webb. Twenty-six year old Webb had been an Olympic teammate of Floyd Patterson's at the Helsinki games in 1952. He lost his light middleweight contest to the Hungarian Laslo Papp, one of the greatest amateur boxers of all time. As a professional, Webb had built up an impressive record and he came with an aura of formidability, which accounted for his British billing as the man 'other American middleweights would have no part of.' Indeed, Terry Downes, who would go on to fight Webb later on that year recalls Webb as been recognised on both sides of the Atlantic as the "uncrowned middleweight champion of the world."

While awaiting the fight, Tiger busied himself with a range of publicity chores. His new found celebrity status made him the subject of a four-part autobiographical series in the *Liverpool Echo* which traced his life from the water pump fight encounters in Aba to his victory over McAteer. He dedicated that triumph to Vairo, Foran and his masseur, Johnny McHale. Accompanying pictures showed an affable looking young man relaxing about his bed sit posing with his Empire trophy, his pet bird and playing records on his gramophone.

On May 20th he was in London, feted along with Hogan Bassey at a cocktail party held in their honour at the Nigerian embassy. Then in June, the cameras were invited to Maurice Foran's lair to witness the finishing touches to his canvas painting of Tiger. The portrait, Foran informed the newsmen, would remain "incomplete" until he was able to insert the world title bout he was convinced that his friend would win one day.

The fight with 'Spider' Webb would serve as a testing ground in regard to his credibility as a potential contender for such a laurel. A win would confer upon him the sense of legitimacy, which he lacked in the all-important American market. A loss on the other hand would give his detractors ample grounds for dismissing his calibre as being pedestrian. Most observers were apprehensive of his chances of beating Webb. According to one commentator, "Dick Tiger is not busy enough in between the punching periods to rattle up any great points advantage and Webb's record is too good to ignore or forecast an upset against him." The promise of the occasion for Tiger however, was underlined by promoter Harry Levene's pledge to "move heaven and earth" to make a world title fight with Sugar Ray Robinson if only he came out victorious.

One week before the bout, Tiger injured his left arm while sparring. Vairo was in a dilemma as to whether the fight should be cancelled or should go ahead. He kept the injury secret, opting for a daily course of therapy from McHale, the 'soother and charmer of aches and bruises.'

The fight at the Empress Hall did not provide for many sparks and was evenly fought. Webb, Tiger found to be very skilful and also quite an elusive man. His best moment came in the seventh when he followed up a body punch with a right cross to the American's face. Webb staggered backwards into a neutral corner where momentarily, he clung onto the top rope for support. He appeared ripe for the taking, but to the crowd's astonishment, Tiger failed to follow up. The injury preyed on his mind and had inhibited the use of his most potent weapon; the left hook. For much of the fight he was forced to rely on his right.

62

The chance was lost. Webb mounted an effective recovery and went on to receive the verdict.

'FAR FROM DISGRACED' ran *Boxing News*'s match report, which viewed the loss in terms of being a learning curve rather than a derailment. Tiger knew that it had been a narrow and relatively painless defeat and could see the positive side. He had afterall held his own against a man many considered the world's best middleweight.

Offers, for his services continued to land on Vairo's desk coming from promoters like Johnny Best, Stan Baker and Reg King. Another from Australia involved him fighting a series of bouts in Sydney. While Vairo mulled over them, he was hopeful that Tiger would be able to fight the winner of the impending contest between Terry Downes and Phil Edwards. Later, he would enter into negotiations with representatives of Clive Steward, the Australian middleweight champion, with the view to defending his Empire title in Sydney. Despite the welter of activity, it was apparent by August that none of the promoters were in a position to deliver Tiger with an adequate opponent: "There is neither anyone on the continent that wants Dick Tiger nor anyone available they want to put in with him," Vairo sighed.

The frustrations caused by the lack of suitable opposition and the searing ambition kindling in him had by now convinced Tiger of the need to make wholesale changes in the handling of his career. While he may have deferred to Vairo in public, the true state of relations between both men was far from being all sweetness and light. Much of this centred on Tiger agitating for Vairo to provide him with meaningful American opposition, that is, of the sort that would enable him to break into the world rankings. This he realised would not be achieved by engaging in 'dead end' excursions against the likes of Downes and Steward.

It had always been impressed upon him from the time of his arrival in Liverpool that if he truly wished to win the world championship, his ultimate destination would have to be the United States. Peter Banasko, whose indifferent career had perhaps in part have been shaped by the realisation that he would never be able to fight for the national title of the country of his birth, had been fond of telling his black fighters that sport, and in particular, boxing, was one of the few areas in American life where the issue of racial discrimination had been resolved to the to the extent that it compared more favourably to the situation in Britain: If you were good enough, you would not be denied the prizes or the purses.

On that score, Hogan Bassey was in a position to attest. The world featherweight champion, by now fighting regularly in America, was embarked on lucrative non-title bouts against the likes of former world champion Willie Pep, topping up the earnings he received for his championship defences. Bassey was instrumental in bringing Tiger to the attention of his American representative, Wilfred 'Jersey' Jones. In 1957, against many odds, Jones had contrived to get Bassey into the world championship elimination series that had been organised after Sandy Saddler had been forced into retirement because of injuries he had sustained in an automobile accident. As Tiger later recalled, "It was Hogan Bassey who suggested that I come to America and have Jersey Jones handle me. Bassey was (British) Empire champion at the time, but that didn't mean anything in America and Hogan was unknown. Jones had some strong opposition getting him into the tournament –there were so many other featherweights with better records- but he did it and Hogan went on to become world champion. Bassey convinced me that what Jones had done for him, he probably could do for me."

The transaction with Jones meant that he would not only be leaving England but would also have to sever his association with Vairo whom his friend, Foran had grown to dislike. "Maurice thought the world of Dick and vice versa," relates Jim Jenkinson, Treasurer of the Merseyside Ex-Boxers Association, "He didn't get on with Vairo because he said Vairo got him a job in a bloody paint factory. Of all the places to put him, with the fumes and everything." Foran for his part insists that he did not have a problem with Vairo, claiming, "it was Dick who didn't get on with him."

That aside, money may well have featured as a point of contention and although Tiger would not outwardly assert to being ripped off by Vairo, the brief measured reflection of his stable mate, Harry Scott speaks volumes. "Vairo," he says, "was a shrewd man." Adding the all too familiar pugilists lament that "boxers retire poor while managers get rich."

By the beginning of Autumn, Tiger and Vairo had settled on two matters: An opponent, Yolande Pompey was lined up on a Jack Solomons' package to take place on October 16th at London's Wembley Pool. Afterwards, he would depart for Nigeria for a long awaited break; this Tiger had insisted upon after turning down Vairo's proposal that he face Clive Steward in Australia, a month after tackling Pompey.

Pompey was a London based Trinidadian who two years earlier had made an unsuccessful attempt at wresting the world's light heavyweight title from Archie Moore. More recently, in his last contest, Pompey, who at this moment was the number eight-ranked contender in that weight division, had humiliated the great Randolph Turpin in a second round stoppage victory. The fight effectively ended Turpin's career.

Faced once more with the predicament of taking an overweight contest, Vairo had insisted that Pompey come in at no more than 12 stones. The punches exchanged with Pompey were particularly fierce and directed largely at each man's mid-section. At the end, it was Pompey, his face bloodied after ten hard fought rounds who came out the worse for wear and the referee raised Tiger's hand in victory.

The following morning's papers were unanimous in their praise of his performance; most seeming to place emphasis on his physical strength. Harry Carpenter of the *Daily Mail* wrote "There can be few men stronger than Tiger in this country today" while the *News Chronicle*'s Gerard Walker noted that "every time Tiger got home, there was genuine power behind the punch." The *Daily Telegraph*'s sportswriter opined that while "Tiger's performance may not have been spectacular, it was workman like and relentless."

At the end of the month, Tiger stood on the deck of the M.V. Tarkwa and waved goodbye to a few well wishers and pressmen gathered to see him off at Liverpool Harbour.

He arrived in Lagos after a two-week journey that took him through Las Palmas and parts of the West African coast. From a vantage point on the ship, he could see the enormous crowd lined up at the Elder Dempster Wharf. The Tarkwa had stalled some distance away in Lagos Lagoon and so as not to inconvenience the disembarking passengers; Tiger was allowed to leave the ship on a tugboat. As he stepped ashore, he was greeted by a number of government officials, members of the Nigerian Boxing Board of Control as well as by an assortment of boxers and promoters. He walked through the crowd, shaking hands and exchanging greetings while pausing at intervals to answer the numerous questions that were fired in his direction from the press. Then he beat a path towards a car that had been put at his disposal. A litany of honking cars and bikes followed the procession that lead to a hotel reception laid on for him by the Amaigbo National Assembly.

Clearly moved, Tiger told the audience, "It is a great experience to come back to one's fatherland after a three year stay in a distant country." Later on that evening he made an appearance at his old stomping ground, Glover Memorial Hall as the guest of honour at the Nigerian Welterweight title fight between Rocky Noel and Ezzard Benson.

The first day home was merely a taster of things to come. He would be feted at many functions and gatherings in Nigeria's southern cities. His itinerary in Aba over the course of a day took in a motorcade tour, a four-hour long civic reception at the City Sports Stadium followed by a cocktail party at a local hotel, finishing with a guest-of-honour spot at a boxing tournament. Similar schedules were rehashed in Port Harcourt, Enugu and Calabar.

Tiger had been compelled to come back home, not merely because of the homesickness that had gripped him throughout his stay but also to become married. In January he took the hand of

Abigail Ogbuji, a 23-year-old kindergarten teacher. She like Tiger was Anglican, the ceremony taking place at Aba's St. Michael's Church. When years later an American reporter asked him whether he had married for love, Tiger's reply was blunt and unsentimental. "You marry to get to have a family and to have a wife in your house. It is not good to marry for love." He also scoffed at what he perceived to be the intolerably subservient role that men played in Western marriages. "I see women tell men 'Get this! Do this'!" he would tell Jimmy Cannon of the *New York Journal-American* in 1966. "Maybe he just want(s) to help the wife, and he (does) it. It is funny, but it is the wife who gives him a smack if he does not do it. I say to myself, this is not good. But this is how the country is. Women have ten laws for them in this country and (men) only have one. I have seen men who work hard from Monday to Saturday; (then) they hand over to the wife. She is the one who opens the envelope to give him the money. Hand the wages over to a wife? To give a woman what you work for?"

Although imbued with a heavy streak of conservatism, he was not totally immersed in the old ways. For even as his wealth and status developed over the years, he would never take another wife or resort to concubinage, a well-worn practice of upwardly mobile Nigerian men. Abigail would go on to bear him a brood of children that eventually numbered eight. First to arrive were the twins, Richard and Grace nine months later. They were followed by Victoria in 1960, Justina was born in 1962, Charles a year afterwards, Joseph in 1966, Gloria in 1967 and George in 1969.

It seemed that Nigeria could not get enough of him and he felt obliged to add unplanned appearances on an almost daily basis. Thus what was planned as a five-week break would turn into a stay of four months. Back in England, there were those who were critical of him, seeing his extended stay as a misjudgement. Four months represents a large chunk of time for a fighter approaching 30 and they felt that he ought to have been 'cashing in' at this moment, the highest point of his career. A concurring Douglas Collister writing for his *Daily Time*'s column claimed that Tiger had "thrown away" three good purses. It had been reported in the sports grapevine that several promoters including Jack Solomons and Harry Levene had wanted to feature him on bills that they had scheduled for the New Year but Vairo had had to decline them on account of the uncertain length of his visit.

Unperturbed by the criticism, Tiger continued his tour, travelling to Ibadan where the Western Nigerian Council of the N.B.B.C had arranged for him to give an exhibition with Jimmy Asani, a popular middleweight. His day began with the now familiar procession through city thoroughfares after which he was the honoured guest of the regional political powerhouse, Chief Obafemi Awolowo. Three days later, promoter Jack Giwan, hastily arranged another exhibition. Mindful perhaps of the need to get himself into better physical condition, Tiger used Joe Quadri less as a spar than as a human punch bag but from the moment in the second session when he sent Quadri's mouth guard flying on to the ring apron until the sixth, he was forced to support his hapless opponent.

On Monday, February 16th, he and Abigail finally flew to London. The following day, Vairo received them at the airport and accompanied them on the London to Liverpool intercity carriage, arriving at the train station at 4.30 in the afternoon.

Vairo, Tiger discovered had been working furiously at securing him a series of fights against world title contenders. In January he had written to Britain's representative on the World Boxing Championships Committee, Onslow Fane, imploring the Old Etonian to ensure that Tiger receive a fair hearing in the event of a need to stage the world title eliminators that were expected if Sugar Ray Robinson was stripped of his middleweight title. Vairo turned to Johnny Best who was busy making preparations for Liverpool Stadium's annual Grand National Week Show, bouts which were held around the week of Britain's premier horse racing event, the Grand National. Best cabled Lew Burston, a New York City based agent, requesting that he send a 'top class' American as opposition for Tiger. Best by this time had given up hope of luring Sugar Ray Robinson to meet Tiger at the stadium and informed Vairo that the most he could hope for was to get Tiger a spot on the bill of the proposed super contest between Robinson and Archie Moore touted to take place in New York at the end of June.

Burston did deliver an opponent for Tiger, the Brooklyn born Randy Sandy. Tall and leanly built, Sandy boasted a solid if not spectacular record; the sort that Vairo hoped would provide the stern but tameable opposition that Tiger needed to overcome in order to break into the world rankings. Tiger would be conceding five inches in reach and height but would have reasoned that the American's eleven stone seven weight spread over a six foot plus frame would be no match for him in the area of physical strength. This proved to be the case. He plotted his way past Sandy's long jab, pummelling his torso with "complete gusto and relish." By the end of the sixth, he had succeeded in inflicting a cut above Sandy's eye. But to Tiger's amazement and the audience's dismay, it was Sandy's hand that the referee raised. Many in the crowd rose, voicing their collective disapprobation with slow handclaps and foot stomps.

Observers noted the calm, stoical manner in which Tiger took the loss and contrasted this with Vairo's outbursts in Tiger's packed dressing room. His world appeared to be in tatters when announcing that the decision "has made me seriously consider whether to quit boxing."

"It has been my life's ambition to manage a world champion," he continued, "and in Dick Tiger, thought I had the chance to achieve this."

For Vairo, however, the anguish continued. Two years had passed since he had signed Tiger and their contract was now up for renewal. Vairo, who had recently re-signed Sandy Manuel, now on a tour of Australia, may have expected Tiger to do the same, but when he broached the matter, Tiger informed him that he had made alternative arrangements. Michael Valerio: "I remember that he went back to visit his family in Nigeria and whilst he was away, my uncle Tony who had a co-promoter in New York, a chap named Mickey Vance,. was negotiating a bout with Sugar Ray Robinson. In that interim period while Tiger was away, he had actually clinched a deal with him. But unfortunately, Tiger signed with somebody, which made him ineligible to go ahead with the fight. When he came back, he hit my uncle Tony with the news that he had signed with another manager. And I remember this because my uncle Tony said that it was the only time in his life that he knew he had a world champion. But it took Dick Tiger another (three) years to get a crack at the title."

Some years later, a writer to *Boxing News* would claim to have seen a copy of a contract detailing the terms of a proposed bout with Sugar Ray Robinson. The agreement, which according to the writer was dated in 1958 apparently bore the consenting signature of George Gainsford, Robinson's manager. Yet even if true, the agreement would appear not to have been binding on the notoriously difficult champion, at the time in debt to the United States Inland Revenue Service, who consistently haggled with promoters over purse sizes far in excess of the maximum monies that would generate out of a fight with Tiger. It is unlikely that Robinson would have considered Tiger, then virtually unknown in America, as a viable money making exercise, and also, perhaps not worth the risk.

Talk that Tiger had thrown away the chance of a fight with Robinson would do the rounds in Merseyside for years, but what is more likely to be the case is that the supposed document purporting to be a contract to fight Robinson was in fact a contract giving Gainsford the right to be Tiger's American representative when as Vairo expected, Tiger would relocate over there. The fact that Tiger did not renew his contract with Vairo, automatically invalidated it.

Tony Vairo was devastated and felt bitterly let down by Tiger, although his nephew insists that there were no lasting feelings of betrayal. "He definitely knew that Tiger would be the champion and that was the most ironic part about it," he says, "but, I don't think there was any bitterness later on. They had made up as far as friends were concerned because business is business, money is money."

This may well be a sugar coating of the realities; Vairo afterall had been the one to assume responsibility over Tiger when other managers had shunned him. It reminded Peter Banasko of the unfulfilled promise of guiding his fighter to the denouement of ring glory: "Tony," he wrote years later, "must get all the credit for Tiger's rise to the top like me with Bassey but neither of us was there as we should and could have been when both became world champions."

The return with Sandy was held three weeks later at London's Wembley Pool. On this occasion, Sandy, having learnt a lot from the first meeting, went about matters in a manner designed to stifle Tiger; keeping his distance and constantly grabbing Tiger into clinches. His other tactic centred on mirth. "Sandy," wrote an onlooking correspondent, "often had the crowd roaring with some amusing antics. At times, Tiger was left standing in the middle of the ring while the American strolled round the ropes twirling his arms windmill fashion." Sandy joked in between the furtive, painless jabs he was throwing going as far as playfully patting Tiger at the back of his trunks at the end of the sixth. Tiger was visibly outraged. Although Tiger's persistent display of aggression won him the fight, the decision drew boos from sections of the arena convinced that Sandy's tactics had won him the bout. Sandy's manager was convinced that his fighter had won and he stormed towards the press section to solicit help in finding an official of the B.B.B.C. with whom he intended to lodge a complaint.

Tiger was nonplussed. All that mattered to him was that the loss had been reversed. For the last time in his career, he stepped out of a British ring and would now step onto a far greater stage: that of America.

Six
NOT A VISITING APPRENTICE

On May 22nd, with bags and trunks packed, Tiger and Abigail took an air flight from Manchester bound for New York City. Awaiting them was his new manager, Wilfred 'Jersey' Jones, eager to purvey Tiger with some good news. His planned bout with one Rory Calhoun would be going ahead on June 5th at Madison Square Garden but after that there was the prospect that he could soon be fighting for the championship. The National Boxing Association were on the verge of withdrawing recognition from Sugar Ray Robinson and were considering staging an elimination tournament of the sort which he had managed to enter Hogan Bassey.

Slightly built and gravel voiced, Jones was a youthful looking 61-year-old with a varied but long time connection to boxing. He had seen the sport from both sides of the lens; first as a small time boxer in his native New Jersey and then as a press officer with Mike Jacobs' Twentieth Century Sporting Club. Apart from handling a sprinkling of non-descript fighters, his vocation was in journalism, serving for many years as an Associate Editor of *Ring* magazine.

Alongside Jones, Tiger hired the services of New York born Lou Burston, an atypical cigar-chomping impresario. Burston was a veteran in the fields of prize fighting and show business. A soldier during the First World War, he had hung around in Europe after demobilisation, settling down in Paris where he would build up a lasting network of boxing contacts on the European continent and French West Africa.

During the 1920s, he developed his specialty business of importing fighters into the United States from areas other than Europe: the best known were the Puerto Rican lightweight Pedro Montanez and the great middleweight, Marcel Cerdan. His exotic connections perhaps unsurprisingly led to his involvement with the two best African imports; Hogan Bassey and then Tiger.

Burston and Jones hired Jimmy August to serve as Tiger's trainer, the role he had fulfilled during Bassey's recent excursions into the American market. Of Lithuanian stock and confirmed bachelor status, August's world had revolved around the fight gyms and neighbourhood fight clubs of New York City ever since he had been invested with his trainers licence in 1922. While most of the fighters that he had seconded had been decidedly of the run-of-the-mill variety, his career was speckled with loose associations to a number of world champions. In the 1930s there had been a one-night stint handling the middleweight Ed 'Babe' Risco and a longer one with Melio Bettina, a light heavyweight. In the 1950s, he began training a 17 year-old Puerto Rican, Carlos Ortiz, who later would develop into one of the great lightweights. Although one reporter assessed August as cutting the figure of a "dumpy, white-faced man with a rather sad air," most were struck by his congeniality and quick wittedness. His working relationship with Tiger, while fraught by the occasional arguments, would be a good and fruitful one.

Little more than a few days after his arrival, Tiger undertook his first training sessions on American soil at Lou Stillman's Gymnasium. Situated on Fifty-Third Street, this was the place for all the great champions – as well as the not so great. A daily procession of fighters walked up a straight flight of stairs and come to an open door from where two massive rings would be sighted. Over to the left, sitting on a stool would be Stillman himself. Above him hung a massive training clock. Working the bells round by round, all day long, Stillman would direct his guests to the 'appropriate' ring. A great fighter or a potential champion was designated ring one while 'lesser' fighters or those to whom he did not feel too keen on were referred to ring two. Around the corner of the ring were the benches where all the fighters and champions ranging from the newest aspirant to the great Sugar Ray Robinson would sit and wait their turns. Upstairs, the fighters could jump rope, punch the speed and heavy bags and indulge in callisthenics.

Attired in trademark all-grey, the sweating, alternatively

ferocious and smiling figure of Tiger became an establishment regular, sparring with the likes of Victor Zalazar, an Argentine middleweight and future opponent as well as the mob controlled Isaac Logart. This for Tiger was paradise. He was embarked on a learning mission not limited to his gym experiences: "In America," he later recalled, "I got good training and sparring, but, best of all I could go to many fights. I went to everyone I could. I watched and I learnt."

The likes of Logart and Zalazar were he found "more rugged and durable" than most of the men he had faced in the professional ring. "They keep me constantly on my toes," he said, adding, "you can't sit down (because) they are always pushing; fighting." His brief experiences around New York gymnasiums gave him first hand insight in to why the American fighter was largely superior to his European counterpart. "It is the training," he told a writer who visited him at a Manhattan gymnasium a few days before the Calhoun fight, "rugged, constant training that does not stop when you leave the gymnasium. In my country, you do some roadwork and fight others who like yourself know just the bare fundamentals. But here in New York, my manager has paired me off with all kinds of sparring partners: the aggressive, strong type; the veterans who know all the tricks; the fast defensive boxer hard to hit. Outside the ring, you work just as hard jumping rope, punching the bag and doing exercises to build up your muscles and reflexes. Outside of the gym, you diet, learn to relax and live clean." This aptitude for learning would continue throughout his career.

Looking on, with August was Jersey Jones. Although impressed by Tiger's grit and quiet confidence, he was quick to counsel August on those aspects of his game in need of 'improvement.' He acknowledged Tiger's possession of a "fine left-hook" but the priority now, he felt, was for Tiger to develop his ability to throw effective punches to the body. Although this may have been a true enough assessment, Jones, it seems pertinent to note, had an exaggerated concept of the English game as being one in which the fighters were almost loathe to throw punches to the area below the neck for fear that they would be penalised for 'low blows.'

"Things don't come quickly to him," he observed of Tiger, "But when he grasps them, they're here to stay." Tiger, he felt, needed "good, strong fights." Only by beating the topmost contenders would Tiger prove his credentials to an often times cynical American fight public which over the decades had grown accustomed to the 'horizontally' prone British fighter.

Over the years, some fighters had come over to America from the British Isles on what might be termed 'visiting apprentiships;' that is on mini-tours designed to match them against available, top American opposition. Most of these ventures (and highly speculative they were) met with little success. Pat McAteer, Tiger's nemesis, arrived a couple of years earlier as both national and Empire champion to embark on a three-match tour. He lost all of them. Tiger was well tuned to the realisation that his Empire title counted for little in American circles. Ownership of the title for instance was not enough to grant him the world contenders status that he craved. He was proud of his title and would make sure that journalists mentioned it, but he would never consider himself to be a typical British fighter. As he once put it: "I am thankful to England for improving my language, but that's all. I never heard of defence until I saw England in 1955 (but) since then, the Britishers have gone the way of the American slam bangers – and so did I." America however did not provide him with all the answers related to fighting knowledge and Jones' comments about Tiger taking time to grasp things may have alluded less to Tiger's lack of guile than to Tiger's strident separation of the methods and tactics that he felt were worth learning from those which he refuted. For instance, Tiger's view that he "copied" his opponent's style, that is, reacting to what his opponent did in the ring rather than trying to impose his own tactics, ran counter to the received wisdom taught in boxing gymnasiums. Later, when he was asked why he trained his sights on an opponent's gloves rather than on his opponent's eye, which boxers are taught to do in order to predict the launch of their opponent's punches, Tiger famously retorted "nobody ever hit me with their eyes."

The match with Rory Calhoun now came. It was the day Fidel Castro's five-month old regime announced the expropriation of large-scale American interests in Cuban sugar mills and plantations. For the first of many occasions, Tiger stepped into the illustrious setting of Madison Square Garden. Someone informed him that the Garden, as was the case with Liverpool Stadium, had a cache of its own superstitions. A fighting debutant, one parable went, was liable to be 'bewitched, bothered and bewildered.' He smiled his usual sweet smile and set about his business.

The fight itself turned out to be anything but a baptismal of fire. He impressed the curious Friday night crowd with a solid display of persistence and aggression. He consistently beat Calhoun to the punch, his salvos inspiring intermittent applause. The decision however ached; the judges scoring it a draw. This however was unpopular with the crowd and with most of the fight reviewers.

The rematch the following month at the Syracuse War Memorial Auditorium followed much the same pattern. Tiger was the dominant party in the exchanges, yet it ended in still more disappointment for him, this time a split decision loss. The crowd here was more demonstrative of its feelings than the Garden audience had been. Loud boos echoed around the arena as fight programs and items of paper landed in Calhoun's corner.

Tiger paused to take it all in. A draw and a loss were not the best of starts. In the recesses of his mind he may have begun thinking that this was Liverpool all over again. But he could find comfort in the fact that his performances were not at all bad.

Jones proceeded on the basis that he would match Tiger with any of the available top contenders. There would be none of the calculated opponent picking typically indulged in by managers – there simply would be no time for that. Tiger was past his 30th birthday and with no foreseeable route to a championship fight, it would be a question of him impressing the boxing fraternity by beating as many of the top contenders as he could lay his fists on and in effect 'force the issue.'

His next couple of opponents bore this out. First was Gene Armstrong, rated fifth in the world rankings and so far unbeaten as a professional. The fight proved that August's lessons were bearing dividends. Tiger's efforts seem to be concentrated on mounting a persistent attack around the ribcage of his foe. In the third round he floored Armstrong for the first time in a 17 fight career that was spread over four years. The overwhelming points victory that ensued signalled his arrival into the official world rankings.

Next came Joey Giardello, a seasoned campaigner, and like Tiger 'ageing' and anxious for a tilt at the championship. This would be the start of a series of four contests between both men. Nobody fought Tiger for as many rounds as did Giardello who has nothing but the fondest of recollections of the man.

"When I first fought him I said 'Dick Tiger? Who the hell is Dick Tiger? They said 'You wanna fight Dick Tiger?' and I said 'I don't care but who is he?' I didn't know who he was but by the fifth, sixth round, I saw who he was! He was very, very tough and always in good shape. We went two fights apiece and I'm glad. I thought he was a gentleman. If you hit him low or something, he never ever put the baloney on. I always thought he was a great guy." Like his opponent, few in the Chicago Stadium audience were familiar with the name of Dick Tiger and even less with his fighting history. His introduction by the Master of Ceremonies barely elicited a response. Although he swung a fair amount of off-target left hooks, he landed enough solid blows to impress the judges enough to award him a unanimous decision. Then came a set back. Jones accepted the rematch proposal from Giardello's managers and Tiger lost the decision. Many in the audience of the Cleveland Arena booed and whistled. Tiger sustained a rare cut, the result, he claimed, of Giardello's sneaky head butts.

The crusade continued. Tiger won his next three bouts decisioning Holley Mims and Gene Armstrong at Chicago Stadium and then his erstwhile spar mate Victor Zalazar at the

Boston Arena. They were all top-ten contenders and served as confirmation of the legitimate claim that he had to fight for one of the titles. Jones' entreaties however to Gene Fullmer, recent victor in the bout to determine the N.B.A's successor to Sugar Ray Robinson were rebuffed.

The title had now fractured. The middleweight division, even in times when the games sanctioning bodies appeared to operate with relative cohesion, now had two champions. Fullmer had garnered N.B.A. approval after beating Carmen Basilio in August of 1959, while Paul Pender, a fireman from Boston, won recognition from the state of New York and the European Boxing Union (E.B.U.), when he outpointed Robinson on January 22nd 1960. Pender, like Fullmer, was not interested in taking Tiger on, admitting to one sportswriter that Tiger "is one of those fighters who just keeps coming. They are the kind you don't fight unless you have to."

Tiger in the meantime was in the process of becoming one of the most recognised faces among American fight fans; this courtesy of the 'box.' It was still the era of saturation coverage. Although a number of the networks had stopped their telecasts; CBS and ABC had dropped their slots in 1955 while DuMont had gone out of business in 1958, NBC continued to broadcast its 'Fight of the Week' programme on Friday evenings.

This partnership between boxing and television was one that would not have achieved the intensity that it did but for the influence of the International Boxing Club, a cartel headed by Jim Norris. After inheriting the monopoly which Mike Jacobs' Twentieth Century Sporting Club had held over the heavyweight championship, the IBC proceeded to fashion a stranglehold over much of the game and the agreements reached between Norris and the television companies served to buttress this grip. The consequences were decidedly in the negative. Many assert the malign influence of television in bringing in fickle audiences while robbing the neighbourhood clubs and local arenas of their natural constituency. Even the Garden suffered. In 1950, the year in which the IBC was inaugurated, attendances had averaged

8,849 per bout, but by 1959, they had plummeted to 2,371. Fighters purses were also hit, although ironically, Tiger would only have noticed the great improvement American wages were when compared to the almost derisory sums he had only recently being earning in England. The $6,500 earned from the Calhoun fight exceeded every single payment he had received from a promoter.

That bout had been covered by NBC and at the end of 1959, all six of his bouts had being televised, more than any other fighter, save the ubiquitous Mexican welterweight, Gasper 'Indian' Ortega. However, Tiger ranked 12th in the end of year top T.V. fighter poll that was headed by Sonny Liston.

Tiger's English fans caught up with his progress on the BBC's Saturday afternoon sportscase, Grandstand and avidly devoured all of his fights. One newspaper journalist however spotted a drawback to the level of exposure which he was receiving on American television. Each succeeding performance, while strengthening his title claims, heightened the threat that he posed to the champions. Hogan Bassey's passage to a championship shot was decidedly the easier since he was relatively unknown to his foes. With Tiger, it was perhaps a case of the potential opposition knowing too much about him too soon.

He and Abigail set up home in a small suite in the Colonial Hotel, a modest establishment situated in Manhattan's Upper West Side district. He would continue to patronise this place, on and off, for the next decade. The rooms were sparsely furnished and they cooked their meals on a hotplate. Abigail, who had left Liverpool in the early months of her first pregnancy gave birth to a set of twins in September 1959, in the week that he faced Joey Giardello. The boy and girl were christened Richard Chimezie and Grace.

Tiger would go on record as stating his preference for America to England, one British journalist quoting him as saying that he did "not like England." New York City, with its glamorous skyscrapers, the green expanse of Central Park (which would

79

form a constant training patch for Tiger) and its overall amenities shaped up to be more than a few rungs above Liverpool. Abigail found Americans to be more open and friendlier.

On occasion after finishing his training at Stillman's, Tiger would meet up with his old foe, Patrick McAteer, who was now settled in the States with his American born wife. "We had a few coffees at the Madison Square Garden cafeteria and enjoyed each other's company," McAteer recalls. "Stillman's gym was up on 58th Street, the Garden was down at 50th Street and right across the street on Eighth Avenue was the Garden cafeteria. We'd talk about old times in Liverpool, we'd look at the girls and say 'How 'bout that cutie over there.' His accent was strange to the Americans, (but), I think everybody respected him. It was hard not to respect Dick. He was a nice guy, patently just a nice guy."

Americans were indeed fascinated by the "short, chunky man with blue tribal tattoos etched across the knotty muscles of his chest and back." A curiosity piece, in the ring as well as out of it, Tiger would provide the sports hacks of New York with a steady amount of copy. His image, the like of which they had not seen before, was striking: A dark skinned African man frequently sighted with a trademark homborg hat and Anthony Eden coat. They wrote often of the incongruity of on the one hand his tribal marks and on the other, the formal, quasi-Anglicised accented speak.

Throughout his career, he endured a seemingly never ending ritual of questions and commentary about the African continent by journalists and others, intrigued by popular tales of the 'Dark Continent.' Wrote Milton Gross, the syndicated sports columnist in the wake of Tiger's death: "He listened and patiently tried to answer some of the stupid questions put to him by boxing reporters. To many of us insulated and isolated in what had been our affluent society, Tiger was a curiosity from a world which few of us understood or really tried to understand...He tried to explain the geography, economics and language of his country." To little apparent avail. Tiger, Gross observed, however, did not succumb to emotional outburst, writing that he would occasionally "be annoyed by our inanities, sometimes amused but never angry."

It became part of the daily grind and he developed a repertoire of responses. To those who presumed that his moniker related somehow to exploits in the great jungle, he informed that "there are no Tigers in Africa – only in Asia" and "I never saw a Tiger until I looked at one in Liverpool zoo."

If we are to believe comments made in the later part of his career, Tiger accepted what he termed his 'Tarzan image' because it made for good business at the box-office. In 1962 he told Nat Loubet that he considered the jokes and the banter about jungles, cannibals and headhunters as "good-natured joshing." So when people asked him what he had eaten for breakfast, he replied with exaggerated flourish "Hew-mon Bee-inks, medium rare." On the occasion when a very largely built New York City policeman visited his training camp, he was asked if Nigerian constables were that large. Smilingly he replied, "Oh sure, 'cause for breakfast, they eat guys like him." The incessant queries about cannibalism prompted the quip "We quit that years ago when the Governor-General made us sick."

There were occasions, however, when his response did not refer to humour. Days after the infamous slaying of black civil rights martyr Medger Evers, he referred to the "cannibals who shoot you in the back." The reality all along was that Tiger was offended and in certain instances felt quite aggrieved by these jokes. The level of ignorance with which he was confronted disappointed him. In 1965, he would go so far as to announce that he would refuse under any circumstances to be photographed standing near trees. He began correcting Americans when they spoke in unconsciously patronising ways. When for instance a person referred to "the natives" of his homeland, he was quick to interject with "people." There were instances when he was sorely tested and found it necessary to direct sharp comments towards the likes of Jones and August when he felt that their words were out of order.

Another area that journalists seized upon, and with a good

measure of justification, was Tiger's perceived frugality this, a reputation immortalised by Charlie Goldman's quip that "Dick Tiger wouldn't pay a quarter to see an earthquake." Tiger, they wrote, had a penchant for inexpensive suits which one journalist would describe as being akin to "Salvation Army hand-me-downs." The recollections of Sam Toperoff in a *Sports Illustrated* article about a walk in the company of Tiger around Manhattan prove illuminating. "His brown suit," wrote Toperoff, "was on the shabby side, the jacket a shade lighter than the pants; his black shoes had grey scuffs."

After Tiger delivered a parcel at a post office, both men stopped in front of a tailor's shop. As Toperoff relates, "He went inside, and I followed. He pulled off his suit jacket and showed the man behind the counter a long tear in the satin lining. The owner persuaded Tiger that it would be better to select a second hand jacket from the racks in the rear than to have his own jacket repaired. Tiger and the tailor disappeared. When they returned, Tiger was wearing another brown jacket, a shade darker than the pants this time. The man wanted $5. They settled on $2.50, his old jacket and a ticket to the (Rocky) Rivero fight."

"He was always considered a very tight man with money and intimacies," wrote Robert Lipsyte in 1969. And Les Matthews, a columnist with the *New York Amsterdam News* recalled that Tiger "enjoyed walking because it saved money."

"He was a very frugal guy," recalls Gil Clancy, trainer of Emile Griffith, "You know, he's still wearing the same old winter overcoat for about three years despite how much money he made. He'd send it all back to Nigeria; he was a very stolid, steady guy."

"He always wore that same overcoat and hat," remembers Tommy Kenville, a publicist at Madison Square Garden. "I don't think that he ever bought another overcoat or hat in his life."

But Tiger was steadfast in refusing to measure his worth in this manner. "Clothes will not make me a better man or a better fighter," he once reposted. "Which is more important –how I dress or how I fight (and) look after my children?" On other occasions a wit and down-to-earth practicality came through.

Once, after he had won the championship, Jones and others were ribbing him about his penny-pinching ways. Now that he was a champion, they suggested that he buy his wife a mink fur coat. "Guys," he replied, "I told you that I was from Nigeria, not Siberia." Ron Lipton, a friend and sparring partner will hear nothing of claims of 'tightness.' "I don't think its true," he says. "He knew that some day, the boxing would be over and he was somewhat afraid that he wouldn't earn a decent living. I don't think he was tight with money because he didn't spend it on himself. I think he really took care of his family and I couldn't stand anyone saying he was cheap. He was a very decent, generous person."

Many were struck by the outwardly calm demeanour referred to by Gross and he exercised great restraint in the face of a great many provocations. But like any other man, he was capable of the odd angry mood. "Dick did have a little bit of a temper," Lipton recalls. "It wasn't a screaming temper but his face would change. If he got upset his whole body and face would change. You knew when he was upset with someone because he was always smiling, so when you saw him cloud up like that, you knew like you better step away from him for a while. I was sitting next to him at the Johnny Persol-Henry Hank fight in 1964 and then somebody walked by and mentioned something about one of the middleweights, 'Oh, he'll kick your ass' or something like that. He was smiling at me and then he looked up. I could see the change in the face. He knew that it was just a stupid fan but you could see (him thinking) 'I'd like to hit this guy a left hook.' He would never do that but I'd say 'There it is.' I was always wondering what would push his button."

Impressions of the man would over the years develop into a positive one. For if Battling Siki, the first world champion from the African continent, epitomised crude, stereotypical notions of the inarticulate savage, filled with sexual and social malevolence, then the genteel restrained bearing of Dick Tiger represented his antithesis. Tiger, like Hogan Bassey, placed great emphasis in projecting images of gentlemanly refinement that was reflected in the way they spoke and dressed. "I would say Sir, that Mr. Pep has most unusual ideas about the rules," Bassey told a startled sportswriter when questioned about the unorthodox (read: illegal) tactics the former featherweight champion had employed against him during their 1958 non-title bout at Madison Square Garden. Tiger's characteristic reticence though, contrasted markedly with Bassey's natural ebullience and his quietness led some, like Joey Giardello, to believe that he was unable to speak the English language, at least in the earlier stage of his U.S. career. He had been campaigning there for five years when after his bout with Rubin Carter, a group of New York writers went up to the English boxing broadcaster, Reg Gutteridge, to ask if Tiger spoke any English. Later, in Tiger's dressing room, Gutteridge informed him of the query:

"Womba,womba Mr.Ihetu, they want to know you speaka English?"

Grinning widely, Tiger quipped:

"Tell them much better than they do"

Tiger barely had time for rest between his fights. In the ten months elapsed since arriving in America, he fought on eight occasions. He decided that it was time for a break. After fighting Victor Zalazar in April 1960, he took Abigail and the children to Aba. Jones announced at the time that Tiger would not fight for the next "two or three months." He was finding it hard to set up fights for Tiger. He told the British press that Tiger had been "quite excited" when Mickey Duff had sent word of his willingness to stage a bout with Terry Downes, but that no more had been heard from Duff.

A couple of weeks after Tiger's departure, Jones received news of an edict issued thousands of miles away in London by the Empire Championships Committee ordering Tiger to defend his Empire title, dormant for two years since he had won it from Patrick McAteer, within 'three months' failing which they would declare the title vacant.

Jones was approached soon after by a consortium of

Canadian businessmen headed by a promoter, Moe Gundersson. They reached a tentative agreement for Tiger to defend the title against Wilf Greaves, the Detroit based Canadian Middleweight champion and gold medal winner six years earlier at the Empire Games held in Edmonton. Jones then entered into a verbal contract with Greaves' manager, one C.W. Smith, a tool-manufacturing magnate, under which Tiger and Greaves would split 60% of the proceeds from the gate with Tiger receiving the larger share.

Tiger returned from Nigeria in late May to put his signature to the agreement. He arrived at Edmonton Airport on June 15th, with August in tow. He smiled for local pressmen as he posed with a soft toy Tiger perched on his luggage. Then he made his way to the city's luxurious Airlines Hotel, which would serve also as a training camp. He retired early and was up at 6 a.m. to commence roadwork. In the afternoon, he sparred with a local fighter called LeRoy Flammond before completing a routine set of exercises. He kept this up until the weekend.

The local press, eagerly covering the fight build up, hungrily gathered titbits on the stranger in their midst. In his column for the *Edmonton Journal*, Tom Harris wrote that Tiger "speaks English amazingly well, carries a good conversation which he punctuates with wide grins and an intense look of concentration, and has a penchant for goulash and spaghetti." Harris perhaps was unaware that Tiger came from an English-speaking nation. But while Harris' impressions of Tiger's speaking ability were high, some of his colleagues preferred to quote him using an accent more appropriate to a Tarzan movie. At a photo session at the Airlines Hotel kitchen, a writer asked Tiger which parts of the menu he wanted to eat. Tiger's reply was quoted as "I not want dessert now. We feed piece like that to cat back home."

On the Monday afternoon that preceded the Wednesday fight date, Tiger had to abandon plans for his last scheduled work out. Instead, at Gundersson's instigation, he visited the local racetrack in order to promote the bout, which was being plagued by slow ticket sales. The sixth race of the day was named the 'British

Empire Purse' and Tiger dutifully presented the winning jockey and trainer with tickets for the fight.

The crowd of 3,360 spectators who turned up at the Edmonton Exhibition Gardens was well below the 9,000 Gundersson had envisaged. Tiger fought tentatively: He had never before been scheduled to go 15 rounds. Not even Greaves' obnoxious pre-fight promise to chase him out of the ring "all the way back to that homestead of his in Nigeria" appeared to have riled him enough to make a faster start. This gave Greaves the edge in the early stages. But Tiger rallied as the bout wore on and the bout ended with him subjecting the Canadian to immense pressure.

When it was over, referee Johnny Smith and the judges, Louis Schwartz and Les Wilcox handed their scorecards to the officials representing the Edmonton Boxing Commission. They were tabulated and the decision was announced as a draw. Tiger had retained his title. Or so he thought.

Few eyebrows were raised at the verdict. The crowd remained calm while the outward expressions of Greaves and his handlers betrayed to onlookers no more than the usual disappointed countenance. The spectators were beginning, slowly, to drift out of the arena and two journalists working for the *Edmonton Journal*, sports editor Hal Pawson and boxing correspondent Tom Harris, were eager to join in the exodus. Pressed against them as they struggled to get out of the congested press row area, were two top officials of the commission. Pawson turned in the direction of the commission table where before his eyes lay the fight scorecards. He recounted the subsequent happenings in his 'Sporting Periscope' column in the next day's edition of the paper:

"The check was not so much intentional as impossible to avoid (with) the four of us squeezed so closely together by the mob around ringside. It was help with the cards or the pickpockets; we were that jammed."

"It was only a matter of seconds before we realised something was wrong with the decision as announced. Dr. Louis

Schwartz's card, for instance, was marked and announced as nine to six rounds in favour of Tiger. One glance made it plain that something was wrong, for at least six rounds stood out as even."

"The quick recheck showed that judges card really to be six rounds for Tiger, three for Greaves and six even. That called for further investigation. Dr. Les Wilcox's card came out as announced, seven rounds for Greaves, five for Tiger and three even."

"That left it up to the recheck of (Johnny) Smith's card. It came out on first quick check as six rounds for Greaves, four for Tiger and five even. However, it was sweat soaked and blood smeared and later checking with Johnny, it boiled down to one round, which at first glance appeared even being in Tiger's favour, making the final count six for Greaves, five for Tiger and four even. His points came out as seventy to sixty nine for the home boy."

Excited by their discovery, Pawson and Harris sought C.W. Smith who then informed Graham of the discrepancy. Graham now called members of the Edmonton Commission to an emergency meeting, while the Commission's Secretary, William 'Spud' Murphy, took hold of his briefcase and scrambled for a copy of the organisation's rulebook.

Quick to get wind that something was wrong, Jones began running towards Graham and his colleagues, shouting, as he approached. He was told to wait alongside C.W. Smith until they finished with their deliberations. Referee Smith, Schwartz and Wilcox were all summoned and asked to recheck their scorecards.

Half an hour passed before the door opened. Jones and C.W. Smith were called in and informed that the original decision would be set aside and that Greaves would be declared the winner of the contest. Jones protested but to no avail. Quoting from the rulebook before him, Graham explained that no decision was official until the commission ratified it, even if, as had been the case here, it had been announced in the ring. The new decision was relayed to members of the press, still camped around the arena, one hour after the fight ended.

The decision threw Tiger. An air of bewildering unreality pervaded the dressing room. He brooded for a time before emerging to speak to the journalists waiting outside.

"I've never heard anything like it," he said, voice betraying more than a hint of stunned incredulity. "It doesn't make sense. I thought it was close and that I got the worst end of the verdict. But at least, that would have meant that I kept my title. Now this happens."

It was bizarre. So typically unlucky.

He arrived in New York, his mind racked with a sense of injustice. These feelings would intensify over the months because of Greaves' subsequent conduct. The contract with Greaves contained a clause stipulating a return match within 90 days if he lost the match and Jones had already announced that it would take place in Edmonton, "despite what they have done to us."

Gundersson pencilled in a provisional date of August 26th but this was quickly rescheduled for September 14th after Greaves pleaded a training injury. Then stunning news followed. Without giving any reasons, Greaves announced that he was pulling out of the fight. He surfaced later to announce that he would be meeting Obdulio Nunez, a Puerto Rican middleweight, in New York claiming that he was using the bout as a 'tune up' for the defence of his Empire title.

Tiger was mortified. He agreed with Jones that beating Greaves and regaining the title would be the priority. Jones announced that "All these postponements are costing him money" and referring, perhaps, to the imminent arrival of another child in September, he added, " He's got a family to support and the money has got to come from somewhere."

He wrote to the B.B.B.C. urging them to suspend Greaves until he fulfilled his obligation to defend against Tiger. He also contacted the commission in Canada who proceeded to advise the New York authorities not to sanction the Nunez bout that had been scheduled for October 15th. New York obliged and suspended Greaves. This forced C.W. Smith into meeting Jones and concretising arrangements for his fighter to face Tiger in November. With only hours left to the proposed bout with Nunez, the New York State Athletic Commission relented and restored Greaves' licence. Greaves lost the bout on a split decision.

At precisely 9.55 p.m. on Thursday, November the 24th, a chilly Canadian winter's day, Tiger's plane arrived at Edmonton International Airport. The first words he uttered to the waiting pressmen concerned his loathing of snow. His mood got darker when an officious Customs Officer proceeded to hold him up for an hour while he decided whether Tiger should pay a toll on his used boxing gear.

He made it plain that Greaves had offended him. "It makes me angry inside," he told one reporter, "For five months I haven't worked, waiting for this one." In all, Jones reckoned that Greaves' prevarications had cost Tiger "up to $30,000" in lost income. Greaves, for his part, was dismissive, saying: "I can't bleed for Dick Tiger because his camp didn't know enough to get him fights while I was out with bad ribs. If it cost him $30,000, his camp should answer to him," adding, "The title is better off in Edmonton where it will do more good than in Nigeria."

The papers would focus on the feud between Tiger and Greaves, picking on the most innocuous of happenings to confirm this 'hostile animus.' Both men were camped at the Kingsway Hotel, with Tiger training at 6 p.m. and Greaves following at 7 p.m. and reporters watched, hawkeyed for any problems:

"There is still animosity between the two parties, both upset at developments since the last meeting," one report began. "For instance, over the weekend, Tiger had finished his workout and Greaves entered the downstairs banquet hall to begin his hours training. Tiger and trainer Jimmy August were still there and Greaves refused to begin until the opponents had left."

Tiger's preparations were not limited to the relatively cosy surroundings of the Kingsway Hotel's basement. Roadwork had to be done in the bitingly cold Canadian winter. He ran through early morning temperatures of ten degrees below zero. By the time he arrived back at the hotel, icicles were formed on his forehead. This, he concluded to himself was worst than what he'd experienced in Chicago. Damp and muggy Liverpool simply did not compare. The Edmonton Gardens had only 2,500 spectators on the night of the fight, the promotion on this occasion, having largely being overshadowed by the Grey Football Cup. This time, Tiger was better prepared to meet the challenge of a 15 round bout. August had had a good look at Greaves' style and proposed that Tiger would break him down sooner by utilising a three punch combination move: Throw a jab then follow up with a right cross and left hook.

It worked well. In the third, he rocked Greaves with a crushing right hand to the jaw and by round eight, his blows had inflicted deep gashes above both of Greaves' eyes. Greaves' condition worsened in the next round, Pawson writing, that the Canadian was "glassy-eyed, his jaws slack, mouth agape and his face punched somewhere over the vicinity of his right ear."

Tiger had him pinned in a corner when, John Smith, refereeing again, stepped in to wave the fight over. This did not accord well with one outraged ringside spectator. "You donkey Smith," he wailed, "you can't stop a title bout until you count the bum out on his back."

There was a decidedly vindictive ring about Tiger's post fight chortle that he had merely being "warming up" when Smith intervened. It had, nevertheless, being a great performance, one which Jones would later acknowledge had convinced him that Tiger was not just a "tough, good middleweight who could give anybody trouble" but was a fighter of depth and facility. If he held this form, he would be champion.

A mix of frustration and resentment had fuelled the punches that Tiger had thrown at Greaves. The bruised knuckle he discovered after unwrapping the gauze, needed time to heal. This meant that the bout which Jones had arranged with Hank Casey, scheduled to take place on December 14th in New Orleans, had to be aborted.

Gundersson, apparently recovered from the dismal revenues

from the Tiger-Greaves fight which had been poorer than the first bout, announced that he had started negotiations with Gene Fullmer's manager with a view to staging a championship contest in Edmonton. Nothing, however, was to come of this; Fullmer signed to fight Sugar Ray Robinson in March 1961.

Hopes rose temporarily after he outpointed Gene Armstrong in a third meeting when Robinson, as was characteristic of the later part of his career, threatened to pull out after a dispute over money. Jones quickly offered Tiger as a substitute opponent, but the matter was settled.

The Garden next matched Tiger against his old foe, Spider Webb. After beating Tiger in 1959, Webb went on to make an unsuccessful world title challenge; a points loss to Gene Fullmer. He retired to join the ranks of the Chicago Police Force but agreed to face Tiger 14 months later at New York's St.Nicholas Arena. Tiger stopped him in the sixth.

A New Orleans based promoter, Lou Messina, now revived the proposed bout with Hank Casey, held in abeyance since December. Tiger signed the contract, but Casey decided to stay put in California. Jones scrambled around for a replacement. One missive was sent to Joey Giardello's handlers. But there was an obstacle here –New Orleans, a city at the heart of Southern culture, had no record of an interracial boxing match since George Dixon, the black featherweight champion defeated his white challenger, Jack Skelly. Blacks could fight other blacks on the same bills as whites but could not engage white fighters.

It is inconceivable that Jones, a noted boxing historian, would have been ignorant of this and he was perhaps issuing a mild challenge to the mores of a region, which at the time were being assaulted by the bourgeoning Civil Rights Movement. He had in fact approached Rory Calhoun's handlers "in case there is any trouble." As things turned out, Casey relented and Tiger won a split decision.

Tiger continued to be ignored by both Fullmer and Pender. The former had been inactive since his March win over Ray

Robinson and Tiger, as the number three-rated contender to the title, expected to get the nod to challenge him. Instead Fullmer bypassed him in favour of Florentino Fernandez, ranked at number seven. He got nowhere with Pender who having beaten the ageing Carmen Basilio now signed for a rematch with Terry Downes. Pender was booked to fight in July while Fullmer's engagement was scheduled for the following month.

His career thus plunged into stagnation; Tiger turned his mind to other matters. He decided that the time was apt to resettle his family in Aba. Although the press releases mentioned Abigail's 'homesickness' and the difficulty of bringing up children in a hotel suite, she still did find living in America quite appealing. Tiger, however, was insistent and they all left for home in June. While in Nigeria, Tiger began the first of his ventures into the property market. He found time for family, friends and the community but there appear to be few discernable hobbies or pursuits outside of boxing and business.

"My mother used to say that he was so dedicated to his profession and she didn't know of any," says his son Charles. "There was nothing in particular like say playing tennis. He would hang out with friends, his brothers and extended family." Family and community meant a great deal to Tiger. His brothers and their families enjoyed his largesse. For instance, he financed the university education of two nephews and never forgot to dispense gifts to relatives. A few years later, George Girsh of the *Ring* would write, "Every time Dick Tiger fights in the United States, he spends a few days relaxing around the pawn shops of the area in which he happens to be, especially if it's New York. He buys gifts for his numerous establishments (mother), wife, six children, cousins, uncles, aunts…. When he returned to Nigeria after winning the light-heavyweight title from Jose Torres, he took back enough gimcracks, jewellery and what not to incur an average of $175 in air charges."

The truth worth of a man in the traditional Igbo society is said to be determined not solely by his ability to enrich himself materially, but, also in his aptitude in cooperating with the wider community for their collective betterment. The deeds of Dick Tiger reflected this and over the next few years, he would aid several projects within the Amaigbo community. 'Handsome contributions' were made towards the building of a hospital and postal agency. And when the village market, schools and churches needed reconstructing, he was on hand to dig deep into his pockets.

Tiger's absence from the ring did not go unnoticed. It moved one Frank Shields in New Orleans to write to the *Ring* and bemoan the scenario of a fighter of Tiger's calibre and popularity being "allowed to escape from the United States and return in disgust to his native Nigeria because he isn't given what he so richly deserves –a chance at the world middleweight title."

Jones cabled him at the beginning of October to tell him of a bout that the Garden had lined up for him with the Cuban, Florentino Fernandez, whose challenge of Fullmer had being unsuccessful.

Tiger arrived at the end of the month to begin training for the December date. Fernandez, however, sent word from Cuba that the post-revolutionary conditions were preventing him from leaving the island. His replacement, Billy Pickett, a popular campaigner around his native New York and Eastern Canada, was beaten by a huge points margin.

Tiger finally met Fernandez on January 20th in Miami. The city had already become the focal point for Cubans fleeing the Castro regime and the local Convention Hall, filled with most of Fernandez's compatriots, throbbed to the sounds of the joyous Salsa beat that a band of supporters played between rounds.

Tiger absorbed a few and blocked many of the murderous punches Fernandez lobbed at him before replying in kind. He broke the Cuban's nose in round five and his trainer, Angelo Dundee, prevented him from answering the bell for round six. In a rare burst of exuberance, Tiger turned to the band to raise his hand and dance a hip-swaying jig. He journeyed to his dressing room with the sound of an ovation ringing in his ears.

Next came a match against Henry Hank, the fifth ranked middleweight. Hank possessed an exceptional strength of punch, among his 36 knock out victims was a light-heavyweight contender named Jesse Bowdry whom he had stopped two months earlier in New Orleans.

Tiger's contest with Hank was billed as a duel between 'uncrowned champions.' Although a foreign boxer, he was by now recognised as what Harry Markson, the Director of Boxing at Madison Square Garden, described as a 'standout fighter'; so much so that the Garden now remunerated him with a $10,500 television appearance fee that more than doubled the average fee of around $4,000.

The Garden drew 7,500 spectators who witnessed a surprisingly one-sided affair. Only in the inaugural round did Tiger have to contend with anything resembling meaningful opposition. Both men exchanged jarring hooks to their faces but Tiger surprised Hank with two stiff right hand leads which landed on his nose. Jolted, Hank countered with two left hooks. Tiger shrugged them off and came back with a short right to Hank's head before following with a powerful sally of left hooks.

Hank emerged for the second, a changed fighter. When Tiger walked to him, he backed away. At other times, he shuffled hesitantly, tightening his stance, as if waiting to land one of his trademark haymakers. Tiger hit him almost at will, but he also defended well. The shots that Hank aimed at his head, he intercepted with his gloves, while his arms blocked those strikes that were destined for his mid-riff.

By the end of the bout, Hank had according to the watching *New York Times* correspondent, been "hit with just about every type of punch that is legally permissible or imaginable in the prize ring." Tiger's dominance had been so complete that referee Arthur Mercante scored every one of the ten rounds in Tiger's favour. The two judges could only award Hanks a round each.

What more, Tiger thought, would he have to do in order to get that title shot?

Seven

THE BEST MIDDLEWEIGHT
IN THE WORLD

"Win this one and you'll get a shot at the title." Teddy Brenner, the cigar-chomping matchmaker at Madison Square Garden was speaking to Tiger before his third encounter with Gene Armstrong. It was February 1961. Two months later, before stepping into the ring with Spider Webb, Brenner told him much the same thing: victory would equal a title challenge. Victory came but the challenge failed to materialise. When Brenner resurrected the same promise before he faced Florentino Fernandez, Tiger looked him straight in the eye and snapped, "I've heard that line before."

By the spring of 1962, the chances of meeting either Fullmer or Pender in the near future did not appear to be likely. Tiger was in pessimistic mode. Most fighters he reasoned were fading by their 30th year and by 35 few were "still good."

"The boxing writers and the T.V. and radio announcers have been very good to me, and I know that the public wants me to fight for the title," he said putting his case to Nat Loubet in the April edition of the *Ring*. "I'm sure everything will turn out right, but I cannot help wondering how much longer I'll have to wait. If as you say patience is a virtue, I guess I'll end up being a saint."

Outwardly, at least, he appeared to have attached no blame on the state of affairs to Jones' managerial performance. Yet, he had seen the likes of Fernandez and Terry Downes obtain title shots ahead of himself. Within British circles, the argument that he could have secured a title opportunity, had he chosen to remain with Tony Vairo, had gained considerable currency. A number of Jones' decisions, they argued were flawed and served his fighter's interests no end. They pointed to the decision to grant Joey Giardello a rematch after Tiger had beaten him on points in their first fight in 1959. It had, after all been Giardello and not Tiger who went on to challenge Gene Fullmer the following year. Again the debacle in Canada with Wilf Greaves, although hardly his fault, was dredged up as an example of Jones' amateurishness.

Much of the criticism appeared however to be unduly harsh. Jones was attempting to strategise a balance which ensured that each fight that Tiger engaged in would in someway serve to maintain his claim to either title and at the same time be viable enough to enable him to earn a living. He most certainly had not been pricing his fighter out of bouts with Fullmer or Pender but rather could not help the fact that Tiger was being avoided. His policy of steering a course that tried to minimise an over reliance on the Madison Square Garden Organisation, by now firmly shorn of its IBC derived monopoly in world title contests, appeared sound given the Garden's inability to secure the elusive title bout.

For long, Jones had continued to reassure Tiger that the match with Fullmer would happen. But even his optimism had limits. He expressed his doubts in his *Ring* column, using Tiger's predicament as the inspiration for a piece entitled 'Best Men Not Always Champions.' The "capricious gods of ring destiny," he hoped, would spare Tiger the same 'nearly man' fate suffered by the likes of Sam Langford and Jimmy Driscoll.

In fact, there was a great deal of sympathy for Tiger. Fans and sportswriters alike in America and Britain felt that the time for his challenge was well overdue: The applause which filled the Boston Arena, scene of the third Pender-Downes encounter in April of 1962, after his introduction, testified to this. Feelings of injustice on Tiger's behalf, not surprisingly, were widespread in Nigeria where it was commonly perceived that every dangerous contender had been put in his path in a concerted attempt aimed at obstructing and permanently derailing his chances of winning the title.

He had watched the Pender-Downes contest, fearful of a Downes victory, which would have triggered off yet another rematch. Yet, the points win granted by the judges to the American brought forth a stillborn hope: the after fight chatter in the gyms and newspaper columns was of a unification bout between Pender and Fullmer that was being touted for the coming summer.

Tiger had his sights focused on Fullmer. Pender he knew would be under no obligation to defend against him or any other contender until later on in the year in October. After beating Florentino Fernandez earlier on in the year, Jones had issued a formal challenge to Fullmer's title through the National Boxing Association. Fullmer's last title defence against a rated contender, Fernandez, had been on August 5th the previous year. He had fought last in February, beating welterweight champion Benny 'Kid' Paret.

At the end of May, Tiger put pen to paper and issued a public challenge published in the London *Boxing News*:

Dear Gene,

> **By the time you read this, I'll be back in my native Nigeria awaiting the arrival of my latest 'Tiger cub' and some news (I hope) on my challenge to you issued through the National Boxing Association last January when I knocked out Florentino Fernandez in Miami Beach. Accompanying my challenge was a certified check of 2,500 dollars posted through my agent 'Jersey' Jones. It is now nearly three months (sic) since the challenge was posted so far I have heard nothing from you. I realise that your attention at the moment is centred on a possible showdown with Pender to determine which of you title claimants deserves to be recognised as undisputed world middleweight champion. As I see it, the chances of getting together with Pender in the more or less immediate future are remote. There are too many problems to iron out – promoter, site, terms etc. – and it may be months before any satisfactory deal is**

completed.

Meanwhile, what of my challenge to you? The six months period of grace since your last defence of the N.B.A. title will expire June 9. That's little over a month away. Times-a-waistin' Gene. I hardly need remind you that in all major ratings, I am listed as number one contender for both yours and Pender's laurels. Naturally, I'd also like to meet Pender for his share of the title but Paul has until October seventh before his period of grace expires. He can afford to wait a little before accepting my challenge unless, instead, he prefers meeting you first.

I know you don't want any part of me in the ring Gene, but you have a reputation to maintain. You were recognised in 1961 as the 'Fighter of the Year.' What are they apt to call you in 1962 if you continue to dodge your outstanding challenger?

Lets hear from you Gene. Say the word and I'll set a speed record getting back to the United States to you.

Dick Tiger
British Empire Middleweight Champion.

It would not be the last time that he would attempt to tease and cajole a seemingly weary opponent into the ring.

Then came some good news. In June, the N.B.A. issued an edict instructing Fullmer to defend against Tiger by August 5th failing which he would be stripped of the title. Quick as a shot, Jones made contact with Marv Jensen, Fullmer's manager. Soon after, both were in agreement that two restaurant owners, Norman Rothschild and Bennie Foord, would promote the fight. Three possible sites were put under consideration; Bozeman, Montana; Las Vegas and San Francisco.

Pale skinned and ice blue eyed (writer A.J.Liebling would describe him as having a "Nordic and chamber of commerce look"), Jensen drove a hard bargain. Fullmer would receive sixty-percent of the gate profits and a similar take from closed circuit outlets. Out-carded, Jones was forced to accept on Tiger's behalf, a straight guarantee of $25,000 along with $2,700 for training expenses. Events, however, would shape up to make this a good deal for Tiger.

He had been in Aba for less than a fortnight when he received the first of Jones' cables keeping him informed of the state of negotiations. He shivered with excitement when the second named a date and location: August 27th at San Francisco's Candlestick Park. This gave him less than six weeks preparation and so he packed his essentials and bolted off to America.

He arrived in New York at July's end and commenced training at the Catholic Youth Association gym, his regular haunt since the closure of Lou Stillman's establishment. Situated in a building on West 17th Street in New York's drab Westside neighbourhood, the C.Y.O. suited him fine. Clear aired and sparsely populated, it was bereft of the grubby, claustrophobic ambience of Stillman's and a million other gyms that were frequented by fighters.

Surrounded by pictures and fight posters depicting the likes of Floyd Patterson, Rocky Marciano and Hogan Bassey, all of them previous customers; he embarked on a thrice-weekly ritual of sparring, skipping and callisthenics. On alternative days he went on a three or four mile jog around Central Park.

It was the start of a regime that would suffer from a number of aggravating interruptions. He had been in New York for only a few days when word reached that the fight would be put back to September the 12th. Events on the other side of America were playing havoc on the fight. The American west coast, and in particular, the Bay area, was in the midst of a violent season of rain and hail storms. Not the best of conditions to hold an open aired event. Meteorological considerations apart, the flurry of excitement surrounding the first time appearance of the local baseball team in a World Series Final was hampering Rothschild's efforts at promoting the fight. And when Rothschild discovered that the series was in fact scheduled to run right up to the day on which he had rescheduled the bout, the date had to be put back yet again, this time to October 16th. The delay was also linked to the fact that the promoters of the impending Heavyweight title clash between Floyd Patterson and Sonny Liston had sewn up many of the preferred sites Rothschild intended to use for the closed circuit showings.

Tiger was most certainly put off by these delays. The long haul of disappointments to this point had created the mindset that he would not permit himself the luxury of believing that his chance had come until he was staring across a ring at Fullmer. He confessed later that the second postponement had led him to the depths of pessimism: "I was beginning to think that my big dream was just that, a dream and that maybe after all, I would never get the championship match."

In order to aid the promotion of the fight, Rothschild suggested that Tiger break up camp in New York and relocate to San Francisco. He left New York on September 24 but stopped off, at Rothschild's invitation, in Chicago to watch the Patterson-Liston title bout. The following evening at the city's Comiskey Park, he was one of a parade of past and active fighters that included Joe Louis and Rocky Marciano, who climbed through the ropes to milk the cheers of the 19,000 strong audience. He touched glove with the soon to be combatants before making his way out as quickly as he had entered. Then he made his way to a fourth row seat where he watched Liston obliterate Patterson in just two minutes and six seconds.

The following morning he continued to San Francisco taking up residence at the 'Governor,' a small hotel on Turk Street. His room adjoined August's, an arrangement that was aimed at ensuring that the trainer would keep tabs on his morale.

He began a diurnal of workouts at the West Coast Seaman's Union Gymnasium. Willie Turner, a Fresno-based middleweight was employed as his sparring partner. A Chinese-American local known simply as Yip also joined the entourage. Yip trained young boys but served as a dogsbody; when he was not running errands or wiping the sweat off the back of Tiger's neck after workouts, he chauffeured Tiger, August and Jones around town in a rickety station-wagon.

August, his visage seemingly permanently etched with a worrisome look, oversaw proceedings. Feeling that Tiger was tending to overdo his chores, he punctiliously kept an eye on the timing of each sparring and exercise session. He also restricted Tiger's daily jogs because he feared a fall in the slippery conditions that had been brought about by the weather.

The heavens were in rebellion. Rain had not fallen in such quantities for more than half a century. There was widespread flooding and daily reports of landslides, some of which proved fatal. Tiger watched on anxiously as Rothschild again rescheduled the fight for October 23rd. Ticket sales had remained sluggish and Rothschild felt that a breathing space between the end of the World Series and the fight might help. He also wished that Tiger would be less sedate and more braggadocios in manner. A challenger's utterances after all traditionally played a part in the overall 'sell'. But Tiger loathed playing along those lines.

Gene Fullmer, encamped on another side of town, was together with his manager, a partner in the promotion and was of course anxious to sell the fight. He often regaled the onlooking reporters with a yarn or two. Once he claimed that a gambler had rang him up and called him a 'bum' after he had been knocked out by Sugar Ray Robinson. The man, who had apparently staked heavily on Fullmer, now asked to be reimbursed. "I asked him if he had ever won money on me," recalled Fullmer, "and when he said he did, I asked him to share his winnings with me. Of course, the smart guy hung up."

Born and raised in the State of Utah, Gene Fullmer was an elder of the Church of Jesus Christ of Latter-day Saints, a denomination more commonly known as the Mormon Church. He made a living as a Mink farmer but had boxed since he was a boy. He had first won the middleweight title in 1957 when he outpointed Sugar Ray Robinson. He lost the return, knocked out by Robinson's 'perfect' left hook punch but reclaimed a portion of the title in 1959 after winning the elimination bout that had ensued from the N.B.A's stripping of Robinson.

His bull necked; full-calved physique was as stocky as Tiger's. Some even considered him to be the strongest middleweight since the 'Raging Bull', Jake La Motta. Like La Motta, he developed a reputation for toughness; his mean-streaked, rough style earning him the tag of the 'Utah Bully Boy'. His style, or lack of it, was unique. He stalked his opponents reposed in an awkward stance that he punctuated with a delivery of punches that travelled from what appeared to be the most improbable of angles. "A type of uncultivated skill," opined Jim Jacobs. A.J. Liebling's descriptions in the *New Yorker* were more vivid and fulsome.

"At times, before throwing a punch, he pulls his right elbow back behind his ear, as if he were drawing a longbow at Crecy. At others, he leaps forward with his left elbow ahead of his advance, his fist retracted at an angle of ninety degrees. If the elbow connects, he brings the fist down to complete the demolition, with the motion of an old subway guard chopping tickets. Mostly, though, he swings blows from the side, at the ribs and the temples; a tiring opponent, shrinking in toward him, will catch them on the kidneys or on the back of his head. They are not proper hooks because Fullmer does not bend his elbows sharply but throws the blows as if he were beating a carpet, and the striking surface is as often the inside of his forearm as his fist. He exploits these barbarisms by inexhaustible strength, seconded by what Egan called *bottom*, mauling his adversary on the ropes and hauling at his arms until they go limp, like strands of overcooked pasta.' In the words of the classicist Dave Shade, who was baffled by Slapsie Maxie Rosenbloom, a Fullmer-like adversary in the 1920s, 'He does everything so wrong that it must be right'."

In late September, Tiger wrote a letter inviting Maurice Foran from Liverpool. "I don't care how much money it will cost to bring you here as my guest because I always remembered my past years when I was a nobody." Gleefully, Foran showed the letter off to all and sundry and parts of the letter were published in the boxing press. This alerted Harry Ormesher, benefactor to Bassey and an occasional adviser to Tiger, who sent word that he also wanted to be there.

They arrived soon afterwards and were booked into the Governor. Tiger spent a lot of time with them reminiscing about the old days in Liverpool. Jones welcomed the presence of both men because he felt that it took Tiger's mind off the tedious, daily grind.

Another arrival was Hogan Bassey, now firmly ensconced as the trainer of Nigeria's amateur fighters. Tiger privately informed August that he would like a similar job when he retired. The two talked frequently, often meeting in one of the booths of the Governor Hotel's coffee shop. One day, espied by the ubiquitous Liebling, as they sat devouring a light lunch, a woman assistant approached their table, eager to expand on her knowledge of global culinary tastes.

"And what do you eat in your country?" she asked.

"Human beings," responded Bassey nonchalantly.

As she hurried back to the counter to share this piece of information with her colleagues, Bassey turned to Tiger:

"They think we have tails," he said.

"But we have not," replied Tiger.

She returned soon after with a colleague who expressed the wish that both men would take August back to Africa and "throw him in the pot." The inquisitive one now asked Bassey about sartorial requirements back home.

"We go naked; in the jungle," he retorted.

This appeared to be going too far for Tiger's liking and he told both girls not to believe him.

"He is mischievous," he assured them with a smile.

The Nigerian government also decided that Tiger could do with some official company. A delegation led by the Federal Minister of Labour and Sports, Chief Modupe Johnson arrived a day before the fight. Their arrival heartened Tiger because it underlined the level of expectation and goodwill among his countrymen. His fight would be a national landmark. At the same time, however, he did express some cynicism about the politicians, a reflection perhaps of increasing public distrust of the post-independence breed of politician. To Tiger, they embodied the 'easy life' of the educated class who only needed to "read a book and talk." The life of the early rising, physically labouring fighter was decidedly much harder and perhaps, from his perspective, a more valid means of making a living.

A cable of support from the nation's Governor-General, Dr. Nnamdi Azikiwe also arrived on the eve of the showdown:

It is with great pleasure that I send this message of cheer, comfort and goodwill on behalf of myself, my government and the people of Nigeria, your beloved country.

I know you will do your best and you will observe the rules of the game as you enter the squared ring to vie for fistic glory.

No matter what happens, let your worthy opponent know that he has fought the fight of his life.

May fortune smile on you but hit hard and defend yourself in the tradition of the manly art.

Good luck Dick Tiger.

The morning of the fight was the morning after the evening of President Kennedy's jolting address to the American nation informing them of the presence of Soviet missile sites on Cuba. The unnerving mood that Armageddon might be around the corner was perhaps reflected in the thick, black fog that had descended on the whole of Southern California. The airport had to be closed, barring last minute customers arriving from Las Vegas and other places.

Tiger was first to enter the 20 foot ring imported from Utah. The cool, raw evening air wafted into his face as he stood, impassively, waiting for August to complete the 'gloving up' process. There was the ritual introduction of fighters and he broke into a brief smile each time he momentarily extended a fist when greeting the likes of Rocky Marciano and Cassius Clay.

Watching every move and gesture of his were members of the Nigerian delegation, the "men in agbadas" as Liebling dubbed them, all of who where seated behind the working press seats. Jones, who was keen to provide a larger and decidedly more proletarian rooting section, had arranged for an extra row of 30 ringside seats to accommodate Nigerian students he had rounded up from a number of local universities, each paying an affordable two dollar fee.

The anthems and introductions and the pre-fight instructions passed quickly. He was back in his corner locking eyes with Fullmer when the timekeeper sounded the cry of "TEN SECONDS". On cue, August, Foran and Jones began scrambling out of the ring. Jones, the last in file, clasped his right glove as if in an act of benediction.

"Fullmer," Tiger would recall, "must have planned to get a quick jump on me." Right at the bells sound, the Mormon bulled forward, swinging blows and then attempted to manhandle Tiger into the ropes. Tiger stood his ground. Holding his nerve well, he blocked Fullmer's shots before countering with stiff combinations that he mixed to the head and body. He began to beat Fullmer to the punch and during the third, opened a cut above the champion's eye.

In the fourth round Fullmer, in an attempt to regain parity made a desperate surge. Their arms became entangled and a wrestling match ensued. Tiger firmed his grip and shoved Fullmer to the canvas. It was probably the defining moment of the match, for it showed that Tiger was the stronger man. Fullmer pulled himself up and proceeded to back away, retreating with a single step almost as soon as he finished pawing out an awkward jab. Fullmer backing off. It was a sight that astounded the on looking fans; it was as if Charles Atlas himself had suddenly turned sissy. Pointing a finger upwards at the screen in a darkened pay per view joint somewhere in the Los Angeles

Metropolis, a viewer drawled in disbelief: "I ain't never seen that BEFORE!"

Dodging and blocking the haze of leather thrown at him and countering with the energy consuming left hooks that sank deep into Fullmer's sides, Tiger wondered if he and Fullmer could keep the pace. The first round had been the "wildest round" he had fought and the succeeding three had been no less rowdy. Fullmer apparently was also thinking along the same lines, because Tiger noticed his caution from the fifth. He also noticed, for the first time, the trickle of blood oozing down the champions brow.

In the eighth, Tiger's head collided with Fullmer's and the nick that had worsened progressively now began gushing blood by the bucket load. The referee, Frank Carter, became concerned and in the following round called on the ringside physician to review the gash. After three minutes, which included the mandatory minute's rest in between rounds, he decided that Fullmer could continue. Jones raised no protest.

This was a reprieve of sorts. Fullmer's restorative capacities would have virtually cancelled out the damage that had been inflicted over the previous rounds. Tiger, who thought that the bout was going to be stopped, had to steel himself for some more rounds. At this point he knew that nothing but an accident would prevent him from winning the title.

The Nigerian contingent provided small but vocal support, "chauvinistically impervious to pity" in Liebling's assessment. As Tiger trailed his opponent, assorted voices came through the quietened audience, bellowing advice and encouragement. "Belly, belly, Tigah," one monotonised; while another intoned; "What a punishment you are receiving Fullmer, what an ordeal you are undergoing."

"The first time I fought him," Fullmer recalls, "I didn't feel that great. I had a hard time losing weight and I kinda weakened myself, which is no excuse you know, he probably would have whupped me anyway." The story of rest of the bout was one of Tiger stalking and Fullmer retreating. Feeling frustrated in the 11th, he motioned his gloves at Fullmer, inviting him to come forward and fight. At the final bell, the Nigerian officials rushed into the ring to hoist him on their shoulders before breaking into an impromptu West African stylised 'highlife' song.

The decision was a formality. Carter had Tiger winning by a whopping ten rounds to one, while the ringside judges, Jack Downey and Vern Bybee respectively scored it nine to five and seven to five, to make it unanimously in Tiger's favour.

Back in Nigeria, the radio service, which normally signed off at midnight, had worked overtime into the small hours. (The country was eight hours ahead.) Many of the thousands who had kept vigil trooped out into the streets to sing and dance in unabashed jubilation. The celebrations continued into the daylight, with newly awoken fans swelling their ranks shouting and waving placards that read CONGRATS OUR PROUD SON and NIGERIA VICTORIOUS. Tiger left the ring still riding high on the shoulders of his kinsmen, virtually unmarked, save a few ridges on his cheekbones and temples. He showered before heading for the Governor where he changed into his own dove-gray agbada which was fastened with small silver pins, to join the government representatives at a party at the Mark Hopkins Club. Drinks flowed from the bar and the buffet was well stocked. A live band played Cuban rhythms, the nearest presumably that could be got to African music. Tiger looked on, almost sheepishly, as Chief Johnson raised his glass to him and thundered: "To the CHAMPION!" Then turning around to the multinational audience, he boomed, "OUR champion! YOUR champion! EV-ERY BODIES champion!" Then everybody joined in singing 'For he's a jolly good fellow.'

Tiger spent a few days sightseeing around San Francisco in the company of Hogan Bassey. Afterwards he made his way to London where Jack Solomons, the doyen of European promoters, arranged a reception for him at Isows restaurant where he was pictured taking an exaggerated bite from a specially prepared cake. The English fraternity considered him 'one of ours,' and he was not short of admirers. He held talks with Bobby Diamond, an associate of Solomons and they reached an arrangement whereby

Diamond would function as his 'European agent.' Tiger's career would continue in the main to be steered from New York but Diamond would soon be instrumental in setting up one of the highlight events of his career.

He returned home where a strenuous bout of festivities awaited. The din in Candlestick Park had hardly died when the Aba Urban County Council hastily appointed a seven man ad hoc committee to accord him a grand welcome. On the morning of Monday, November 5th thousands lined a seven-mile stretch of the Onitsha-Aba highway right to the gates of his house on Clifford Street, cheering his arrival. The following afternoon, he stood in an open-roofed vehicle at the head of a motorcade that began at his home and took him to the Aba Sports Stadium where he sat, proudly listening to congratulatory speeches and a round of entertainments that included traditional dance troops from various Igbo areas.

The following week in Enugu, capital city of the Eastern Region, he was greeted by the governor at a similar event held at the City Sports Stadium. He ended the day refereeing a few bouts at a local amateur boxing tournament. The two day visit was completed with a dinner party at one of the city's finest hotels and a ballroom dance at the Sports Commission Hall.

He rested until the end of the month when it was the turn of the Western Region to succumb to 'Tigermania'. Dressed in suit and wearing the perennial homborg hat, he rode along the thoroughfares of Ibadan, smiling and waving to the thousands of hand-waving, sing-songing people many of whom waited up to three hours to catch a glimpse of him.

Tiger was now a national icon, the adored object of a nation and would, for the rest of his career, continue to be subjected to reverential treatment. From street corners, they would call him 'Onyeisi' as he went about his daily business. "Even thirty something years later, I can see the magnitude of his fame," recalls his son Charles. "I remember when I was younger, we would be driving in the car and people would line the streets and wave and I'd be waving back. I knew that he was somebody special but I did not have a grasp of it."

His stay continued to be punctuated by invitations, many of which he accepted, to fetes and social gatherings. Tiger was quick to realise that his upgrading in social status brought with it a certain amount of influence and responsibility. At a meeting of the Amaigbo Community Association, he addressed the issue of rising levels of youth unemployment, and called on the government to do more for the urban poor by investing in the undercapitalised palm wine making industry.

1962 ended on two splendid notes. First, a local community group made him the offer of a chieftaincy, and then news came from America that the New York Boxing Writers Association had awarded him the Edward J. Neil plaque for 'Fighter of the Year.' Named for a journalist casualty of the Spanish Civil War, the award had been inaugurated in the 1940s to honour the fighter voted to have made the greatest contribution to the sport over the course of a year. He was following an illustrious line that included Joe Louis, Ray Robinson and Henry Armstrong.

The boxing journals relished the tale of Tiger's improbable transformation from the bedraggled, unacclimated journeyman fighter of Liverpool to that of world champion. Yet, there remained an element of incompleteness: He was, he realised, *a* world champion and not *the* world champion.

Still, he was keen to promote the view (tongue-in-cheek) that his was a more solid claim than Paul Pender's. Writing for the *Ring* magazine he told its readers that "My manager tells me that by counting the countries controlled by the W.B.A. (World Boxing Association, as the N.B.A. was now styled) to those covered by the British Empire, I am Middleweight Champion of three fourths of the world (and) I'd like to add the fourth as soon as possible."

This came sooner than he envisaged. In November 1962, the New York State Commission, the British Boxing Board of Control and the European Boxing Union all issued collective edicts withdrawing recognition from Pender as world champion. The reason given was his failure to make a mandatory defence against the Puerto Rican, Jose Torres.

The move, while largely popular, did not accord well with those who felt strongly that a fighter should only lose his title in the ring and not in a boardroom. Sounding indignant in the editorial column of his influential magazine, Nat Fleisher wrote, "The *Ring* is not forced to accept the dictum of the ruling bodies who toppled Paul Pender from his world championship pedestal and declared Dick Tiger his undisputed international successor." "Tiger," he concluded, "is an excellent representative of boxing. He is a gentleman in whom boxing must feel proud. He is a fine fighter, a crowd pleaser. The *Ring* is pleased to see him on top. But we dislike the manner in which Pender has been treated to gain for the Nigerian, universal recognition except in Massachusetts."

Pender, unsurprisingly, was gutted. He felt that he had a superior claim; after all it was he who had won the title by beating the incumbent Ray Robinson. He was the 'linear' champion while Fullmer on the other hand had only won an elimination contest. "Tiger," he argued had "won a title which never existed."

Disappointments piled for him. Proposed fights with Joey Giardello and Jose Torres fell through because television sponsorship, already a vital component in raising monies for fights, did not materialise. He would also fail to get Tiger. In Peter Heller's book, '*In This Corner,*' he complained bitterly about the alleged role which Jersey Jones played in thwarting his pleas to fight Tiger. When Fullmer began to look doubtful for a third meeting with Tiger in Nigeria, Pender journeyed to New York accompanied by his lawyer to hold a conference with Jones and the Garden's Harry Markson.

"Let's put me and Tiger together," he remembered telling Jones, "I'll tell you what Jersey, I'll fight him in Africa."

Jones, who according to Pender, had intimated that he considered Tiger an ageing fighter who would be better disposed at making money against 'safer' opposition, is said to have replied: "You couldn't fight him in your own house."

"You mean to tell me that you're never going to put us together?" Pender came back.

"No chance," Jones affirmed.

"Well then," said Pender, "I quit."

He announced his retirement in May of 1963.

Tiger returned to New York to make arrangements for his next fight. Though the ever present rematch clause existed with Fullmer, this did not have to happen immediately. Jones weighted the options. Offers had come in from Jack Solomons and Harry Levene, England's premier promoters who wanted to match him with Terry Downes. The fight would possibly have broken all sorts of records if it were held in England and would continue be touted for the next couple of years.

Tiger felt somewhat obligated to Fullmer "who was sportsman enough to give me a crack" and was prepared to delay a return match if Fullmer needed more time to recover from the facial wounds he had inflicted. There was pressure on Fullmer to retire from his family -his father-in-law had suffered a heart attack and died while watching the fight at Candlestick Park. There were, however, other pressures, which were guiding Fullmer to continue his career much of which was financial. Both he and Marv Jensen, silent partners in Rothschild's promotion, had lost heavily. It was rumoured that the latter owed them $35,000. Terms were soon agreed upon with Jones and the return was scheduled for February in Las Vegas.

In 1963, Las Vegas was still in a relative infancy as far as prizefights were concerned. But the hotel and casino owners acting in tandem with boxing promoters, were beginning to figure out the gold minted opportunities of generating huge returns from the high rollers attracted to the big fight atmosphere.

Tiger, avoiding the plush hostelries of the strip, checked into the relatively modest El Cortez Hotel in the city's downtown district. He quickly settled into a regime that had him averaging 20 miles of roadwork and 12 hours of gym chores a week. The prospect of facing a fighter who many experts considered 'washed up' did not faze him and he announced that his training was geared to enable him to go the full championship route.

Fullmer may well have willed Tiger to believe the hype. Soon after the fight at Candlestick Park he had mentioned that he had discovered something in Tiger's style "that will suit me next time." He felt that he had held Tiger off rather well in the later rounds of the first meeting when he was desperately hurt, by becoming a jabbing, feinting, moving target. Most observers perhaps did not notice it given Fullmer's wretched physical state. The man, who in Paul Pender's words "couldn't outbox your girlfriend," had managed to do that for as many as "ten rounds." An overblown assessment, maybe, but one that Fullmer agreed with namely that lateral movement troubled Dick Tiger. "Awkward and clumsy" was what Fullmer understood as the public's perception of his fighting, but he felt that they had forgotten that he had approached both of his winning bouts against Carmen Basilio as a 'boxer' and not as a 'slugger.'

But press as well as public could not see this happening. 'TIGER SOLID PICK TO RETIRE FULLMER' spouted the sports page headline of the *Los Angeles Times* on the morning of the fight. "Gene Fullmer's farewell to boxing is expected to be written in large, bright and bloody letters here tonight." Tiger, the paper's staff representative forecasted, would score a technical knockout win over the "broken-faced bull" that was expected to lose "several pints of plasma."

Tiger seethed with frustration at Fullmer's tactics. Each spell of feints, jabs and lateral shifts ended with a suffocating clinch and he expended large amounts of energy releasing himself from Fullmer's grip. In the sixth round he manhandled Fullmer on to the lower strands of the ring rope and the crowd, many of them local Mormons, booed him. Tiger hereafter plodded on after Fullmer, refusing to give chase. On occasions when Fullmer appeared to be close, he swung full-blooded punches at Fullmer's head most of which missed.

During the final minutes interval, as Marv Jenson quietly whispered "the fight is all yours" in Fullmer's ears, Jones at the opposite end was frantic, berating Tiger for "aiming too much for the head" when he ought to have followed the pre-fight agreement to work on Fullmer's body.

The verdict was a draw. Tiger, within a whisker of losing his hard won title was honest in his appraisal:

"We both boxed like amateurs, not champions."

Eight
IBADAN

The unsatisfactory conclusion at Las Vegas immediately signalled the prospect of a third meeting with Gene Fullmer; indeed Fullmer was insistent that he could not retire with a draw and that if Tiger was "man enough," he would grant him another match. The bidding began from the moment both men reached their dressing rooms. Norman Rothschild and George Parnassus each pitched in purse offers of $100,000 and $150,000, while Harry Markson appealed to Jersey Jones "not to make a decision" before conferring with him. The Vegas match, a Garden co-promotion, had done well financially and Markson, now overseeing the Saturday re-lauch of the 15 year long series of televised bouts that had been on Fridays, was confident that a third bout would do even better. The most intriguing offer, however, to come to Jones' attention was from Nigeria. He reacted firstly with scepticism when the matter was broached to him by a journalist, feeling it merely to be a publicity stunt but his mind would gradually be changed over the coming weeks.

In Nigeria, a mood was steadily building that the country was ready to stage a world title bout. In Lagos, three days after the fight in Las Vegas, Basio Osagie, a journalist with the *Daily Times* called a press conference to announce the formation of the DICK TIGER-GENE FULLMER FIGHT CAMPAIGN COMMITTEE, which had the objective of bringing the fight to Nigeria. Early the next month, the committee called on the assistance of the only organisation capable of sponsoring such an event: the Federal Government. Chief Johnson responded by agreeing to underwrite the cost of the event to the tune of £20,000, a figure that left Jones distinctly unimpressed. Johnson, his imagination captured by the proposed event, then began 'working' on the governments of the country's regions. Before long, the government of the East, Tiger's home region, offered to put up a guarantee of £15,000. The Western Region backed this up with a guarantee of the same amount, and also offered the facilities of the newly completed Liberty Stadium. A final pledge from the North brought the total guarantees to £65,000. Johnson placed a call to Jones on March 17 informing him of the progress made and Jones' response was positive. He had been gravitating, up to this time, towards the Garden's plan, which envisaged the Gillette Company paying $100,000 to sponsor the bout as part of its massive annual advertising campaigns around Fathers Day. A date, June 8, had tentatively been pencilled in. But sensing, perhaps, that history was in the making, he finally decided on the Nigerian option. He had one reservation about Johnson's plan, which related to Hogan Bassey's designated position of 'promoter.' Noting that Bassey had no experience of promoting a bout of this scale, he requested that Johnson draft in an established figure to oversee the fight.

This is where the English connection came in. In London, Tiger's representative, Bobby Diamond laid the groundwork for the involvement of Jack Solomons. To many Nigerian followers of the game the 62-year-old Solomons was considered as something of a magus among boxing promoters. Born into a Jewish family of East End fishmongerers, the young Solomons first cut his business teeth at the famous Billingsgate Market. In the 1930s, he began promoting small-scale boxing events at the Devonshire Club but quickly outgrew these surroundings to rise to the elite of promoters. It was to Solomons that the post World War revival in British boxing was largely credited, staging hugely successful bouts involving Freddie Mills and Bruce Woodcock; two favourites of British fight fans. His crowning glory came with the world middleweight championship bout he staged at London's Earls Court in 1951 between Sugar Ray Robinson and Randolph Turpin. Solomons was never afraid to venture into previously unchartered territory, whether it involved trawling the war ravaged European continent in search of foreign opposition for his fighters or by bringing over American stars. So it was no surprise that he took a grasp of Tiger-Fullmer mark three. Promoting Black Africa's first ever world championship bout would be in keeping with his audacious spirit.

Meanwhile, Tiger, in New York to receive the trophy awarded to him as 1962's 'Fighter of the Year,' brought along S.O. Adebo, Nigeria's Ambassador to the United Nations to the ceremony where Adebo made a plea. "We have had two world champions, but neither has boxed as champion in his homeland. You have championship fights all the time in the United States. Don't you think we're entitled to one? We want Dick Tiger to fight for us while he is still champion."

Johnson extended an invitation to Solomons, Jones and Marv Jensen to visit Nigeria to discuss the match. They arrived together with Diamond on the 27th and were taken on a tour of the proposed venue in Ibadan. Back in Lagos, he held a conference with all parties who appeared satisfied with all they had seen. He began the meeting by informing them that despite a smattering of anti-fight sentiment emanating from some quarters (The Lagos *Daily Telegraph*, though saluting the proposed bout as being a "grand idea" thought it "poor economics" while one member of the Nigerian Parliament had called it a "waste of money" which ought to be held overseas so that Tiger could bring his earnings home) he was determined to go ahead with the bout and was happy to entrust Solomons with the entire production. Afterwards, Solomons gave the Chief a detailed estimate of the envisaged costs settling on a figure of £100,000 ($280,000) and a further amount to cover his expenses. Johnson appeared temporarily stunned –it was more than he expected and he called a few of his aides to his desk where they huddled over, calculating the possible losses. Surprised, Solomons interjected. Addressing Johnson and his aides he made an enquiry; "Hadn't it occurred to you gentlemen that the show could be a winner?" he asked. "Instead of figuring how much you could lose, why not give some thought to how much you could win, after all, if Nigeria is excited about its own Dick Tiger as one of the principals, why shouldn't the show be a success?"

That said the matter then turned to setting a date for the contest, in this case at an open-air venue in the middle of the West African rainy season. The meeting favoured a July date, but this

116

would be left open until Johnson had finalised the contractual arrangements, which he would mail to Solomons. The deal was finally closed a month later in London where Johnson represented the Nigerian Government at a royal wedding.

Tiger returned to New York and on Thursday the second of May began a schedule of light training at the Catholic Youth Association Gym. The gym, normally closed at this time of the year, was opened specially for him. Jimmy August enthusiastically informed a visiting journalist of Tiger's legendary appetite for work. Any work."I give him the day off and he doesn't like it," claimed August. "He gets restless. He washes his own clothes too –just to be busy, I guess."

August, who knew little of what to expect in Africa, was apprehensive of making the trip, going so far as to express his distaste for the whole idea. Tiger was amused by his trainer's lack of enthusiasm and confided that August "thinks everybody over there is a cannibal."

There were welcome diversions from the daily rituals of pain and exhaustion. On June 7th, Buckingham Palace announced that his name was among the list of honourees for the Queen's 'official' birthday. As with Hogan Bassey five years previously, he was made a Member of the Civil Division of the Most Excellent Order of the British Empire (M.B.E.), for his 'distinguished services to the sport of boxing.'

Before heading for Nigeria, Tiger squeezed in an appearance on national television. The perennially popular prime time scheduled *What's My Line?* aired on June 16th featured Tiger as one of the games challenger's. He shared the role with a man who sold bridal veils and a helicopter stewardess. The mystery guest was the actress Geraldine Page.

He departed with August. The Pan-American Airlines plane made a brief stop over at Dakar International Airport in Senegal. August, feeling mightily oppressed by the African heat, turned to Tiger who to his astonishment was still wearing his homborg hat. Some time later, he presented Tiger with a panama hat that he had purchased from the airport gift store and Tiger accepted it without comment.

The plane touched down at Lagos' Ikeja Airport on the evening of June 24. "There were huge signs and everybody was cheering," August remembered. "I got off the plane before Dick and waited with everyone for him to make his appearance. It was thrilling (and) I was very happy for him." Staring up the airplane stairway, he heard the roars of the crowd when Tiger finally emerged. His head still bore the panama, but on top of it August recalled was the "darned black homborg."

He was up early the next morning. After seeing off a departing sports official at the Lagos docks, he paid a breakfast visit to Hogan Bassey's home. Then in the afternoon, he picked up Jimmy August enroute to the Abalti Barracks, his designated training camp. Both men stood by directing the workmen as they erected a host of materials that had been shipped out of New York. All was completed before the day was through.

Training started in earnest the following day. The routine was the same as ever: Road work in the early hours, breakfast in the late morning, gym workouts in the afternoon, dinner at six and retirement at ten. The difference of course was that he was fighting among his countrymen with six hundred of them congregating daily to watch his sparring sessions. They were a constant source of irritation to August. "Why do they have to scream every time he throws a punch?" he asked one local pressman. A few days later, he arrived at the barracks with Bobby Diamond only to miss Tiger's sparring session because they found it impossible to negotiate a path through the mass of bodies. It infuriated August so much that he insisted thereafter on having a police guard around the ring.

Tiger was oblivious to all this, his concerns centering solely on the fact that Gene Fullmer did not appear to be making any obvious plans to embark for Nigeria. Fullmer had sent a message to the promoters at the beginning of July, claiming to have injured a foot ligament as he trained on June 21st which was not healing "as fast as expected." But few believed him. The ink had hardly dried on the contract when the Nigerian press began running stories on Fullmer's reservations about the quality of food, water and sanitary conditions that he and his entourage expected to face in Africa. It was said that if he did decide to come, he would be bringing copious supplies of food and water. While he denied making such statements, claiming he was misquoted, Tiger's people were convinced that Fullmer's messages were ploys aimed at avoiding Africa, especially when a second missive expressed doubts over the idea of holding an open air fight during the rainy season.

Jones, newly arrived in Lagos was contemptuous telling the *Daily Times'* correspondent Ajibade Thomas that Fullmer "will not fight in Nigeria –I know he won't. If he doesn't want to fight, let him come out and say so. He's just thinking of excuses. Now it's his foot, next it will probably be his hands or eyes." Soon, he was talking openly about drafting a substitute, perhaps Joey Giardello or possibly Laslo Papp.

"Gene is merely bluffing," Tiger proffered to Thomas after a hard days toil. "Maybe this is a way of trying to avoid coming here, but I know that he wants that title bad, and if he is serious…" He grinned as he loosened his gloves.

Who would he prefer to meet if he stayed put, Thomas asked.

"Oh well, there's a lot of them there," he replied. "There is Joey Giardello, Laslo Papp (but) I would rather choose Joey, I have a score to settle with that guy."

Back in America, Lou Burston met with Fullmer and Jensen and received an assurance that they would arrive on Sunday, July the 19th. Solomons too, added his weight and after speaking with Jensen by telephone, it was agreed that the fight would be postponed to August 10th.

Few, at the time, knew the true reason behind Fullmer's prevarications was that Jensen's wife had come down with an illness. Oblivious to this, the ever sceptical, Jones kept up the pressure, informing a gathering of journalists that Joey Giardello was "anxious" to take Fullmer's place if the former champion withdrew. If he did not show up, Jones continued, Fullmer would never get another world title fight against Tiger.

Fullmer finally arrived on July 19th, a warm Sunday evening, at Ikeja Airport with a small entourage of Jensen, his father Tuff and a sparring partner, Milo Savage. The following evening, at Victoria Island's Federal Palace Hotel, Solomons and Bassey played host to 150 guests at a dinner in honour of the combatants. The evening's conviviality was disrupted by a comic-serious argument between Marv Jensen and Bobby Diamond, the former demanding an apology for Diamond's frequent comments describing Fullmer as "yellow." Solomons quickly jumped in to calm things while Chief Johnson, irrepressible as ever, offered to put them on the fight bill, "Maybe I'll take on both." All thunder and bluster, the good chief was always one to talk a good fight –or two. As skilful in the act of promoting as he was in politicking, he had for several weeks been telling all and sundry of his intention to square up to two Ghanaian government ministers on the Tiger-Fullmer bill (Nigerian rivalry with Ghana, dating from colonial times, was intense). He even took to stripping to his shorts to engage Tiger in 'sparring' workouts. When the Nigerian Boxing Board of Control informed him that his 'application' for a fighter's licence had being turned down, Johnson immediately 'lodged an appeal.' "I will fight in Ibadan next month" he insisted, "they won't be able to stop me. If they don't give me my licence, then I will apply my powers as minister of sport and suspend the boxing board." The assembled pressmen burst into laughter; he was obviously joking. Still, many wondered.

Thirty-six years on from the bout, Gene Fullmer has appreciative memories of Nigeria. "The people were great," he says, "they gave us a welcome like I've never been welcomed in any place." The morning after the dinner, a huge crowd gathered to watch him pay a visit to the palace of Lagos' Oba, Adeyinka Oyekan and a few hours later, an even larger one of 150,000 lined the principal streets of Ibadan to serenade his name enroute to the official reception organised by the Western government at the Liberty Stadium. Everyday for the duration of his preparations fans milled around the camp he set up at the gym of the

University of Ibadan, paying the shilling (14 cents) entrance fee to watch him go through his paces. Within the week, he was happy enough to write home to Utah confirming that the "food is good, the weather is kind and the people are very friendly."

Meanwhile, Tiger was every bit the celebrity among his countrymen. His image saturated billboards and newspaper advertisements endorsing products ranging from Quaker oats to Dunlop tyres. There were daily digests of happenings around his training camp. On one occasion he posed beside his recently delivered gleaming top of the range Mercedes Benz automobile while another time they covered a small ceremony in which Johnson presented him with the *Ring's* Gold Championship Belt. Nat Fleisher, the caption went "could not make it."

A documentary made the previous year by the United States Information Service, titled *'Dick Tiger: Profile of a Champion'* was completed and together with full length versions of the two previous bouts with Fullmer, was showing at several cinema outlets. *'Profile of a Champion'* provides a fascinating look at its subject casting Tiger in the 'rags to riches,' 'poor–little–boy–grows–into–prosperity-by-dint-of-hard–work' mould; in other words, the American Dream writ in African. "What made Dick Tiger persist in circumstances which would have made lesser men yield?" An American narrator asks in the introductory passages as clips of Tiger's visage, smiling broadly in one and in another turning his face from side to side as though surveying the peaks of mount Olympus, fill the screen. The narrator instructs that a review of the subject's roots in his homeland will provide the answers as to why this young Nigerian now bestrides the world middleweight division. Starting with fast moving aerial camera shots of the African jungle landscape that are accompanied by equally pacey African drum beats, the film starts in Amaigbo, Tiger's birth place where the sketchy details of his early life are spoken over scenes of Rebecca Ihetu in animated conversation with Abigail in the front porch of her home as Tiger's children play around. The viewer catches glimpses of the village school and the areas the infant Tiger would have played

121

in as well as the road he used to walk to school. The upshot is that Tiger grew up poor but that this less than privileged environment nevertheless provided him with a protective family network that ensured that his physical and moral wants did not go undernourished.

The story quickly shifts to Aba Township where scenes of Aba Market, its Town Hall, a Bank, Cinema and government buildings provide the backdrop of modernity, a startling contrast to Amaigbo's rural trappings. Here the theme is the influence of Aba's unabashed collective optimism on the developing mind of the young Richard Ihetu. This communal urge to progress to greater and better things the narrator adds is borne through the inscriptions on buses and trucks which profess religious (the Christian) faith and more secular expressions like 'Let the Good Times Roll.' The scenes which follow chronologise Tiger's route to self betterment: There are the signposts of businesses to which he delivered goods and a short segment on his old school where the bespectacled principal, Mr. Aliminu is captured holding an open air lesson. There are also glances at the edifice of the Emy Cinema, location of Tiger's first professional bout. The reward of these exertions; commercial, academic and athletic is displayed in the form of 'Dick Tiger Lodge,' Tiger's large homestead, impliedly purchased long before he began earning boxing purses in England and America.

An interview with Maurice Foran, Tiger's Liverpool trainer forms a brief reference to Tiger's experiences in England before the viewer is transported to a New York City gym where a hard at work Tiger engages in a vigorous sparring session under the watchful eyes of Jimmy August. The film then seeks to present an impression of Tiger's life in America; one that is apparently consumed by constant, almost ceaseless training which is punctuated only by few instances of rest and relaxation. Tiger is shown having dinner with what appear to be an upper-middle class New York family. He is also shown signing autographs for a large group of fans, two of whom pay glowing tribute to his fighting abilities as does Harry Markson who speaks from his offices in Madison Square Garden.

The film then begins to focus on the build up to his impending World title fight with Gene Fullmer. Tiger is seen waking up in the small hours in his room at the Governor hotel before going on his daily jog around the San Francisco Waterfront. Later on that day, August, Jersey Jones and Foran watch him spar. A comical interlude then ensues with the 'visit' to Tiger's hotel room by Chief Johnson, Hogan Bassey and Rafui King all of whom trot through shaking his hand as they enter. Then everyone settles down to watch Johnson, at his theatrical best, 'ham' things up. Background music plays over the film as Johnson animatedly 'advises' Tiger on how he will proceed to exact defeat on the hapless Fullmer. Raising his palms in the air in the manner of Cassius Clay, he appears to predict a seventh round kayo for Tiger.

En route to Candlestick park, the venue for the bout, Tiger is shown touring San Francisco with August on a cable car, viewing the city's bay area and famous Golden Gate Bridge from the 21 storey apex of the Carlyle Hotel. Homage is paid to his image as a familyman as he is captured shopping for toys at a department store while his spiritual side is noted when he is filmed entering the local Episcopal Church to worship two days before the fight. The last segments of the film highlight the fight with Fullmer and after his victory, a clip of the post fight interview and the after fight party held at the Carlyle.

"Let the good times roll," intone the narrator's final words.

Fight fever had gripped Nigeria. Or so it appeared. For the apparent enthusiasm of press and public was not translating into a flood of ticket sales. This was partly a consequence of the uncertainties caused by Fullmer's initial prevarications and although his arrival had served as a boost, sales were by the beginning of August, still well below the 40,000 envisaged by Solomons. This was not through a lack of effort. The Government sponsored publicity machine had been active right from the outset. In early July, when the fight was still scheduled for July 27th, Dr. Azikiwe held a ceremony at state house at which he formally purchased ten ringside tickets. Dutifully, the press took photographs of him posing with Tiger, Hogan Bassey, Bobby Diamond and Chief Johnson.

The regions also played their part. The Deputy Premier of the Western Region staged an occasion similar to the President's, buying tickets for his civil servants while in the Eastern parliament a 'political truce' was declared between the opposing parties. A resolution also granted the region's civil servants a two-day holiday. This was taken further in the North where ticket sales were at their slowest, the government granting a four day long holiday for its public service employees. In fact the theme of holidays and the granting of economic concessions to the public became the overriding promotional feature. The respective regions all negotiated cheaper fares with public and private transport services so that buses and railcars offered low rates to those travelling to Ibadan. The national airlines also announced that it would be offering cheaper airfares to those travelling from any West African capital city.

Along the way, there were incidents worth reporting for the gathered foreign media, among which was an intriguing public row between competing 'rain doctor associations,' who tried using the threat to the fight of heavy seasonal rain to their advantage. In one hilarious encounter, Solomons was accosted on the street by a Lagosian 'doctor' who assured him that he could guarantee clear skies for twenty hours, all at a price, of course. When asked what the going rate would be for such a feat, he informed the promoter that it would cost him $2,800.

"I'll give you $3,000 if you can rain ice," Solomons retorted, as he re-clamped his bulbous cigar in his mouth.

On the eve of the match there was a near tragic accident involving Solomons and Jack Hart, the fight referee. Travelling from Lagos to Ibadan along the so called 'murder road,' a nickname said to have been inspired by the authoress Elspeth Huxley, their car smashed head long into a stray cow. Happily for them, although nor for the disembowelled carcass, they escaped unhurt.

Ibadan was clear skied, if a little damp on the morning of the fight. Both fighters made their way to the Obisesan Auditorium where the weighing in ceremony was due to commence at 11.00 a.m. A huge crowd had been developing and Tiger, wanting to keep his feathers unruffled, parked his Mercedes some blocks away and stealthily entered the building through a back door. Fullmer arrived a few minutes afterwards and when the ceremonies were completed, Tiger again chose the rear egress. Fullmer, on the other hand, made his departure from the front and was immediately swamped by the pressing crowd who chanted 'FULMA, FULMA.' Ten minutes passed before a detachment of riot police waded through to get him but he still could not get to his car, and had to make do with a lift from a local journalist.

The eyes of the world, it seemed were now trained on Nigeria. The morning papers carried a full spread advert placed by the Western Region's government in which Tiger's visage, bestriding the length of a superimposed African continent, was accompanied by the caption 'TOWARD THAT NOBLE AND REWARDING VENTURE OF NATION BUILDING.' The enormity of the occasion, however, was fraught with attendant risks and so as to minimize the threat of disorder and if need be to cope with any disturbances, strict measures were taken to police the event. Special police and army units, both containing veterans of recent operations in the Congo, were drafted in to patrol parts of the city. Over 250 members of the elite Queen's Regiment dressed in scarlet and yellow jackets which were topped off with red Fezs, though designated as stadium ushers, were primed to act as the first line of maintaining order. Outside the stadium was a sizeable though undisclosed number of steel-helmeted riot police, each armed with a wicker shield and five-foot long Billy club.

As the burning sunrays dimmed and evening dawned, the dignitaries began to arrive. Governor-General Azikiwe, the governors of the Western and Eastern Regions and the American ambassador sat in the front row. The foreign press were intrigued by the flamboyant traditional attires on display: The men came in robes of green and blue, some of which were completed with bejewelled caps, while the women came in lace that was embroidered in assorted patterns. Stealing the limelight once again was Chief Johnson, resplendent in green and gold robes and waving a white feather tail. Standing the full length of his six foot three frame, he acknowledged the cheers of the stadium when it was announced that he had been awarded a 'walkover' because neither of the Ghanaian 'opponents' had turned up.

At 8.30 p.m., the moment arrived. A fanfare of trumpets blasted around the stadium as the lights temporarily went out. A minute later, the lights returned to reveal Gene Fullmer bouncing on his heels. The crowd roared. Another blackout followed and when the lights resurfaced, Tiger, wearing a blue and silver robe had joined him. This time the crowd's response was deafening. Referee Hart entered the ring after a rendition of the national anthems to give the barely audible pre-fight instructions. Tiger stared at Fullmer, fully confident that he would finally take care of him. He remembered August and Jones' fears that he might become "overanxious" while fighting before his countrymen. Both had told him to remain steady, not to get wild or careless but to fight his normal fight. When the bell sounded he rushed toward Fullmer and soon backed him into the ropes. Fullmer managed to extricate himself out of the cul-de-sac but as he made his way to the centre of the ring, a right hook thundered off the side of his jaw. Fullmer was stopped dead on his tracks and Tiger followed up with a left-right-left combination. Encouraged by this success, Tiger threw a succession of wildly delivered punches but Fullmer made him pay for this lapse and caught him with two stiff counter-punches. Hart was alone in scoring the round even and it was the last one in which Fullmer would come close to anything like maintaining parity with Tiger.

In the second, there were several toe-to-toe exchanges with Tiger getting the better of Fullmer each time. Tiger began developing a steady pattern of attack which was to move in with the jab and follow up with punch combinations to the head and body. By the third, Fullmer appeared to be shorn of much of his energy. Tiger continued the punishment, chasing Fullmer from corner to corner as busily, he continued dispensing hooks, uppercuts and straight right hands.

Astonished ringsiders let out gasps as each blow hit the target: "Is this Fullmer human?" An incredulous Nigerian official asked. The American was game noted Kofi Badu, the Ghanaian journalist seated beside him, but, "What," he wrote verbosely, "is raw naked courage against the fury and ferocity of a tiger, the remorseless, pitiless, destructiveness of a human caterpillar; the irresistible might of an African avalanche?" The battering continued until a half minute from the round's end, Fullmer sat slumped on the ropes in a sitting position, his gloves positioned defensively above his head, "as if attempting to solicit divine intervention." The bell saved him on that occasion. As he sat slumped in his corner, blood oozing from above his brows, his eyes closing fast, Jensen and his father pleaded with him to quit. Fullmer responded by vigorously shaking his head from side to side.

They let him out for the fourth and the fight got better for Tiger and worse for Fullmer. When a few, fleeting jabs managed to penetrate Tiger's upraised fists, Tiger immediately responded with two heavy left hooks. Fullmer then moved to clinch and made a grab for Tiger's head as if to wrestle him into a headlock, but Tiger countered by grabbing Fullmer by the waist and lifting him onto his shoulders. Hart, concerned by Fullmer's condition but mindful of the tradition of giving desperate opponents every chance in a world title bout, viewed the hunched Utan postured shakily somewhere half way standing up and half way on his way to the canvas. He pulled Tiger away just as the bell sounded, saving Fullmer if only for a little while longer.

The crowd, sensing that the end was nigh, erupted, chanting "TIGER, TIGER, TIGER." The lone voice of Jensen's barked at Fullmer to "Fight, fight, fight." By the seventh round, Fullmer's face was a mass of red gore –red as his trunks and redder than the crimson coloured gloves he was wearing. Mouth agape, he moved mournfully in circles as blood trickled down his nose, littering the canvas with specks of plasma. "Fullmer's face," wrote Peter Wilson, the London *Daily Mirror* correspondent as the round ended, "was a rubbery caricature of a human countenance, a contour map of disaster with bumps and lumps for mountains, ridges and meandering red streaks for the rivers."

By now Jensen had seen enough and beckoned for Hart to stop the fight. "I didn't have any strength in that fight," Fullmer remembers, "I mean I stuck my left jab and it wouldn't even go out, it just looked like a limp hose. He cut my eye in the seventh round and cut it real bad. So the referee said, "We're going to have to stop the fight or you'll endanger your vision" and I told him, "I hate to see you stop it, but I can't whip this guy with two eyes let alone one."

"I had nothing," Fullmer told author Peter Heller in the early seventies, "He beat me. My father and my mother could have been judge and referee and I couldn't have won a round, wouldn't have won a round. I mean he beat me that bad."

Hart proceeded to Tiger's corner to raise his hand and thirty thousand voices erupted in unison. A handful of spectators bounded into the ring, breaching the security cordon as they shouted "YOU GOT HIM TIGER, YOU GOT HIM." Pursuing police quickly rounded them up.

Ten minutes passed before Tiger's victory was announced through the public address system. Chief Johnson waded through the melee and offered Tiger his large hand. Then lifting his jewel-studded cap from his head, he placed it, reverentially, atop the champion's head. Johnson completed his quasi-coronation by thrusting his feather tail into the champion's hand and Tiger waved it high at his adoring audience, each movement acknowledging the gust of cheers. The match had been over for thirty minutes when Tiger, now tiring of the adoration, 'begged' for a path to be cleared to his dressing room. Hours later, as he peered out of his limousine, he was moved by the sight of the thousands who had waited to cheer his departure.

Tiger's victory signalled the start of a night of celebrating around the country. So called 'victory dances' were held at virtually every nightspot. Once again, Chief Johnson led the way, sponsoring the party at Ibadan's Paradise Nightclub, instructing his invitees to 'Bring your own dame and avoid disappointment.'

Amidst the revelry however were voices of dissent. Nigeria was after all a developing nation with a multitude of social and economic wants and the fight had been a money spending exercise which did not break even, the crowd for one being short by fifteen thousand of the expected attendance. Tiger and Fullmer's purses had to be paid, as did the expenses of Solomons, Bassey and Hart. The cost of erecting the ring, renting chairs, installing lights, paying temporary staff and miscellaneous matters added up to something in the region of $170,000. Tai Solarin was an educator as well as a journalist who revelled in his reputation as the conscience of the Nigerian nation. In his *Daily Times* column he asked whether any tangible value had accrued from the "tremendous chunk of prestige we have hewn for ourselves from this fight." The cumulated costs and losses were he insisted a national own goal.

"We have gone out of our way to look for a national prestige which paradoxically must have been worn threadbare by our flamboyant and our most ostentatious search for it. Foreigners must be trying (desperately) not to laugh publicly at our profligacy. We would have if we were in their shoes." Methodically listing the "waste" caused by holidaying civil servants, absconding workers and the concessionary fares effected by the public transportation service, Solarin with the aid of an economist he had 'consulted,' estimated a total national loss in the region of £120,000 –quite enough money he assured his readers to have educated 40,000 young Nigerians to degree level. "Would our prestige have suffered in anyway had the fight been staged in Canberra or Tristan du Cunha or Honolulu or San Francisco, when we would not have been called upon to foot the bill?"

Still, most of his compatriots begged to differ, the *Nigerian Outlook* editorialising on the "spirit of unity and national brotherhood" that the fight had helped to foster. Speaking for himself, Tiger cabled the *Ring* insisting the fight had worked wonders for the country. "There is no saying what this fight has meant to Nigeria with the worldwide publicity and prestige it received. Financially that publicity or prestige couldn't be purchased for millions of dollars and of course, my victory made a perfect end to the story."

His success had wider ramifications. From Black Africa's chief proponent of nationalism came the following cable:

Accept my hearty congratulations on your successful defence of the world middleweight crown in Ibadan, Nigeria on Saturday. Your victory over the idol of the U.S. has added another testimony to the ability of the African to scale the highest ladder of human achievement. I hope your example will inspire the youth of Africa and give new fillip to the quest to assert the African personality not only in sport but in all fields of human endeavour. I wish you more grease on your elbow.

Dr. Kwame Nkrumah.

Nkrumah accompanied this with a personal invitation to visit him in Ghana. But for Dick Tiger now at the summit of his popularity, all did not remain well. A side consequence of the fight would produce a rare episode of public disapprobation. When the Eastern Nigerian Tax Authority ruled in September that he pay an assessed amount of £12,548 in taxes on his total purse of £35,000, Tiger balked, making it clear that he thought the sum "too excessive." He had apparently been told during the fight negotiations that all taxes would be waived. Reacting with scorn, an editorial in the *Nigerian Outlook*, warned that the "idea of people thinking that they should be given preferential treatment on state matters should cease." Asking whether Tiger had ever protested about the taxes levied on the purses he had received for his bouts held overseas and refuting the notion that Nigerians had suddenly taken the fancy of treating their sports men as demigods, the paper called on Tiger to be "man enough to settle his account with the state."

Portrait of a fighter. A young Dick Tiger strikes a pose.

Tiger poses in a Liverpool gym with spar mate Tony Smith

Tiger's breakthrough fight came in May of 1957 when he administered a merciless beating to Terry Downes, the loquacious 'Paddington Panther.' In only his third professional bout, Downes had been expected to beat Tiger, whom Downes' brain trust perceived would be an easy fight. When asked, after the fight, whom he wanted for his next opponent, Downes shot back: "I'd like it to be the bastard who suggested Dick Tiger."

With Bessie Braddock. The formidable 'Battling Bessie' was the Member of Parliament for Liverpool Exchange.

Maurice Foran took up the reins as Dick Tiger's trainer at Tiger's lowest ebb. Here he points to his painting indicating that the portrait will not be complete until he is able to superimpose the world championship belt of the middleweight division.

The family man. Dick Tiger proudly displays his daughter Grace, while wife Abigail holds Victoria and Hogan Bassey, Nigeria's first world boxing champion, carries Grace's twin, Richard. (Circa 1961) He and Abigail had eight children in all.

The 'Pugilistic plenipotentiary.' Tiger as described by an American journalist. American sportswriters picked up on Tiger's enthusiasm in promoting the emerging nation. He is with Simeon Adebo, Nigerian Ambassador to the United Nations.

Winning the world's middleweight championship from Gene Fullmer.
Candlestick Park, San Francisco, October 23 1962.

With manager Wilfred 'Jersey' Jones, on the left, and trainer Jimmy
August.

Hamming it with Emile Griffith at a press conference before their world middleweight championship contest in 1966.

Battling Jose Torres and winning the undisputed world's light heavyweight championship at New York City's Madison Square Garden. December 1966.

The Soldier. In December of 1967, six months after declaring his allegiance to the secessionist state of Biafra, Tiger received a direct commission as a second lieutenant of the Morale Corps of the Biafran Army. His fight contracts stipulated that the rebel anthem be played before his bouts where MCs introduced him as "Dick Tiger of Biafra." Later, in December of 1969, he would return the MBE civil medal to the British Embassy in Washington D.C. charging the British, who aided Federal Nigeria, with complicity in the 'genocide' of men, women and children.

Bob Foster connects to Tiger's jaw knocking him out for the first and only time in his 81-fight career. May 24 1968.

138

Near the end. Tiger, his body displaying the beginnings of an emaciated physique that is a symptom of his recently diagnosed cancer of the liver, arrives at Lagos airport on July 18 1971 with his son Richard by his side.

The coffin of Dick Tiger is borne to its final resting on Sunday December 20th 1971 in Amaigbo.

Nine
A GARDEN FIGHTER

Tax disputes not withstanding, Tiger turned his attentions to making some more money. He was on top of the world now, and was relishing the prospect of making a money spinning bout with one of the top middleweight contenders. Of these, three were no longer in the reckoning; Fullmer, of course, he had bloodily dispatched into retirement; Paul Pender had announced his retirement and Laslo Papp, the Vienna-based Hungarian who had dominated amateur boxing, was on the verge of having his professional career terminated by the Hungarian authorities who had become increasingly displeased by the 'un-socialist' levels of purse money he was receiving.

Madison Square Garden, eager to resume its association with Tiger, threw in an offer of $100,000 for him to meet the winner of an impending bout between Rubin Carter and Joey Archer, but, perhaps still smarting over a recent spat he had had with Teddy Brenner, Jones ignored it. Instead, he steered his attentions across the Hudson River, towards the handlers of the official number one contender, George Benton. Negotiations were at a pace when suddenly, they were terminated by the intervention of Lou Duva, a small time promoter based in Patterson, New Jersey.

Duva, who later would join forces with Benton to become one of boxing's most successful manager/trainer teams by guiding the likes of Evander Holyfield, Pernell Whitaker, Mark Breland and Meldrick Taylor to world titles, was in 1963, the boxing obsessed boss of the local teamsters union, looking for his big break. But in order to be able to do this, he would need an established fighter, a promoter partner as well as money and the help of 'people with influence.'

His first task was to solicit the agreement of Joey Giardello, Tiger's erstwhile opponent, who decidedly, was not a name at the top of many a promoters lips. Giardello, a crafty boxer-puncher had been born Carmen Tilelli (he appropriated his ring name from an army buddy) in Brooklyn thirty-three years previously. A ring veteran of fifteen years, his talents had not garnered for him the world championship belt that might have been his. The perception among many in boxing was that Giardello, dubbed 'Kid Disillusion,' was a spent force who had denied himself the opportunity of winning the title. In 1954, he had been jailed for his part in a 'riotous assault' at a Philadelphia gas station. Primed, at the time, to challenge Bobo Olson for the world's middleweight championship, a mystified magistrate told him, "Joe, I never saw anyone throw away a million dollars before."

At the time Duva approached him, Giardello was 'persona non grata' in New York, the N.Y.S.A.C. having barred his licence. The Garden had even refused to use him for off premises bouts that were held in other states. As with Sonny Liston, his debarment stemmed from the question mark that hung over his associations with 'undesirables' who were said to be making the decisions in his career.

"Everybody had dumped him. He was down and out until I talked him into letting me promote (the fight with Tiger)," Duva would tell the sportswriter Dave Anderson. But although Giardello remains grateful to Duva's magnificent effort, it is apparent that his gratitude extends by no less measure to Dick Tiger.

"I fought for twenty years," explains Giardello. "I had 129 fights and it would have been terrible if I hadn't been the champion. I was number one since 1952. They wouldn't fight me in those days; Robinson wouldn't fight me for the title, Basilio wouldn't fight me for the title, Bobo Olsen wouldn't fight me. I fought Fullmer in 1960 in his hometown and I got a draw. A draw! I had him bleeding, I shook him. But when Tiger won the title, he told Robinson that he would fight the winner between myself and Robinson. So I beat Robinson, and then I fought Dick Tiger. (Tiger) was the man, because he figured that the guys who deserved it, (would get a shot at the title). He knew that he was in trouble with me a little bit, but I thank him very much for giving me my chance."

As boxing commission rules forbade the dual role of trainer and promoter, Duva, who also trained fighters, joined forces with Murray Goodman. Goodman had made his name as a publicity man, but together with one Sam Bartolleta, had begun staging a series of largely unsuccessful promotions around New York and New Jersey. Nevertheless, Goodman had a name familiar to the boxing fraternity. Duva also utilised the help from those familiar but nameless persons attached to the boxing industry: "I sat down with the right people and worked out the right deal," he would tell Dave Anderson in *'Ringsiders,'* Anderson's tome to boxing's greatest trainers. "I never sat down with (Frankie) Carbo (the Mafia's underboss of the boxing business) but there were other people I sat with."

Armed with money; a lot of which promised to come from television rights and a name fighter few considered a threat to Tiger, Duva approached Jones. "We made the match after I outbid Benton's handlers. They didn't want to fight no Georgie Benton because they knew he was a tougher fight. They would rather have fought Joey Giardello. They didn't know what his condition was like. But as far as I was concerned, Joey was in excellent condition."

The fight was set for December 7 at Atlantic City. Notable to Americans for being a summer resort, the city had never before staged a world championship. Boxers like Jack Dempsey, however, had used it in the past as a training depot.

For the first time, a relaxed, more playful side to Tiger began to emerge. Although he refused to totally let down his guard, he was more at ease with and more adept at handling sportswriters, even making time for amusing repartees with those who gathered daily at his training camp. One day, a reporter offered to spar a few rounds with him. Tiger 'agreed' and beamed at the sight of his decidedly portly challenger, with great effort, squeezing himself through the ropes.

"Don't hurt me," he begged Tiger, adding self consciously, "I should be a heavyweight." Sizing him up, Tiger cracked: "No, middleweight is alright for you. All your weight is in your middle."

The bookies installed him as the three to one favourite. While his opponent's gifts as a fighter were still apparent, his commitment to training remained highly suspect. The Giardello camp were doing nothing to squash the rumours, that their fighter was back to his habitual routine of gorging himself full of pasta and then washing it down with large quantities of beer. Not the kind of boxer many believed was capable of troubling Tiger, a champion whom Robert Lipsyte described as training for the bout "as if the losers of prize fights are thrown to the beasts."

On the night of the fight, the Atlantic City Convention Hall, a venue with longstanding associations with Miss America Beauty Pageants, had a big fight atmosphere. At ringside, boxing legends like Joe Louis and Rocky Marciano mixed with political dignitaries. As if they were not satisfied with the 'ageing has been' they thought they had lined up for the champion, the Tiger camp aimed to unsettle Giardello, whose supporters now thronged the aisles. First, two men dressed as African 'witch doctors,' confronted him, both issuing oaths and curses as they waved oversized feather's in his face and rattled "bones in their bags." Tiger also decided to delay his ring entrance for a full 15 minutes.

But Giardello remained unfazed, soaking up the adulation of his supporters as he sat waiting and no doubt recalling the grand plan that he had already shared with anyone who cared to listen to him. "Tiger," he had informed the sportswriters, "eats up guys who stand there and fight him like Florentino Fernandez and Fullmer. He's going to have to chase me and that's the way I'm going to win the title." He was as good as his word.

In the first round, Tiger found himself punching the air which Giardello had filled half-seconds previously. And on the occasions that he got to him, he had to struggle to get out of the challenger's smothering arms. Then a powerful overhand right caught Tiger full on the face, and his legs buckled. This for Giardello was the defining moment. "I hit him with a good shot," he recalls "A right hand and he almost went down. I think that made the whole fight different."

Tiger became hesitant, bidding his time. Giardello was

moving so swiftly, it appeared that he could only punish his opponent when wrapped in the clinches. In the second, his left arm was locked between Giardello's right arm and right side, for a time he struggled, before suddenly using his strength to spin the challenger around and firing short blows to Giardello's body. It was frustrating for Tiger, but he remained stoic in the belief that Giardello had to come to him if he wanted a part of his title. In order to do this, he changed tactics in the third. Electing for a stationary stance, he dropped his shoulder and tilted his head sideways. This brought Giardello within his reach and he countered a number of the challenger's jabs.

For the most part, however, Giardello succeeded in keeping him off balanced. Here was Giardello reviving the depth of his talents particularly his mastery of range fighting, that is, of keeping his opponent at a measured distance and making him miss by fractions of an inch. He pawed out his left hand, feinted his man off balance and then counter punched. In the fourth, a succession of stabbing jabs jolted Tiger's head backwards. Angered, Tiger bolted forward and swung a right at Joey's head. The punch missed its target and the momentum sent Tiger tumbling on to the canvas. Tiger got up and when referee Paul Cavalier waved them on, Giardello came forward, throwing a right to the side of his body and another right to his head. Tiger repositioned his stance to meet Giardello's jab with a straight left when the bell sounded.

Tiger kept up the pressure and waited in expectation ofGiardello's thirty-five year old legs giving way. But this did not happen. The challenger, whom Tiger knew had a propensity for opening in cuts survived the critical periods of rounds seven, eight and then nine. He did not tire markedly and he did not bleed. His supporters, perhaps as surprised as the boxing pundits, began to roar a chorus: 'TAKE HIM CHUBBY, TAKE HIM CHUBBY.'

When both men did the ceremonial touching of gloves in the final round, Giardello was in tears, already believing that he had won the thing his heart desired most. Tiger tried to initiate exchanges, but Giardello would have none of it. "To go in and fight it out would have been suicidal," he remarked later. He remained on his toes and kept on retreating until the final bell.

Tiger stood quietly in his corner to await the decision. Flanking him were two Nigerian delegates, each waving a miniature copy of the national flag. Cavalier, the sole arbiter of the match, scored it eight rounds to five for Giardello.

At the post fight interviews, Tiger complained that he had been robbed. "Fancy giving the verdict to the runner instead of the fighter and the one who did all the chasing. Look, I haven't got a mark on me. I was convinced that I won. How can you give it to a man that back-pedals? I tried to fight like a champion, but as the challenger, he should have come to me."

The fight, as with his other encounters with fighters who had 'run' from him, generated its fair share of debate, but on the whole, opinion appeared to favour Giardello. In the audience that night, was Larry Merchant, then a youthful sports editor of a Philadelphia daily. "Both of them were past their prime," he recalls. "Giardello landed very hard punches early in the fight and afterwards, if my memory serves me correctly, Dick was not too eager to engage him. Giardello was able to outbox him after that."

Giardello, all emotion and ebullience, touchingly told the press that his sons could now return playground taunts about their 'jailbird' father with a "My father is a world champion" repost. He made continual references of his gratitude to Tiger for giving him the opportunity that he thought would never return. Walking up to Tiger, he hugged and then kissed him on the cheeks: "You were man enough to give me the chance at the title," he said, "so you deserve a return."They were words that would haunt Tiger for some time to come.

Drained and sick with disappointment, Tiger made his way home. On this occasion, Lagos airport was not awash with the usual flag waving and hand clapping reception committee. His brother, Godwin, waited alone and together they loaded his luggage into a 1952 model Buick. They drove, mostly in silence, for thirteen hours until they arrived in Aba.

While there were the pleasures of his burgeoning family –he had five children in all and had the satisfaction of attending to his businesses, his mind continued to be pre-occupied with the fight. He was troubled and he was angry. The focus of his ire was Jersey Jones, whom he blamed for the discrepancy in the purse money that was promised and what he had received. Jones had assured him before the bout took place, that he would earn at least $100,000; an amount that he expected to be bolstered by the television deal which Murray Goodman hoped to put together with the Madison Square Garden Organisation. Goodman, however, had been unable to obtain this backing. And while the gate receipts had been healthy (Goodman had given Jones assurances that the fight would be a sell out), it had been diminished by the shambolic mishandling of ticket sales; many spectators having been allowed to walk into the arena after paying bribes to various ushers and on duty police officers.

The August 1964 edition of the *Ring* reported that Tiger had received $78,000 for the bout and although Lew Burston insisted that the difference was eventually made up, Tiger's confidence in Jones was severely shaken when he discovered that his manager had failed to insert a return bout clause. His response to a reporter's query a few days after the bout was on the vague side and appeared a guilty admission of his oversight. "We had a general agreement in which Giardello agreed the return but no promoter was involved in the agreement," adding "We understood that the independent promoting group which staged the bout had a return bout contract but it seems that arrangement is up in the air."

The aura of amateurishness in Jones' handling of the fight is perhaps encapsulated by a story that has Jones depositing a $10,000 cheque in Nat Fleisher's safe and promptly forgetting about it. The catalogue of errors and mishaps did not bode well for Tiger's relations with Jones. At the outset of their relationship, Jones, who knew of his disappointments with Vairo and Banasko, had sensed an initial "resentment" on Tiger's part, rooted, he

146

believed, in the treatment many an African fighter had received at the hands of their European managers. In time, however, Jones felt that they had managed to overcome this and indeed was proud to tell people that their association was based on the mutual respect of partners and not one of exploitation. In the beginning, he had insisted on reviewing each of the contracts that Jones had drawn up on his behalf, but as his trust in Jones grew, he tailed off on this. After this debacle, he went back to reading the small print. "No manager," he would soon say, "ever did anything for me. It has all being down to my own luck. All I have is because of me –not because of anyone else." Even August did not escape his wrath: "Don't you take any credit for me," he told him while a magazine interview was taking place, "You never told me anything new to do since I came to this country."

He may have rued Jones's decision to turn down other fights that could have been made. Perhaps the most profitable might have been one across the Atlantic with Terry Downes, vanquished by Paul Pender but still spoiling for a fight with Tiger. The fight, which had first been touted after Tiger had won the title from Fullmer, would never materialise. Downes blamed Tiger and his camp for this. "We did try to make offers," he wrote in his autobiography published in 1965, "but Tiger was pumped up to make replies like 'Let Downes win the British title first,' after I vacated the British title. I still think Tiger was a right mug and wrongly advised not to have cashed in fighting me –we'd have drawn a lot of money- instead of blowing his title for comparatively chicken feed to Giardello, who was probably pushed as a soft touch."

Tiger brooded in Nigeria but hoped that Giardello, the man whom he had given the chance which most would not have bothered to, would give him the rematch which he claimed his ears had heard would take place three months after Atlantic City. A number of cables came through from both Jones and Burston, but since none contained any assurance that a deal was being secured with Giardello's handlers, he pointedly refused to acknowledge them. Giardello for his part was not making any obvious plans to meet Tiger and he would cite Tiger's absence from America as the reason for this. "I don't know where he is or anything about him," he told the *Ring*, quipping: "I've heard he has become a farmer."

It was a bleak period for Tiger. Three months went and still no word on a rematch arrived. A couple of months after and 1964 was approaching its mid-mark. At 34 years of age, he might have pondered on whether his career was headed on a downward spiral, after all there were consequences to be reaped if his absence from the ring was prolonged further.

Jack Solomons, staging West Africa's second world title bout, sent him a message inviting him to Accra, Ghana to see the May 9th featherweight clash between the Ghanaian challenger, Floyd Robertson and the Mexican champion, Sugar Ramos. He looked on from a ringside seat as both men fought a gruelling contest that ended in confusion and bitterness. The hometown crowd reacted furiously when the judges favoured Ramos by a split decision. The Ghana Boxing Association then purported to overturn the verdict, substituting it for a win for Robertson. (The world governing bodies would later reinstate the original decision.)

While in Ghana, Tiger spoke with Solomons who urged him to go over to England where Bobby Diamond would make the arrangements for a few 'tune up' matches that would prepare him for the return with Giardello who was talking of defending against him that summer "preferably in New Jersey."

He left for England before the month was out and headed for Liverpool to begin training. It was a time to meet friends like Maurice Foran and also to renew many acquaintances. Johnny Best invited him over to watch a promotion at Liverpool Stadium where his presence elicited a heart-warming ovation. He responded with a deep bow. He was also the guest of honour at a function held by the local Nigerian Social Club. He loved the affection shown to him. To one American reporter he referred to Liverpool as his "second home." "In England," he said, "I am

148

respected. People smile at me on the streets, they are polite to me. I am invited everywhere for tea. People stop me in the streets and wish me well."

But as the days passed, his stay on Merseyside began to bring its own set of frustrations. A proposed fight with an Italian light heavyweight, Guilio Rinaldi, had to be aborted when Rinaldi announced that he had sustained an injury while training. Diamond tried for a replacement but Tiger was quick to see that there was no middle division fighter keen enough to take him on in this part of the world. In desperation, he wrote to Jones, urging him to arrange a fight for him. But from Jones, perhaps miffed at Tiger's refusal to answer any of the cables he had sent to Nigeria earlier on in the year, no reply came. "I kept writing Jersey," he would tell one journalist, "(but) he never answered me. Maybe he was too busy with other things, but he should have been busy with me. I made him a lot of money." Tired of waiting, in June, he left for New York, intent on securing a fight –with or without Jones' help.

He arrived to be greeted by the bombshell news that Giardello, who had been talking all year about fulfilling his pledge of a rematch, had announced his intention to defend his title against middleweight contender, Rubin Carter. Tiger was insulted. Later, in a contribution piece to the *Ring*, he wrote of his anger. "Why did he wait until then? If he intended to forget his promise and sidetrack me, he could have done it while I was in Nigeria, not when I was back in America. It was poor timing on Joey's part –and of course (poor) sportsmanship. My arrival must have scared him into doing something in a hurry, and the Carter match was the result."

He had being inactive for six months and knew that he could not continue kicking his heels while waiting for Giardello to make good on his promise. Money had to be made for his flourishing real estate concerns and there were familial obligations to be met. He considered his options. One involved taking a number of 'tune up' bouts in small towns against minor, unranked opponents. The other was to fight a high-ranking middleweight, the object of which would be to 'force the issue' with Giardello. Of the former, Tiger did not relish the prospect of waiting for fight offers that may have necessitated his crisscrossing the United States. So he settled for what the Madison Square Garden organisation could offer him. Five of the twenty bouts he had had since he had debuted there had taken place at the Garden and the Garden Corporation had put up money for two further bouts. From this point on until the zenith of his career, Madison Square Garden would provide the location and in two instances, the backing for all but one of his fights.

While he was induced by the prospect of maintaining his base in New York as well as by the meeting of his travel expenses, the Garden were also keen to promote a fighter whom they simply knew to be a 'crowd pleaser.' This attribute, both Harry Markson and Teddy Brenner knew, would be vital as the Garden now prepared its passage into the post-Television sponsorship era. The Garden hosted the first of the series of bouts, which were packaged over the course of a yearly television season, in 1951. By 1963, the Gillette Corporation was sponsoring an annual average of 50 fights, all of which the Garden promoted, to the tune of $5 million. $1,250,000 of this went towards fighters 'appearance fees.' Boxing, had since the latter part of the 1940s, been one commodity used by the American television networks in the battle for viewing figures and it was perhaps, inevitable that the sport would become susceptible to the whims of audiences, who had begun to tire from the overexposure. It was not greatly surprising when Gillette announced in the early part of 1964, that it would not be renewing its agreement when it expired at the end of the television series.

The drying up of television sponsorship now meant that the Garden would have to begin to concentrate its efforts on drawing back to the stands, many of those long lost in the comfort of their armchairs. Dick Tiger, it appeared, was one of those who fitted the bill.

When Tiger climbed through the ring ropes to face Jose

Gonzalez, he had not been in a competitive bout for seven months. Gonzalez was solid competition having beaten the likes of Rory Calhoun, Joey Archer and Florentino Fernandez (twice). He also stopped Rubin Carter in six rounds. He had seen Gonzalez fight at several New York venues and was impressed by the Puerto Rican's speed, his toughness and by what he termed "his aggressive two handed style."

Gonzalez crowded him from the moment the bell sounded, rushing at Tiger and repeatedly unleashing powerful combination blows. But his manoeuvres were mostly unsuccessful, the thud of leather sounding as Tiger picked him off with blows to the face and body. By the third, Tiger was in full stride and repeating the manoeuvre of stepping in with a jab and crashing lefts into the Puerto Rican's side. The effects were quickly apparent as Gonzalez's energetic lateral applications slowed down to limp, burdened movements. Tiger then began to mix his left hooks with right-handed crosses, which caught Gonzalez in the face.

By round six, Gonzalez's legs were unsteady and he was becoming too tired to protect his jaw. The end started when Tiger caught him a short right hand and followed up with a ferocious left hook to the mid-section. The following series of combinations were of such force as to send Gonzalez crashing on to his knees. He struggled to get up and although in a standing position by the time referee Arthur Mercante's count had reached five, one look into Gonzalez's glazed eyes was enough for him to wave the fight over.

Ron Lipton, who had trained with Gonzalez at the Solar Gym on Twenty Eighth Street had a ringside view and saw what few others saw. "Dick shot out a jab, crossed a right to his jaw and followed with a left hook which rocked his head from side to side. The right hand that paved the way for the wrecking ball left hook, was a thunderous short right hand thrown across Tiger's body, tearing Jose's head to the right into an immediate short left hook which tore his head to the left. Both blows landed almost simultaneously and dropped him unconscious to the canvas where he bounced so hard it woke him up. He (Gonzalez) had been dropped on one knee but arose on legs that were shaking. When the referee stopped the fight tears of frustration came from two glazed eyes still burning with the fire to continue but with a body unwilling to continue. He had wanted to win the bout so badly and I could see the reason why he was crying: He had felt such power. He'd trained so hard that he knew in a millisecond that the punches were so hard that this was the one man he could not beat."

Back in his dressing room, Tiger, the glint of satisfaction over his features, told the press "If Giardello beats Carter, he will have no excuses to pass me again." The rift with Jones appeared not to be healed, when he added, "My manager in London will make arrangements for my next fight."

There were a few fights to come before he could get to Giardello, who would not be meeting Carter until December 17th and Tiger accepted the Garden's offer to appear in the very last of their weekly televised fights. When it was discovered that the Garden Arena would not be available on the date scheduled in September, the venue was relocated to Cleveland. This of course had not been unusual. On occasions like this a promoter would be sought and the arrangement would be for the Garden to pay the main event fighters, keep the television rights and for the promoter to have the takings from the live gate.

Tiger's selected opposition was Don Fullmer, brother of Gene. Fullmer had been a last minute replacement for an Argentine fighter, Rocky Rivero, who had been unable to obtain a United States visa in time. It was one of Tiger's more frustrating bouts. Fullmer constantly circled him and then scurried backwards when he tried to engage him. He caught up with him on a few occasions, and in the eighth, bloodied his nose with a hard left. Mostly, however, he chased in vain, at one point dropping his hands to his sides and shrugging his shoulders.

He wrote about his disappointment at not being allowed to give the fans value for money, injecting his article with a teasing humour. "Don was the best replacement (for Rivero). For one thing, the publicity could centre around his determination to square accounts with me for what I had done to Gene. I honestly expected a hard fight with Don. I thought that he would try to restore the family prestige by beating me. It didn't turn out like that. Instead of fighting, (he) elected to box, using hit-and-run tactics and trying to stay as far away from me as possible. Maybe this being an Olympic year, Fullmer decided to make this a running event, turning the bout into a 15,000-meter race. I wanted to make boxing's last appearance on weekly T.V. an exciting one and I am genuinely sorry that it wasn't."

His next opponent was announced as Joey Archer, a Bronx-born contender ranked highly by the governing bodies and *Ring* magazine. "When he beats Archer," said the back-in-the-fold Jersey Jones, "Giardello will have to fight him." Others, however, were not certain that all would be straightforward. One sportswriter apparently took Tiger aside and advised him not to take the fight. "You'll have to knock him out to win," he warned. "Archer will run from you, he'll stab his left and run. It's not a good fight for you Dick." But he smiled, and replied, "I'm not worried, I'll win."

It was not that Tiger was over confident. Far from it. He had seen Archer on numerous occasions at the Garden as well as on television and felt him to be one of the "cleverest" boxers around. He had been mightily impressed with Archer's defeat of Rubin Carter and as far as he was concerned, Archer's revenge rematch victory over Jose Gonzalez who had inflicted his only career loss made Archer's the perfect fight record. He spoke of Archer as being "my most formidable rival."

The Archer bout would present the Garden, now without television money, with a test of its own; namely that of attracting paying customers. The October 16 schedule meant that competition would be coming from the ongoing World Series between the St. Louis Cardinals and the New York Yankees. The local New York gridiron teams, the Jets and the Giants would also be involved in matches over the weekend of the fight.

Heading the Garden's publicity machine at the time was John

F.X. Condon, a tough, no nonsense character who was determined for the Garden's boxing programme to hold its own against other competition. His tactics were blunt, occasionally ruthless and sometimes risqué. Indeed a few of them, like the stunt he engineered to temporarily relieve Vice President Hubert Humphrey of the official Cadillac he was to use during a parade down a Manhattan thoroughfare, went outside the boundaries of the law. On another occasion when the middleweight Nino Benvenuti arrived in New York by ocean liner, he made arrangements for the corps of sportswriters to meet the Italian for a press conference on board the ship. He marched them down Tenth Avenue and when all were assembled at the appointed pier, moments before setting off by tug boat, each was promptly informed that the only means of reaching the conference point would be to clamber up the ship using a Jacob's ladder.

"It was hysterical," Tommy Kenville recalls, "to see the power of boxing journalism trying to get up the ladder with their typewriters, press kits and so on, without falling into the ocean." While Condon appreciated Tiger's gifts as a fighter, he was less than enamoured by the man, feeling that Tiger's soft-spoken demeanour contributed little to his objectives. "John Condon wasn't fond of Tiger," says Kenville, at the time a Garden employee in the hockey department but later, a longstanding publicity man at the boxing department. "Dick at times was difficult to deal with. (It was an effort) just to get him to talk to the press. We can make up stories, but there's a time when a fighter has to talk to the press, tell them what he thinks. I worked four or five years with Ali –didn't have to tell the man what to do. He would come into the office and ask me 'What are we doing today boss?' You couldn't get that out of Tiger. Tiger would talk in monosyllabic tones, 'It could be a good fight…'."

For this fight, Condon employed the services of a skywriter to etch the words TIGER-ARCHER over the city. The fans that walked through the turnstiles on the night of the fight generated gross receipts of $36,000. Not an exceptional amount, but Harry Markson would later announce his satisfaction at the takings.

154

Tall, and wide shouldered, Archer's eyes bespoke a steel edged toughness hewn from many ring battles. They were alert, not at all weary and informed the observer that he feared no one. While he may have lacked the rugged muscularity of contemporaries like Carter, Gonzalez and Tiger, Archer conveyed a palpable toughness and an aura which indicated that he was a man invested with great determination and a resolute fighting spirit. Coming into the bout with a career record blotted only by the sole loss to Jose Gonzalez, Archer's lack of fear was derived from knowing his limitations and capitalizing on his strengths of mobility, executing excellently timed punches as well as his ability to absorb the punches thrown at him by opponents.

Archer, his hair slicked back, was the first to enter the ring. Glowing in the manner well trained boxers do, he trod across the canvas bearing the look of the fighter cometh in expectation of victory. Then Tiger came easing himself through the ropes and emerging from the temporary crouch to reveal the smile that never failed to light up the Garden audience. Holding a single arched hand into the air, he walked in a circle, shyly acknowledging the cheers of the fans who chorused his moniker in competition with the equally rousing echoes being made on behalf of Archer. He went back to his corner to disrobe, revealing to the audience a carved-from-stone physique before joining Archer at the centre of the ring for the referee's pre-fight instructions.

From the bell, Tiger stalked and measured his blows while Archer moved and parried, catching some of Tiger's punches with an open glove. Soon, the fight began living up to the nightmare scenario envisaged by the journalist with Archer circling, stabbing out his left jab and clinching with impunity. The crowd booed Archer's tactics, but Archer calculated as many box punchers do that after weathering the storm in the first few rounds, the snap and venom from Tiger's punches would diminish come the later rounds. But he did demonstrate enough power to unsettle Tiger. In the second round for instance, Archer ground the ball of the rear of his right foot into the ring canvas to shift his weight onto the front leg and as Tiger waded in, he angled a pinpoint jab followed by right hand that landed squarely on Tiger's chin. Tiger's thickly muscled legs buckled momentarily – a sight that astounded many. Whereas many boxers would have jumped at the chance of capitalising on this success by stepping in and planting their feet firmly to the canvas in order to throw power punches, the super cautious Archer appeared to restrain himself. He may even have hesitated, surprised at his ability to hurt Tiger. Tiger responded by chasing Archer all over the ring, firing long, leaping hooks at Archer's head, trying to induce an exchange but finding little success. His best moment came in the fifth when he caught Archer with a looping right cross that drove the Irish-American, bended on one knee, into the lower ring rope. The referee, Zack Clayton, however, ruled it as a slip. He had hurt Archer in the third, fourth and ninth rounds, yet Archer had made him look bad on a number of occasions when nifty footwork had made him miss wildly with his left hooks.

The decision went against him but he refused to accept it, saying, " I won the fight –big. But I wasn't surprised at the decision because I hadn't knocked him out." Later in his dressing room, he remained adamant that he had been cheated, hinting at something sinister. "They robbed me," he claimed. "People told me that I was foolish to be fighting Archer. Archer they told me is 'one of the boys.' That I'd have to knock him out to win. I was going to pull out of the fight, but I was told that it would be bad for boxing if I did that. I respected these people, so I fought. But is this good for boxing? What the people told me would happen has happened. Everybody knows that I won the fight –everybody but the boys."

Jersey Jones expressed anger at the decision, but stopped short of contesting it, sighing "It's too late now." When pressed, Harry Markson admitted, "the way I saw it, Tiger won." Even Joey Giardello expressed his "disbelief".

Not all, however, were inclined to sympathy. Writing in *Ring* magazine's fight coverage, Nat Loubet opined that the "Tiger of his prime would have had no problem with Archer. But it was not the Tiger of his prime and more was the pity." Once again, he returned home a bitterly disappointed man.

Although Tiger had left America with an 'I-don't-know-if-I'll-be-back-to-fight-here" parting shot, he returned to New York at the end of January. The New Year did not bring him much promise. Giardello had seen off Carter's challenge but then started negotiating with Ray Robinson. These talks were called off in early February, because as Giardello put it, Robinson wanted "too much (money)." Giardello's actions hurt him a great deal and he continued to voice his disappointment in him. Jones' connections of course, allowed him to use the *Ring* as a conduit for his campaign to get the rematch. He was not averse to pressing his claims at press conferences like the one he called two days before facing the Argentine, Juan 'Rocky' Rivero.

Only four or five reporters turned up, waiting outside the door of his dressing room. They listened to the thud of bouncing feet and of rope scraping the floor until the door opened and all filed in. Among them was a young English language teacher turned UPI reporter named Sam Toperoff who was immediately struck by Tiger's "special quality of voice and intelligence." The tone of the conference was set by Tiger's opening address. "The present champion refuses to meet me again," he announced. "He has defended only one time in fifteen months and again it was in his home city. I put it that this is not the courageous posture for a so-called champion."

"Why," one of the reporters asked, "did you agree to fight Giardello in Atlantic City, knowing that it was his backyard? Especially since you were the champ?"

"To a certain extent, it was because of his problem in New York," Tiger replied. "But that is not the entire story. They offered me more money if I would fight him in Atlantic City. I do not wish to seem the mercenary, gentlemen, but this is my livelihood." He continued pouring out arguments as to why Giardello ought to fight him. Moral arguments aside, there was the financial angle: Giardello, he insisted, would only get a decent payday if he laid it on the line with him. If Giardello did not make him an offer, he threatened to step up to the light heavyweight ranks to challenge the winner of the upcoming championship bout between Willie Pestrano and Jose Torres and Joey could kiss goodbye to the monies a bout with him would bring.

The reporters listened intently, and when he finished his statement, one asked, "You own a fur coat?"

Tiger looked bemused and shook his head.

"You should have one," the reporter continued, "because Giardello will give you another shot just about the day hell freezes over."

"Isn't he just waiting until you're too old, until you lose your edge?" another asked. This riled Tiger, who quickly clenched his fists as his face contorted into a sneer: "He is as old as I!" he responded. "A Tiger never loses his hunger."

Rocky Rivero was formidable opposition. Rivero, Tiger knew had given Giardello "two tough, close arguments" the decisions of which he felt ought to have gone Rivero's way. Rivero came into the ring fully ten pounds over the middleweight limit. He looked it too and when both men started tossing leather at each other, the mass of flesh around his belly rolled above his trunks. Tiger caught most of Rivero's punches on his elbows while the rest simply missed. It suited him rather nicely that the Argentinean appeared incapable of taking a backward step and before long, Rivero's face had been transformed into a bloody mess. In the sixth, a brutally executed left and right combination dropped Rivero to one knee, the first time he had been knocked down in 54 professional fights. The referee quickly called a halt to the proceedings.

Later in his dressing room, Tiger held a private conference with Giardello during which Tiger believed they had both reached an agreement of sorts to stage their return bout at the Garden in May. Giardello thought differently and emerged to tell awaiting pressmen that "Tiger's got to win some fights or he's not going to draw any crowd."

His next opponent was Rubin Carter. Goateed, shaven headed and heavily muscled, Carter presented a figure of unbridled menace. He had grown up poor and undereducated in Patterson, New Jersey where his fists served as a more convenient means of communicating than his stammering voice. He discovered boxing in juvenile hall, but success at the sport, first in the amateur ranks and then as a professional was fated not to bring him the redemption and contentment that he yearned for out of life. In the spring of 1966, he would, on the dubious word of a local petty criminal, be arrested for a triple killing at a Patterson bar and grill. He was convicted a year later and imprisoned for a crime which he adamantly protested his innocence. In the supervening years, the likes of Muhammad Ali and Bob Dylan, who wrote the haunting folk ballad, 'Hurricane' in tribute, would join a lengthy campaign to free him. Two decades elapsed before, finally, the conviction was set aside.

Carter had recently dropped a decision in England to Harry Scott a Liverpudlian middleweight managed by Tony Vairo, Tiger's old manager. But Tiger was among the 3,000 spectators who watched Carter return to winning form by stopping Johnny Torres at the Patterson Armoury in New Jersey. Tiger left the Armoury outwardly gracious in his appraisal of Carter's efforts but inwardly unimpressed. True, Carter had a great deal of hand speed and he punched harder than both Gene Fullmer and Florentino Fernandez but he felt that no middleweight was capable of hitting harder than Henry Hank who he had handled very adequately. Besides, Carter would have to contend with his own power.

Rubin Carter was an old hand in the game of intimidation - he admitted practising 'the look' in his mirror. He was outspoken, not only with regard to political and racial matters but also in relation to his opponents, several of whom he goaded with provocative comments and suggestions. For instance, in a televised encounter with Emile Griffith on the night before their fight in December 1963, Carter poured scorn over the welterweight champion's apparent ice-cool confidence. After an exchange of words Carter sneeringly informed Griffith that while he talked like a champion, "you fight like a woman who deep down wants to be raped." Griffith gritted his teeth. Few needed reminding about the tragic consequences that followed the insults Benny 'Kid' Paret had hurled at Griffith before their world welterweight title fight in 1962. Griffith pummelled the Cuban into a coma from which he never regained consciousness. Paret died a few days later at a New York City hospital. Carter calculated that Griffith would be sufficiently enraged to fight it out with him and true to plan, stopped Griffith in the first round. Tiger, Carter knew was not a man who would be thrown off by the opposition's aggression, but he made it plain from the start that he intended to wage a battle with the utterance, "Dick Tiger is what I want and I'm prepared to get it." Tiger knew what he meant: the name of Dick Tiger, champion or non-champion, remained a badge of honour on any fighter's record of wins.

But there was no animosity between the two men. "They were always cordial to each other," says Ron Lipton, Carter's friend and spar. "Carter had a high respect for Dick and used to tell me he dreamed of fighting Tiger on many occasions while he was incarcerated prior to the murder convictions. In those dreams he always won but by decision which to me revealed his own deep seated doubts about his ability to cope with Tiger's durability."

The Garden publicity machine went into gear publicising the fight with a cheap and semi-comical gimmick. On this occasion, Condon dressed a fellow he knew in a Tiger suit and sent him all over New York to ride the buses, subways and trains. Although, he was arrested four times in one day, Condon managed to get him out of jail on each occasion and back on the streets. Meanwhile, photographers from the press agencies and all the New York papers took pictures of the mascot and to Condon's evident satisfaction, 10,000 people passed through the Gardens turnstiles for the match.

Standing face-to-face in the centre of the ring, both men provided a study of anatomical contrasts. Carter's upper body construct was his most impressive feature; his upper and mid-back being layered with clear-cut muscle forged from an extremely punishing training regime. There are few prizefighters of any era whose tricep and bicep development can compare with Carter's. And then there were his legs; lithe, slim and well defined but which appeared to be more appropriate to that of a welterweight. Tiger, shorter and stockier, was distinctive by the absence of fat from any part of his anatomy. This, all the more laudable given his 'advancing' years and was testament to the Spartan disciplinary code he was continuing to abide by. And while Carter's preparatory chores were no less demanding, they were however punctuated by bouts of smoking and drinking. Once, he had even been knocked unconscious in a sparring session having entered the ring the worse for drink.

Tiger looked at Carter who appeared pre-occupied as referee Zack Clayton issued his pre-fight instructions. Carter refrained from making any eye contact with him, unusual behavior by the 'great intimidator.' Nevertheless, Carter started the fight fast and aggressively and Tiger lost the first round on all the scoring cards. But in the second, the tide changed. Carter signaled a feint, which Tiger did not fall for, and as he pulled his weight back onto his near leg, Tiger threw a powerful left hook that bounced off Carter's chin, depositing him onto the ring canvas with a sickening thud. He remained on the floor, flat on his back with his head outside the bottom ropes. Tiger waited in a neutral corner and watched Carter scramble up to his feet. The referee, Zack Clayton, administered the mandatory eight count and afterwards turned to Tiger to wave the fight on. Wasting little time, Tiger rushed towards Carter and began unleashing a barrage of blows that ended with his left fist again connecting to Carter's face. Once more, Carter found himself lying prone on the canvas. As he wobbled up to a standing position, Clayton motioned his arms and he looked to be stopping the bout. The bell ending the round had sounded when the count had reached two and Clayton began signalling for both men to go back to their corners but remembering that New York rules stated that the bell could not save a fighter, changed his mind and continued with the count. When the count was finished, he proceeded to both men's corners to remind them that the fight was still in progress.

The tremendous wall of noise that was being generated in the Garden continued into the next round. Collective sighs, whoops and gasps followed each blow that Tiger rained on the parts of Carter's upper anatomy. He chased and Carter retreated. The dreams Carter had in prison about fighting Tiger were now a present nightmare as his prime strengths were being neutralized. The frequency of Tiger's head movement as well as the expertise of his body dipping motions were negating Carter's hand speed while Carter's power of punch was severely diminished since he had begun to deliver his punches cautiously and from a distance. In the fourth, both men stood still and engaged in a furious toe-to-toe exchange from which Carter came off worse: Tiger dipped to his left and came up with a left hook which sent him spiralling down. This time, he was slower in getting up. When the count reached five, he was still on one knee and he was not standing until it reached nine.

The seeming futility of confronting Tiger in a close range fight was by now impressed on Carter and he opted to turn 'boxer': circling, jabbing and clinching when cornered. Tiger's worst moment came in the seventh when Carter stunned him with a straight right hand and followed up with a crunching left hook. It was a rare moment of distress. As a stylist, Carter was not in the league of a Joey Giardello or even a Joey Archer. It was alien to his fighting sensibilities and he could not keep it up for extended periods and so each lapse was exploited by Tiger.

"Rubin Carter was a good fighter who could knock you dead with either hand," explains Lou Duva, who sat in the Garden that night. "But the thing is that he was the kind of guy who didn't have so much as far as finesse was concerned. I mean Dick Tiger had the finesse, he knew what he was doing in there while Carter was looking to knock you out with one punch all the time. It was a hell of a fight, one guy is throwing bombs and the other is out boxing him, going to the body a lot and hurting him."

The verdict was unanimously in Tiger's favour. The ringside judges decided that he had only dropped the first round while Clayton's six-two-two score was greeted by hoots of derision. Sporting as ever, Tiger walked over to commiserate with Carter and both men posed for photographs. Tiger relaxed and smiling brilliantly put his arm over Carter's shoulders as his vanquished opponent, lumpy faced and hunched managed a sheepish smile. It was, Carter later admitted, the worst beating that he had taken "inside or outside of the ring."

The press were in general agreement that this had been his best performance in a long while. According to *Ring* magazine's match report, he "looked sharper than at anytime since August 1963, when he knocked out Gene Fullmer in the seventh round of their rubber match in Ibadan, Nigeria. This proves that he is the world's best middleweight, the uncrowned champion."

The following morning, he attended a luncheon Lew Burston had arranged at Les Champs restaurant. Again he addressed the frustrating issue of Giardello in typically restrained tones. "When I first came to your country," he began, "I met many nice people, people who were friendly and kind to me."

"But," he continued, "If I had met Joey Giardello first, I'm not sure if I would have liked any Americans."

"Ask Giardello if anyone else even thought of giving him a chance at the title," Burston fumed, "Would Fullmer have taken him on as an opponent? The answer is in the negative. Giardello is going to keep finding excuses to duck Tiger until he falls down."

Before heading home, Tiger issued a formal challenge to Giardello's title through the W.B.A. and accompanied it with the obligatory cheque deposit.

"You know what it was in those days?" says Joey Giardello thirty four years later. "Champions were losing titles but in a comeback fight would win it back. So they stopped that. The boxing commissions said, 'There'll be no more rematches —otherwise you lose the title.' So I fought Rubin Carter then I fought (Tiger) right afterwards."

163

It is not an argument without foundation: The W.B.A. had in the previous year stripped Muhammad Ali of their version of the heavyweight title because of the return clause made with the previous champion Sonny Liston. Many, however, suspected a political motive behind that decision and the W.B.A. would do nothing to stop Nino Benvenuti from making a first defence in December 1965, against Sandro Mazzinghi, whose light middleweight crown he had taken six months earlier.

Certainly Giardello did have to contend with the distractions of a court battle with Lou Duva (which he lost) and having to pay off his erstwhile handlers in order to 'rehabilitate' himself in the eyes of New York. But it still begs the question of why so many opportunities of making the match with Tiger were squandered. It is tempting to view Giardello's sluggishness in the context of a man keen to wallow in the mantle of champion while taking bouts against decidedly inferior opposition. Putting the championship defence against Rubin Carter to one side, fighting the likes of Rocky Rivero (on two occasions) and the largely unheard of Gil Diaz in non-title bouts, appeared to be Giardello's attempt at formulating his own veritable 'bum-of-the-month-club.' Yet, while the object of such ventures are to maintain a champion's purses at minimum risk, Giardello had barely profited. Severing his links with his previous manager had cost a lot and after ignoring Lou Duva's plans for a money-spinning encounter with Nino Benvenuti, there was simply no other avenue available to him to earn a large amount of money other than by engaging Dick Tiger.

Giardello had swung to this line of thought by the summer. It was around this period that the New York authorities restored his licence and New York was the place that he most wanted to fight in, so in August, he quickly accepted the terms proffered by Teddy Brenner, a $50,000 guarantee as against forty per cent of the profits with Tiger getting $15,000 or twenty per cent of the profits. The bout was scheduled for October 21st.

The news gladdened Tiger, now ensconced in Aba. Almost immediately, he began training in the gym he had installed in his home some years back. In early September he made his way to New York, stopping over briefly at Heathrow Airport where he told British reporters that it was the "happiest trip" he had ever made.

He conducted his workouts at the C.Y.A. gym until September 20th when he moved to the Basement Exhibition Hall of the Garden. It was the first time that a fighter had been allowed to use the complex's facilities to train. Over the six weeks that remained, he would make daily use of room 26 right at the rear of the Garden. A steel plated door provided the entrance to the wall peeling, rusting environment. Among its amenities were a rubbing table, two low benches and an old-fashioned bronze coloured scale. A door led to a small, tiled shower.

He trained mostly behind closed doors. Jimmy August had died and in his stead came Chickie Ferrara, a slimly built, curly haired veteran from Stillman's Gym. Ferrara knew that there was little he could do to change Tiger's fighting style –like any other boxer of experience, he was firmly set in his ways. But there was some opportunity to reformat movement and strategy. And he felt that the best way in which Tiger could take care of Giardello was by neutralising his counter punch: Any time Giardello tried to counter punch, Tiger would meet him with a left handed jab. It was a ploy designed to disturb Giardello's smoothness of movement and to keep him off-balanced.

Tiger also acquired a new sparring fighter named Ron Lipton. Lipton was only nineteen but had already trained with Rubin Carter when Carter was preparing to face Tiger. He had also worked in Giardello's camp and had been friendly with Tiger for some time. A year earlier, both had sat ringside at the Garden while watching the Johnny Persol-Henry Hank contest which had brought down the curtain on the Gillette sponsored fights held at the venue.

Born in 1946 at Manhattan's Polyclinic Hospital, Lipton grew up toughened by frequent violent conflicts with his father. He left home at 17, soon after his parents divorce, drifting around New York homeless before finding sanctuary in many of

Manhattan's famous boxing gymnasiums. It was from these venues that he launched an amateur career and began sparring with many top professional fighters of the day. He was unsurprisingly fearless, feeding off the skills he had developed as a street fighter and judo black belt. By the time he had turned 22, Lipton by his estimation had been involved in "over 300 vicious, hardcore fights" none of which he lost. He competed in the 135–147lb class in Golden Gloves and A.A.U. tourneys winning three New Jersey Golden Gloves titles and losing only three times in forty-two contests.

Lipton never fought a professional bout, and instead turned to a career in law enforcement; a decision, which he explained was based in part on a desire to atone for the excesses of youthful indiscretions. As an officer for Verona New Jersey Police Department and later as detective for the Hudson County Prosecutor's Office, Lipton's work on occasions veered into the boxing world, involving him in the affairs of personalities whom he knew personally. For instance, Lipton had a role in investigating the murder of Frankie DePaula, a light heavyweight with whom Tiger had an exciting Garden brawl and he was given responsibility for arresting Gary Garafola, DePaula's manager and the chief suspect in the crime. He was also charged with investigating the discharge of a firearm at Emile Griffith's residence. But it was his role in the saga of Rubin Carter that would have the most profound consequences; consequences that still reverberate in his life. One day at a police shooting competition, he overheard some officers boasting about how they had had Carter "framed." On another occasion at the Hudson County offices, he overheard further sinister references to the Carter case being made by Officers and Prosecutors including the chilling boast of how they would "bury that nigger and keep him buried at any cost." In January 1974, Lipton went public, disclosing what he had heard to the *New York Daily News* and making a report to Brendan Byrne, the Governor of New Jersey state. Significantly, he would also enlist the support of Muhammad Ali, an act that quickly galvanised a host of celebrities like Burt Reynolds and Bob Dylan into joining a campaign to have Carter released. Lipton would lose his police job and today claims that he is a victim of continuous harassment by vengeful law enforcement officials as well as the Ku Klux Klan.

Such happenings were a long way off in the autumn of 1965 when Lipton gratefully accepted the job of sparring partner of Dick Tiger. Tiger was making good on a promise he had made some weeks earlier to the youngster. But before it happened, Lipton had had to prove his worth to Jersey Jones and Jimmy August. He arrived at the gym armed with articles on his boxing wins and mentioned his work with Carlos Ortiz, Emile Griffith and of course, Rubin Carter. Those were easy enough to check out and Lipton was invited to strip down to his waist for a practise session with Tiger. What they saw was convincing. Lipton moved swiftly, staying out of range and constantly keeping Tiger off balance. He appeared strong and made Tiger work, frustrating him with an elusiveness that made it difficult to strike the young man cleanly. And when Tiger succeeded in connecting, Lipton was fast enough to elude the follow up strike. Jones employed him for an infinitesimal amount of money and did not even think of putting him up in a hotel. None of this bothered Lipton. The thrill of being with Tiger and the invaluable experience he was getting for his Golden Gloves campaigns was enough. He was content to sleep in a cot in the Garden basement and would rise in the early mornings to run with Tiger. Tiger he recalls was "not a fast runner but had tremendous endurance and could run forever and ever."

In the afternoons he sparred with Tiger. Here he observed Tiger's features up close and was impressed not only by Tiger's fighting abilities but also of Tiger as a physical specimen. "Dick had very powerful thighs and he had a very wide set of shoulders. There wasn't much intercellular fat on his body. What I call the 'couplings' the elbows, the knees –they were very strong. The structure of his jaw and neck (were also vital features). His arms were not that big compared to Rubin Carter but they were very,

very strong."

In between sessions Tiger gave Lipton many encouraging words, frequently complimenting him on his speed and his power. "Dick was very strong," he relates, "but he was never able to knock me down because I was very quick. He hurt me to the body. Rubin (Carter) would paralyse you, Emile Griffith would sharp-shoot you but Dick would crunch you." Remembering the way Tiger set his most dangerous punch, Lipton recalls "he would be very relaxed then all of a sudden, his power would just spring out of his stance. He would get his entire body into the punch and then if you started to trade with him, he would get his head out of the way and the left hook would whistle through the air and if you did not move your head, you would have your skull crushed. I'm serious: You would lose your life if you did not move promptly."

"When Dick cornered me there were times he spread his legs, planted his feet firmly and started to try and force me with open glove to be pushed back into the corner. But what I did was to take both of my thumbs and push them into the inner part of his biceps, a trick Giardello showed me, and he would get pissed at the pressure, rip his hands away in anger and in that second, I'd pivot and be moving around him judging his arm length and his ability to jump at me, and stay at least a few inches out of that 'kill zone.' I managed, at the most, to be able to get off three fast hard shots that landed before it became extremely dangerous, as Dick was so refined a professional, that his delivery was so superb, he could accidentally kill you or give you internal bleeding with his rights and lefts to the body if taken flat footed.

"I did shake him to the head now and then and got in some really hard body shots but he was so strong, it was like hitting a brick wall. Once even with my hands taped strongly, I remember I ripped a perfect lightening double left hook to his side. The first one made him grunt and the second one bent my wrist and sprained it for a second. So hard was his body that I did not keep my wrist and forearm locked. Anyone including Rubin would have been stopped in their tracks from that, but Tiger was like a

168

piece of iron coming at you. His eyes viewed up close were absolutely chilling. It sent out alarm bells of danger to a professional fighter. My memory of his eyes was that they communicated deadly focus to win and the spirit of a man at one with his body all welded together with an iron will which refused to be backed up or quit until you were beaten senseless at his feet."

There were few weaknesses but one 'flaw' stood out. Lipton noticed that Tiger always 'set' himself before he punched; this boxing parlance for when a fighter pauses to plant his feet prior to stepping in with a blow. The effect of this was to slow down his pace, which had given the likes of Archer and Giardello ample time to move on out of harms reach or to cover themselves defensively. One day Lipton summoned the courage to inform Tiger of this habit and his suggested amendment.

"Why would you know how to do this better than me if I am champion," he smiled, humouring the younger man.

"Because," Lipton replied, "I know how to get big guys, fast guys and knock them out. Your legs are heavier than mine and they are very strong, but I can tell by the way you 'walk' you could not catch me in this ring."

"The way I WALK?" Tiger replied, incredulously.

"Yeah," said Lipton, "the way you stalk is all with power. Like how you destroyed Fullmer. But you have to learn how to change just a little."

Lipton then proceeded to give Tiger a detailed rendition of Tiger's fighting movements, the steps he used when stalking opponents, the manner in which he held his fists, the facial expressions, everything. Tiger burst out laughing, so hard that tears streamed from his eyes. Then when Jones and Ferrara were absent, he allowed Lipton to guide him. Says Lipton: "Very lovingly and good naturedly he let me show him how I half stepped and punched. I showed him how to go a little crazy in his attack and stop being so refined and 'European' in his delivery." Tiger continued to train intensely, fuelled no doubt by Giardello's antics. It would be presumptive to say that he hated Joey, but it would not be stretching it to say that he was extremely angry with Giardello. Two days before the bout, Giardello, who had moved his training quarters to a part of the Garden, sent one of his acolytes to borrow a swivel to work out with a light bag. Furious at Joey's temerity, Tiger turned to the man and snapped: "No!"

"He is my enemy," he explained, "Tell him I will loan him nothing. Tell him when this fight is over; I will give him the swivel –even a bag. Now? No!"

When informed of the refusal, Giardello let out a stream of Italian epithets. "He's just trying to get me mad," he reasoned.

A crowd of just over 17,000 spectators turned up on the night. The announcer, Johnny Addie presented samplings of boxing's old guard: Jake La Motta, Ray Robinson and Rocky Graziano all took a bow as did some of the rising elite, Emile Griffith, Jose Torres, Nino Benvenuti and Joe Frazier. Celebrity icons like Frank Sinatra, Yogi Berra and Mickey Mantle were also there. There were quite a few Nigerians dressed in traditional garb on hand to give Tiger support, more Africans then Sam Toperoff had seen in one place before.

"They paraded through the crowd," he wrote, "some of them in tribal robes whose colours had such a dark intensity about them that they made the garments seem not only exotic but vaguely dangerous."

The Garden reverberated from the thumping Apesi 'talking drum,' which urged him to 'keep on punching.' Tiger was the first to come out of the dressing rooms, from the '50th Street end' of the arena.

He could hardly wait to rush at Giardello after the sounding of the bell. Twice he succeeded in cornering Giardello and twice he walloped him around the head and body. Unlike in their previous bout when he complained to referee Paul Cavalier, Cavalier had stood back and allowed Giardello to tie him up and keep him in clinches for inordinate periods of time. Here referee Johnny Lo Bianco appeared to pull Giardello loose as often as he could and also allowed Tiger to punch out of clinches with his free left hand.

In the second his assaults had Giardello on the verge of a stoppage, but grimly, jaw hung slack and the left side of his face bleeding, he held on. For a brief moment in the fifth, he found his old form, pushing Tiger's head backwards with crisp counter punches. But Tiger came back in the seventh when pinning Giardello against the ropes, he let loose a barrage of punches, perhaps a dozen, none of which were replied. Mouth ajar and gasping for breath, Giardello managed to escape to the centre of the ring. At the touching of gloves prior to the beginning of the last round, Giardello bent over to Tiger and whispered; "Nice fight."

When Addie read out the second judge's scores, Tiger knew he had won and leapt into the air. He had followed the feats of his legendary predecessors; Stanley Ketchel, Tony Zale and Sugar Ray Robinson in regaining the middleweight championship. At the age of thirty-six, he had also become the oldest active world champion of the day.

It was one of the most popular victories many had seen at the Garden and as he made his way back to his dressing room, he saw a sea of outstretched hands hovering around him, each eager to press the flesh. He entered a packed dressing room where reporters mingled with a flood of Nigerian dignitaries many of who had brought their wives who busily waved miniature national flags.

In the conundrum, Lou Burston called out frantically; "This man went fifteen rounds, he needs a rest now." But Tiger, who constructed a figure of serenity in the midst of all the hullabaloo, was the first to protest. Led by the Nigerian jazz drummer, Olatunji, the revelry continued for a little more time.

Ten
A STEP UP

"Not even twenty four hours he got the title, all of a sudden this ugly duckling nobody wants to fight is a swan. A swan!" Surveying the crowd of managers and promoters that were gathered at Leone's Restaurant, all seemingly beholden to Dick Tiger and to him, the voice of Lou Burston conveyed as much jest as it did irony.

The voices coming from all angles of the room collided around them. "We'll guarantee Tiger $100,000," declared Jim Archer, the brother and manager of Joey. "Emile Griffith beat more middleweights than Benvenuti knows is alive," pitched Gil Clancy. Offers were coming from all over the place. Pittsburgh's Dapper Dan Club offered Tiger $75,000 to meet the winner of the bout that they were about to stage between Archer and Sugar Ray Robinson. (The fight that would finally lie to rest the saga that was Robinson's career.) Jack Solomons wanted Tiger to face Griffith in London while, the Italian promoter, Rino Tomasi, was offering $60,000 to defend against Nino Benvenuti in Rome.

Tiger looked on, luxuriating in all the attention. It felt marvellous to be the King of the hill again. "What I want now is money," he said. "I will fight who will draw." Honour and prestige were not figuring in his mind, only the promise of cash for his burgeoning investment portfolio.

He left the joint after fulfilling several photo opportunities with Archer and Benvenuti. Privately, he knew that Jones and Burston had already narrowed the options down to Griffith and Benvenuti. A fight with George Benton would not draw while the risk of Archer 'running away' to victory was too much. Some weeks later, cognisant that Tiger's people were shunting him aside, Archer placed a chiding advert in the *New York Times*:

<u>Dear Dick Tiger</u>:
Here's why I think
I deserve a shot at your

Middleweight crown:
The last time we fought
I beat you

Respectfully
Joey Archer

Before leaving for Nigeria, he signed an open contract with a Puerto Rican promoter, Eddi Martinez to meet Luis Rodriguez, a local middleweight in a non-title bout to be staged in San Juan. The agreement guaranteed Tiger a $15,000 fee plus round trip expenses.

At home he maintained a high profile. The government invited him to the Northern city of Kaduna to stage a couple of exhibition bouts on New Years day at Ahmadu Bello Stadium. The first was with Abraham Tonica, the national middleweight champion and the other with the Liverpool based Sandy Luke. While in Kaduna, kinsmen from the Orlu Youth Club presented him with an inscribed silver cup.

He returned to New York at the end of February, announcing a few days later at a press conference that he would fight Griffith at the Garden in April. The warm up bout in Puerto Rico was called off in favour of one in Dortmund, West Germany.

Peter Muller was a 38-year-old veteran with a reputation of a nutcase. In 1952, he made headlines after manhandling the referee in a German championship bout. Tiger watched stoically as Muller strolled around the ring, bearing a countenance that alternated between an affected grimace and a moronic smile. When Muller wasn't clowning, he was clinching. But a right dug in to the pit of the stomach wiped the smile off his face, then when in the third a careless lunge created an opening for Tiger; a right hand exploded on the German's chin, dumping him on the canvas where he was counted out amid the boos of the 7,000 strong audience in the Westernfallen Halle.

It was a rare easy fight in a career not laden with 'bum of the month' title challengers. In a review of Tiger's career, Jones would refer to this trip as having being a "jaunt." The Muller fight notwithstanding, Tiger was respected by the American fight fraternity for not having shirked from taking on all manner of opponent. They had also come to respect him for being an honourable and decent person. To Ted Carroll, writing in the April 1966 edition of the *Ring*, Tiger was "living proof that nice guys finish first."

"For all his considerable ability, the personal charm of this affable Nigerian remains the most impressive thing about him. A famous singer and television personality long has been referred to as Mr. Nice Guy, a cognomen which in the world of boxing fits Dick Tiger as snugly as the black homborg hat which has become his trademark."

"Whatever the provocation, Tiger rarely raises his voice. While upset over the long wait he had to endure before Joey Giardello finally got round to giving him a chance to regain his title, his criticism was always restrained and never ungentlemanly. It was with such muted statements as this, 'When I came to America, I always understood that Americans were men of their word, I am very surprised and hurt that Giardello is making me wait so long'."

"Tiger thus aired his exasperation over a delay, which would have brought screams of denunciation from one of less refinement. Whether as a challenger, champion or ex-champion, Tiger's disposition remains constant. His smile is friendly, his greeting sincere, his manner modest, his bearing correct, and his conduct exemplary, regardless of the state of his fortunes."

"Dick is always conscious of the image he projects. He caused amazed gasps with his courteous refusal to pose with an attractive model for a publicity dodge."

'I mean no disrespect to the young lady. She is pretty. But in Nigeria the people –and my wife- don't look at this sort of thing as you do over here, and they might misunderstand,' Dick explained.

"A stalking, walk in fighter, Tiger does not discard his manners with a bathrobe once the bell rings. Rarely guilty of any breach of ring etiquette, when such violations do occur his regret is obvious. He extends both hands, and bows to his opponent, to the referee and to the crowd, apologetically. Tiger's courtly composure, which he maintains impeccably, has made him one of the best-liked foreign fighters to campaign in the United States. His triumph over Joey Giardello was one of the most popular victories seen in the Garden for a long time."

"Everybody likes Dick Tiger. 'How can you dislike a guy,' expounds veteran boxing man Charley Rose, 'who likes everybody. Sometimes I get the idea that he really hates to hit his opponents, and does it only because he has no other choice'."

Emile Griffith, the undisputed welterweight champion of the world knew an awful lot about Dick Tiger. They first met and sparred together soon after Tiger's American arrival when Griffith, the Virgin Island born labourer and later milliner cum fighter, was making the transition from a several times Golden Gloves champion to the demands of the professional ranks. He would admit later that he used these sparring sessions to "study him for the time we would eventually meet." Griffith had for some time been waging a campaign of sorts geared to getting Tiger into the ring; asserting three years earlier that "he's been fighting the same way for years and hasn't changed his style."

His credentials as the pre-eminent welterweight of the era had been settled in the aftermath of the final, tragic battle with the Cuban, Benny 'Kid' Paret. Griffith intensified a habit of taking on heavier fighters, beating almost a dozen including the hard punching Florentino Fernandez. The only blemish to these forays was a humiliating first round stoppage by Rubin Carter.

The fact that Tiger had beaten both men handily perturbed neither Griffith nor his trainer Gil Clancy:

"I have a picture in my basement that the two of them took together in the gym, and you know, Dick was much heavier than Griffith but Griffith had such a big upper body that if you saw the two of them together you would think that Griffith was the heavier of them. Dick was such a tough, strong guy that most people thought that I was crazy to put Griffith in the fight. At the weigh-in, I guess a lot of other trainers would have tried to have built Griffith up to a hundred and fifty five pounds to make (the weight differentials) close. But, I thought that the best thing for Emile was to use his speed and keep his efficient weight. The bigger and slower the guys were, the better he was. Dick was really a great middleweight champion but I just thought that he was a little bit slow and I knew that Griffith had the strength not to be overpowered on the inside."

Tiger travelled upstate to train at Grossingers, a community in the heart of the Borscht Belt, staying at a nondescript cottage. Rocky Marciano, a boxer like Tiger with tendencies veering on the frugal had often used it during his championship campaigns. It was dull and drab, the white painted walls were peeled and faded, the carpeting was worn thin and the furnishings that sparsely littered its rooms were markedly aged. To boxing columnist Arthur Daley, it was a scenario that apparently suited Tiger's "disposition and style."

He was disposed to eschew activities like shooting pool and card games, staple forms of conduct in many training camps. He worked out, ate his meals and treated himself to a spot of late night television before retiring to bed. Venturing to watch the floorshows at the local hotel were out of the question.

But coming to Grossingers had not been his idea and years later, he complained about feeling "isolated." Loneliness was a constant companion. A sixth child, Joseph, had been added to the litter of 'Tiger cubs' and he had missed the birth. Breakfasting with veteran reporter, Jimmy Cannon three days before the fight, he admitted that he worried about the burdens that his frequent absences placed on Abigail. "My wife," he said, " doesn't feel happy when I'm here (in America). Leaving her with six children is too much for one woman to carry. She will be happy for me to return."

Work like soul appeared to suffer. "He seems to me to hesitate too much," opined Barney Ross, the former world's light and welterweight champion, as he watched Tiger spar with Candy McFarland. "When he should have moved in to punch, he didn't. He's got to press his man; pin him in the corners or along the ropes. Of course, any fighter that stands and trades punches with Tiger will be in trouble quickly. But Griffith, with his foot speed and fast hands isn't going to stand still for a heavier and dangerous hitter like (Tiger). Griffith will always be on the move like McFarland was. It's getting late for Tiger. If I had to score those three rounds, I'd have given all three of them to McFarland."

Back in New York, the prying writers once again could not but notice the signs that he was having problems sweating down to the one hundred and sixty pound limit. It is customary practice for fighters to take a rest from training a couple of days before a bout. Light workouts are okay but when he continues a robust itinerary that lasts up until eve of the fight, the conclusion is that there is a big problem. The danger is that he will come into the fight drained of energy and will be susceptible to quickly dehydrate.

Tiger, reported the *New York Times* correspondent, had on the day before the fight, roused himself at five in the morning to run three miles around Central Park and followed this up with the traditional nap, breakfast, nap and afternoon sessions on the heavy and speed bags plus three-minute episodes of rope work and shadow boxing.

Nobody bought Ferrara's explanations about his need to "work off the nervous energy."

The following evening, Tiger journeyed through the darkened arena and emerged into the harsh glare of the lights that shone over the ring. Aided in part, perhaps by the television blackout enforced on the New York metropolis, a 15,000 strong audience had turned up at the Garden. They greeted his name with an ovation easily surpassing that which they had accorded Griffith.

It was, Tiger later confessed, somewhat foolhardy on his part to have believed that Griffith would stand and fight. He stalked Griffith but the challenger wisely jabbed and moved –quite well, it should be noted, for a man who only days earlier had his leg shoved into a bucket filled with ice in an attempt to arrest the effects of a mild sprain he had sustained on his ankle.

He played out a game of cat and mouse with Griffith until the challenger started, in round eight, to meet him in the centre of the ring. Blows were exchanged, and he was jolted by a number of Griffith's jabs.

In the following round, he came out of one of many clinches Griffith had initiated and moved a few paces forward when a bolting fast jab caught him dead on his chin. He landed on his knees for a split second before hastily collecting himself. Arthur Mercante, the referee, signalled a knockdown and wiped the resin from his gloves. The count finished and Tiger sprang towards Griffith. A short right somehow penetrated his guard and again he was down. He was down for as long as it takes to blink the eye and chased after Griffith. He pressured Griffith for the rest of the fight. A blow to the jaw late in the rounds buckled Griffith's legs but Griffith's legs got him out of danger.

Tiger stood in his corner and shook his head when he heard the decision, a unanimous one in Griffith's favour. The new champion could hardly contain his joy, hopping around the ring before grabbing Tiger and lifting him off his feet.

Few in the Garden shared Griffiths joy. The silent pause that followed the announcement of the decision gave way to a large roar of dissent with catcalls and hoots of derision being directed at the ring. A small group gathered there to shout 'ROBBERY! HOW COULD THEY MAKE SUCH A DECISION.'

When Tiger left the ring, they cheered him. He remained calm in his dressing room, smiling and shaking the hands of those who came to commiserate.

"It was close," proffered Ralph Bunche, the Nobel Prize winning diplomat.

"Yes, it was close," Tiger replied.

The next morning, he sat alongside Griffith in Harry Markson's Garden office. "I'll only say I'm glad all of you were there to see the fight –to see what happened," he told the gathered pressmen. "In Nigeria, it takes two men to fight, I learnt that when I first started boxing. You can't win a title by running. The way he predicted that he would knock me out, I thought that he would come to me, but he ran away."

Then with a reference to the Giardello and Archer fights, he added, "I've had this before. Go and ask him if he feels that he really beat me."

"That was Tiger, not me on the floor," Griffith retorted. "I don't think that there was any doubt that I won the fight. He's a good fighter, but I was the better man this time."

Tiger was not convinced.

"You're a lucky, lucky boy"

"Why you keep saying that?" asked Griffith, now clearly needled. "Why you keep calling me a lucky boy?"

"I've been fighting longer than you," Tiger replied, a sly look crept on his features. "But I'm a stranger here."

Opinions differed. The *New York Times* saw the fight for Griffith as did the United Press International while Nat Fleisher, was strident in his denunciation of the verdict.

"The majority of the reporters at the ringside apparently were looking at a different fight. They had Dick Tiger retaining his title. The vote was 18 to 5. The vast majority of the spectators indicated clearly by their boos when the decision was announced, that they did not accept the official verdict. I saw it 10 to 5 for Tiger. The verdict was one of the worst rendered in New York in many years, particularly the score of referee Mercante, whose lopsided tally was out of line."

The judges he concluded had been "honest but deluded."

But Jim Murray of the *Los Angeles Times* thought Tiger the deluded one. His post fight column analysis had a biting sarcasm. "Against Griffith, this Tiger's chief stock-in-trade seemed to be his enormous patience. As of this writing, he is still waiting for an opening and the fight ended at 11:15 p.m. Eastern daylight time Monday. Dick learnt his style of fighting from the old 'British squares' of the revolutionary days when redcoats would come out and line up in a block formation where they were vulnerable from all sides, a style of battle which American-Indian fighters found as fascinating as a firing squad formation. Tiger fought from this unwarlike stance all night long and considered it un-cricket to fire unless fired upon. He preferred to hold his punches 'til all systems were go. When he triggered, all systems had went (sic)."

The controversy endured. One writer to the *Ring*, describing himself as a 'boxer from Montreal,' claimed to have interviewed a total of 650 boxers and boxing enthusiasts from "all over the world" and insisted that not a single one had expressed the opinion that Griffith had won.

More than thirty years after the bout, Gil Clancy professes bewilderment at the divergent views. "I don't even know what the controversy was," he says. "All I know is that Griffith won the fight and won it clearly. I thought that Griffith would actually do better than he did in the fight. He did knock Tiger down for the first time in his career. Before the fight, I kept telling Griffith, 'Emile, you'll be able to handle this guy on the inside, don't worry about it.' After the fight was over and he got the decision, it was like a madhouse in the dressing room and he said, 'You know Gil, I was stronger than him inside.' I said, 'Emile, I've been telling you that for two months'."

Tiger never accepted the loss and the depth of his feelings is borne out by his subsequent actions. He wrote to Major-General Melvin Krulewitch, chairman of the N.Y.S.A.C., calling on the commission to arrange for a rematch with Griffith on what he termed as 'neutral ground.' He even went as far as to call on the W.B.A. to nullify the result and to arrange for a return bout for November 1966. Each request was politely turned down.

They were desperate actions made by a desperate man. It was not long before he discovered that both the W.B.A. and the Madison Square Garden Organisation, the latter, for whom Griffith served as the nearest thing to an in-house fighter, were deposed to seeing him go behind a queue consisting of Joey Archer and Nino Benvenuti. They most likely felt that he was finished as a fighter.

In September, Tiger told the *Daily Times* that he had received two "firm assurances" from Griffith's camp, each offering terms for the return he desired, only for each to be recanted. It was, he thought playing into the same painful scenario that he had gone through with Joey Giardello. "It's the old trick," he said, "of giving a promise by these boxers knowing very well that they hardly intend to keep it."

He had recently passed his thirty-seventh year, an age when most fighters careers have been consigned to the faded pages of a record book. Even when active, only but a few are major players at world championship level and the thought of retiring did cross his mind. Some of his countrymen felt concerned enough to publicly urge him to hang up his gloves by addressing the issue in the form of an open letter in a national daily. But Tiger responded by claiming that he would continue to fight until 1972. Life on the surface was grand. The proceeds that he received from the bout with Griffith, about $80,000, had added greatly to his bourgeoning assets. He oversaw his enterprises from a ground floor office in the nine-room, two story mansion, which had replaced the house on Clifford Road. Across the corridor, Abigail ran a cosmetics boutique that incorporated a custom jewellery facility. Four apartment houses dotted Aba, while in Port Harcourt; he owned three apartment blocks as well as a recently completed 2,000 seat cinema he named for Abigail. In Lagos, he had laid down the foundations for an apartment building in the Surulere district. The most valuable investment was in an estate located in upmarket Ikoyi, filled with its luxurious colonial-style residences and foreign embassies.

Fate, however, was about to deal a cruel hand in destroying the 'perfect' world of Dick Tiger.

"The politics of my country are a cause of great concern to me," he once confided to Sam Toperoff. "There could soon be a civil insurrection. The situation is classically Orwellian." He enjoyed '*Animal Farm*,' George Orwell's satiric parable on the pitfalls of revolutionary idealism and drew parallels from the tale with the political machinations he had been observing in the real life story of Nigerian independence. Nigeria, Tiger was all too aware, had been a troubled land from the time its colonial overlord had granted it independence. Hope and optimism were quick to dissipate amid the fraud and mismanagement that had become so widespread among the political and civil establishments. Six years had been enough to accommodate two general strikes, a rigged population census and countless rigged election ballot boxes. Then in 1966, a concatenation of bloodletting began on January 15th when a group of middle ranking army officers led by one Major Chukwuma Nzeogwu staged an armed revolt aimed at ridding the country of "the political profiteers and the swindlers in high and low places." But Nzeogwu's revolution, intended to bring about an end to what he called the "gangsterism and disorder" and the "corruption and despotism" would, over a short period of time, succeed only in precipitating an intensification of tribal hatreds. Nzeogwu like most of his cohorts was an Igbo, and most of the political and military figures who were murdered in the coup were non-Igbo.

The mutiny did not succeed but power was taken by the Army commander, Major-General Thomas Aguiyi-Ironsi, an Igbo, who could do nothing to convince his compatriots in the largely Moslem Northern Region, who had dominated the overthrown civilian government, that his ascent to power had not been part of a grandiose machiavellian plot to supplant Northern leadership with Igbo hegemony.

The Igbos had always threatened. The spread of Western education and culture through the institutions of colonialism had been more amenable among Christianised ethnic groups like the Igbo. The North, by contrast, with its ingrained Islamic traditions and its essentially feudal social structures, had not been the willing recipient of Western values and were conscious that they lagged behind the South in terms of development. They were very sensitive to the Igbo migrants in their midsts who served as civil administrators and who were dominant in petty trading –a source of resentment for the indigenous peasantry who felt exploited. Among their educated class the constant chatter revolved around the Igbos being 'money grabbing vermin devoid of a genuine culture.'

When on May 24th, Ironsi decreed that Nigeria would be ruled not as a Federation, but as a unitary state, it appeared to the North that the plot was complete. An explosion of violence followed as mobs armed with shotguns, daggers, clubs, poison arrows and other deadly paraphernalia, set upon the Igbos. From the ancient city of Kano, the pogroms spread to Kaduna, Zaria, Sokoto and Katsina, claiming upwards of five hundred lives. Those still with life fled southwards in cars, buses, trains and in ox-wagons.

This served only as a baleful prelude to more terror. Two months later, on July 29th, soldiers of Northern origin seized the keys to the armouries in the barracks and cantonments in the Northern and Western Regions and proceeded to exact a terrible vengeance on fellow soldiers of Igbo (and Eastern) ethnicity. Gruesome reports of ambushes, torture and executions filtered out. At Lagos' Abalti Barracks, where three years earlier, Tiger had prepared to fight Gene Fullmer, Igbo soldiers were sectioned off from others and shot. Across town at the Ikeja cantonment, some were imprisoned and forced to ingest a mixture of urine and faeces before facing a firing squad.

In Ibadan, subordinates arrested the unfortunate Ironsi, who was touring the country in a vain attempt to shore up support for his policies. His end was somewhat symbolic of the suffering and humiliation that the Igbos would continue to endure: his captors stripped him naked and flogged him, before ending his life with a burst of automatic gunfire.

For three days, Nigeria had no functioning government. The mutineers, who had killed over 200 Igbos and other Easterners, had had in mind the secession of the Northern Region before they were persuaded to pursue another course. They agreed that Yakubu Gowon, a thirty-one-year-old lieutenant colonel and a Christian from the North, should assume the mantle of Head of State.

On August 1, Gowon broadcasted to the Nigerian people, presenting himself as being the seniormost officer to have survived the mutinies of January and July and announced plans to set up a Constitutional Conference which would decide the country's future. Hours later, another lieutenant colonel, Odumegwu Ojukwu, the Governor of the Eastern Region, gave a dissenting broadcast, which accused the Northern military of the "brutal and planned annilation" of their Eastern counterparts. He refused to accept the authority of Gowon whom he claimed as a usurper being backed by a murderous band of soldiers who had their fingers "poised on the trigger."

An uneasy calm followed and by the beginning of September, a sizeable number of the Northern Igbo community, emboldened by government assurances of their safety, had returned to the homes and businesses they had abandoned. It proved, however, to be only a temporary lull. A broadcast from Radio Cotonou, in the neighbouring country of Benin detailed an untrue account of attacks organised by Igbo mobs on the small numbers of the Northern population in the East.

On September 28, in Kaduna, gangs of Hausas armed with clubs, knives and broken bottles went on the rampage, killing any Igbo they sighted. A few days later in Kano, mutinying Hausa soldiers, supported by machete wielding civilians invaded the Sabon Gari (Strangers' Quarters) district, and killed scores of Igbos. At the airport, they seized an about to depart aeroplane, removed twenty-five Igbos and shot them on the tarmac. An estimated 8,000 lost their lives in the pogrom.

For Dick Tiger, it was a time of deep contemplation. Like others in the East, he heard stories of appalling violence and death; of Igbos who were doused with petrol and set alight, of his kinsmen being buried alive, of pregnant women who had their stomachs opened and foetuses ripped out; of mothers arriving in the East with the remains of their children in the bags they carried.

It is possible that he peeked into the future and decided that continuing to earn money from his career would be an absolute necessity in the period of uncertainty that would now follow. But he had always left clues in some of his past comments, which indicate that he would have prolonged his career even if these tragic affairs had not occurred. It is difficult for fighters to lay down the fighter in their souls and Dick Tiger was no different. He was frustrated by the futility of obtaining a rematch with Griffith and now turned his attentions to fighting as a light heavyweight. It is something of a miracle that Tiger succeeded over the years in making the middleweight division. Back in the 1950s, some had wondered aloud whether his chances of achieving success would be hindered by this. His battles with Fullmer, Giardello and Griffith had been fought against a backdrop of the pressure to make the weight. These difficulties caused a certain amount of friction between himself and Jimmy August and the two had "repeated arguments" on the matter with August attributing the problem to a "mental block." But Tiger knew his body and only he understood the pain that was involved in reducing his naturally bulky physical exterior. "Dick came in the ring the first day I was (at his camp)," recalls Ron Lipton, "and I said to myself, he's going to have to get down to 160 (pounds). I don't know what weight he walked around at. I asked him but he never would tell me. He was heavier than 160, that's for sure. (Rubin) Carter would walk around at 157; he'd have to stuff himself to make 160. Dick had to come down and he worked very, very hard."

Jersey Jones was hesitant about him moving up a division where he would have to meet taller, larger opposition. "Jones was a shrewd type of person," says Tommy Kenville, "Tiger was not a big man, he was very compact and very solid, so Jersey was always looking for an edge in the weights. He was not exactly crazy about him going up."

Jones may have likely had another misgiving, one that related to economics: The potential financial rewards obtainable from fighting in the light heavyweight division compared unfavourably to those garnered by middleweights. Tiger went for the light heavyweight option and soon was informed that a deal had been struck which would enable him to jump the queue and fight the champion Jose Torres. The fight was set for December 16 at the Garden.

Burdened though he was by the tribulations of his people, Tiger studiously refrained from commenting on the political situation. At the press conference that he held in Aba before departing for New York, compliant journalists aided him in presenting a picture of 'business as usual.' The government ought to be providing more amenities for its talented sportsmen one answer went. The *Daily Times* reported him as saying that it was his hope "to bring to Nigeria, my country, another world title."

Yet Tiger was living in a Nigeria that could not guarantee his safety. His normal point of departure would have been Lagos, but this he realised was now off limits. Although a few thousand Igbos continued to live there, the capital city was considered unsafe. The International Airport, he knew was heavily guarded by troops, most of whom were ethnic Northerners and with memories of the previous month's mutiny at Kano Airport still fresh in the mind, he had to find an alternate means of leaving the country.

It would be the first of several circuitous journeys. On this occasion, it began at Port Harcourt Airport where he shared a small twin-engine plane with seven other passengers. After a short stop over at an airfield in Calabar, the plane traversed the border with Cameroon arriving an hour later in the city of Douala. There he boarded an Air France airbus that made the long haul to Paris. A connecting flight went to London where the journey ended for his companions. He bid them farewell and waited for the next available flight to New York.

He prepared in the knowledge that he had been cast firmly in the role of the underdog, three to one being the most frequent quoted odds. Training was different on this occasion as he had less restrictions placed on what to eat and what not to eat. There was no question on the other hand of bulking up to the light heavyweight limit –that he was convinced would slow him and would do little to add power to his punching.

The new regime did not lack for discipline or for cunning planning. He had watched several of Torres' bouts live at the Garden as well as on television and noticed that the champion "winces when he gets hit to the body." It was a habit, Tiger informed the press, which he found to be "unprofessional." Rumours reached his training camp indicating that Torres was suffering from an abdominal ailment and feeling that the champion would be unable to "take it downstairs," he announced that he would be dedicating two weeks of his programme to practicing body-punching manoeuvres.

In Jose 'Chequi' Torres, Tiger was confronting the challenge that would be a constant for the remainder of his career, that is, of having to face an opponent possessed with a monopoly of physical advantages. He was seven years older than the Puerto Rican and would be giving away precious inches in height and reach.

Torres was an Olympic silver medallist and Golden Gloves champion who had been guided in the early part of his career by Constantine 'Cus' D'Amato, the eccentric character who had guided Floyd Patterson to the world heavyweight championship and who later would nurture the young Mike Tyson. He had being a quite active champion since dethroning Willie Pestrano at the Garden the previous year. His fight with Tiger would be his fourth title defence within a year, a feat equalling that of Maxie Rosenbloom in 1933.

He was unusual for a fighter, being a lover of the arts and a budding writer (he was often referred to as a darling of the Normal Mailer-George Plimpton set). His friendly, outgoing nature also accommodated a certain amount of Latin bravado. He was seriously considering challenging Muhammad Ali. "I think I could defeat him," he told one journalist, "because in his eagerness to display speed, he does not back up his punches." Yet, lurking beneath the determined, ambitious, passionate exterior was an equivocative attitude to his career.

"Once I became champion, I lost interest," he recalls,

"Character plays a major role in boxing. I had begun to write and I felt that boxing was a short career. I considered quitting after beating Willie Pestrano (but) I had just got married and boxing was the only way I could make fast money."

Shortly after making a defence against Tom McNeely, Torres had been stuck down by pancreanitis and although he had gone on to make two further defences; some claimed that he had not fully recovered. It was also hinted that Torres worried about Tiger's reputation for attacking the body.

On the night of the fight, the Garden teemed with a large and vocal band of Puerto Rican supporters. The bout was being telecast live, only to a few select areas, notably in the Latin strongholds where Torres was a hero.

Tiger could count on the support of six hundred Nigerians, among them the ambassador to the United Nations, Nathaniel Ade Martins who sat ringside. Before leaving the dressing room, Jones reminded him of the simple plan of action, "shuffle, bob and weave under Torres' best punches, and come up underneath with combinations to the body."

This was precisely what Torres expected and he began the fight with an excruciatingly monotonous rendition of the D'Amatoan 'peek-a-boo' stance of gloves smothering the cheekbones and elbows tucked tightly at the ribs. Tiger easily won the first couple of rounds, if only for his aggression and his opponent's inaction.

It was not until the eighth round that Torres, buoyed by the fanatical encouragement of his kinsmen, began loosening himself from his crab like posture. Jabs and right crosses bounced off Tiger's head as he desperately tried to make up for lost ground. Tiger was hurt a couple of times but fought on doggedly. During one episode, Torres spotted him arm weary, temporarily defenceless and within easy reach. He threw a powerful combination to Tiger's head. As he stepped backwards to watch Tiger fall, he felt a left hook connect to his jaw. When his head cleared up, his eyes focused on the brown colour of Tiger's mouthpiece. Tiger was smiling.

The first card to be announced was referee Johnny Lo Bianco's which had Tiger winning by ten rounds to five. Then judges, Tony Castellano and Frank Forbes were announced as eight rounds to six and ten rounds to four both in favour of Tiger, the new world champion. He had made history, becoming only the second man to have won the light heavyweight title in addition to middleweight laurels. And at a time when such feats mattered, he had also become only the fifteenth fighter in history to become a world champion at two divisions. All of which was noted by the sportswriters of New York, who a few days later announced that he had again been given their Fighter of the Year Award.

The next morning, he sat reclined and relaxed in his room at the Colonial Hotel. It was little over a week to Christmas, New York was cold and his parlour thermostat was as ever set to overheated. He sifted through piles of congratulatory messages that were streaming from Nigeria (one had come from Lt. Colonel Gowon), England and parts of America, pausing to grant short interviews to the journalists who continued to flitter in and out.

"Fighters who wouldn't talk to me are suddenly after me now," he cooed to one. "The people all said that Tiger was finished, that he looks a hundred years old and now they come around and pat my head and tell me I'm a good boy. That's life!" When somebody asked him to comment on Torres' pre-fight prediction that he would knock him out, Tiger was almost sneering: "I heard all that bragging. He made better use of his mouth before the fight than he did of his fists during the fight."

He returned home two days after Christmas again having to pass through France and Cameroon. At Port Harcourt Airport, he spoke briefly to journalists and diplomatically mentioned that he had been boosted by the messages of support he had received from Colonels Gowon and Ojukwu. Celebrations, however, were not as raucous as they would otherwise have been. The Eastern Province was awash with refugees, well over a million and increasing daily. They were ensconced in homes, rest houses, roadsides and bushes; scenes that reminded one British journalist of the gathering of exiles into Israel after the end of the Second World War. It was not an inaccurate parallel given that the Igbos, beaten and brutalised, were now gearing themselves for separation. They considered themselves the outcasts that no one cared for. No one, civilian or military, had been prosecuted as a result of the mayhem in the Northern Region. Colonel Gowon had only expressed his "regret" over the events but stopped short of issuing condolences. He also rejected Colonel Ojukwu's demands for reparations.

Faced with the colossal task of resettling its destitute citizens, Ojukwu's government began drawing up plans to divert monies, which his region was due to pay the Federal treasury. Parts of the community devised their own self-help projects. One group calling itself Mirror Productions approached Tiger with a view to staging an exhibition bout that would raise money for the Eastern Nigerian Rehabilitation Fund. Lending his name to causes and financially assisting projects was, of course, nothing new to him and he accepted. It was a significant decision, which signalled a first public demonstration of support for what would be transformed into secession. While some pillars of the Nigerian establishment including the Chief Justice of the Federation, Sir Adetokunbo Ademola, would on January 25th, meet in the Supreme Court Buildings in Lagos to elect him as the sportsman who had 'done most to raise the prestige of Nigerian sport' during the year which had passed, he was preparing what might be considered a first act of severance with the Nigerian state.

Tiger put a great deal of effort into promoting the bout, travelling around the Eastern Region to remind the people of its importance. Two weeks before the event, Paul Eze Onwuachi, at the time a seventeen-year-old second former at Port Harcourt's Amiara Technical High School, and today a successful boxing coach was among the crowd that thronged the 32 Afikpo Road compound owned by his uncle, Nze G.N. Onyegbule, the treasurer of the local U.A.C. branch and a leader of the local Igbo community. The children he recalls shouted "Dick, Dick," while the elders favoured the repeated refrain of "Agu," Igbo for 'Tiger.' Beaming, Tiger waved back and shook hands before meeting the chief who later announced the date of the bout that would be taking place nearby at what today is known as the Isaac Boro Park in the Mile One area of the city.

The event was organised in great haste, and Tiger did not even have the time to cable Jones or Burston about his ten round non-title fight with Abraham Tonica, the Nigerian Middleweight Champion. He left Aba in the early morning of Saturday, February the 5th at the wheel of one of his cars. Accompanied by Abigail, Richard junior and a posse of relatives, they made the forty-five mile journey to Port Harcourt. Outside the park, they were mobbed by hundreds of fans milling around his car, singing his praises and dancing, until a contingent of security men cleared a path.

The gathered spectators; men, women and children, had come from Aba, Owerri and other towns and cities of the region all "curious about what Abraham Tonica would do." Onwuachi recalls Tonica's confidence in the fight prelude: focused, bouncing and displaying "aggressive moves." Tiger had already informed him that they would be fighting for real and had no intention to 'carry him' for the scheduled ten round duration.

Tonica burst out from his corner to the centre of the ring seemingly confident in matching Tiger in pugnacity. It did not last for long. The moment Tiger's blows began sinking around his body, Tonica's spirit yielded and Tiger began chasing him from one corner of the ring to another. The crowd, who considered the Fernando Po born Tonica as 'foreign' inspite of his Igbo parentage, mocked him with shouts of "Abraham Tonica wake up!" and "404 car" (a reference to the Peugeot model, then the speediest motor on Nigerian highways) and urged him to fight Tiger. The pattern continued for three more rounds at the end of which the referee mercifully intervened.

Jersey Jones heard about the bout through the news despatches. Soon after, a cable from Tiger reached his Garden offices explaining that he would be unable to collect his Fighter of the Year Award at the ceremony that had been scheduled for March 19. His mother, Rebecca, the missive mentioned was "ill." It was around this time also that Tiger joined the ranks of panic selling Igbos who saw no future in Nigeria and were induced by the prevailing circumstances of flight to the East to sell their properties for a fraction of their true values. In Tiger's case the reduction in the cost price of his most valuable piece of property in Ikoyi was exacerbated by subsidence caused by the swampy topology on which it was built. Jones was aware of the troubles. Of the massacre of Igbos, of the re-routed journeys and of the rumours that some of Tiger's properties had been 'confiscated.' The reports horrified him and he remained uncertain about when, or if, he would be returning to the United States. It was Jones' fears, which may have instigated the April 1967 edition of the *Ring*. The surreal painted visage of Tiger that adorned the cover, was accompanied by the startling headline of 'DEATH STALKS THE TIGER.' Part of George Girsch's article read:

"When Dick Ihetu beat (Gene) Fullmer at Ibadan, he was the national hero.... Now Tiger is something less than a hero among at least half of the Nigerian population. The reason? Religious, plus jealousy."

"Here is a professional fighter who has only to fly out of Nigeria to the United States and pick up more money than 100 Nigerians could earn in a year. Those on the wrong side of the fence conceivably regard this as topsy turvey economy. As a result, there are Nigerians who are reported to be stalking Dick Ihetu."

"Lagos is the centre of much of the trouble, and Lagos is the place he has to avoid for his life."

The article, while bearing the hallmarks of a hastily written, tabloid-form shock expose piece, nevertheless did convey a certain truth. While there is no evidence that Tiger had specifically been earmarked for assassination by a stalking death-squad, he would have been aware of the shootings of several prominent Igbos, residing in the capital, in the aftermath of the pogroms of October 1966. In one incident, the manager of the national airline was killed while in another; the principal of a high school was badly injured. The novelist, Chinua Achebe, barely escaped with his life when soon after the Northern inspired coup of July, several gunmen had attempted to waylay him at his home. Achebe wasted little time in fleeing to the East. The impression, deeply ingrained among Igbos such as Tiger, was that outside their native Eastern Region, their lives and property counted for little. The matter of General Ironsi's death in the putsch of July, which was not officially announced by the central government until January 1967, appeared to confirm this as did the signature war song that served as a prelude and afternote to hourly news bulletins emanating from Radio Kaduna in the North. "Let us go and crush them," went the refrain, "we will pillage their property, ravish their womenfolk, murder their menfolk and complete what we began in 1966."

Erring on the side of caution, he was again smuggled across Nigerian frontiers. He arrived in New York in the early part of April. Later in the month, he and Torres signed the official contracts for their bout at a luncheon where he also received his Fighter of the Year trophy. His opponent had in the interim period been placed on the N.Y.S.A.C.'s 'Ill and unavailable list' and it was not until six days before the bout that he was passed as fit. He announced himself as being "one hundred per cent" and able to knock Tiger out. "This time," Tiger retorted, "he will have no alibis."

Although Tiger fought as the eight to five underdog, Torres surprised him again by confronting him with the defence minded 'peek-a-boo' style. Still he managed to stick in heavy blows to the portions of Torres' abdomen that lay exposed. They made Torres wince. "Normally in other fighters," he recalls, "you needed to have an accumulation of punches to have that effect on me."

Both men suffered for their efforts. At the end of the second, Torres returned to his corner sporting a bloodied nose, but he drew blood the following round courtesy of a solid jab that landed on Tiger's cheekbone. In the twelfth, Tiger was stepping backwards after the referee barked an instruction to break, when a fierce body blow delivered by Torres, swept him into the ropes. The follow up cross connected to his chin and Tiger staggered. One more punch would, he admitted, have floored him. He held on, meeting each attack with "disjointed, rhythmless counters."

Tiger stood in his corner at the end of the fight, the top of his brow cut and feeling tender, to hear the decision. All of the scorecards read eight rounds to seven but he won by a split decision. His handlers hoisted him and began parading him around the ring when a commotion began. Bottles, hurled from the balcony seats, began smashing on the ring canvas. Those falling short exploded around the arena's marble floor. Pieces of wood, ripped off from the chairs, also rained down, followed by fight programs and even shoes.

Protection came in the form of police and Garden security who flanked and escorted him back to his dressing room as Ferrara and another man held chairs over his head. This was the second riot in three months to take place at the Garden and as in this case, involved Puerto Ricans protesting a decision made against their fighter. Twenty minutes elapsed before officers despatched from two precincts restored order.

"That was a fearful night," recalls Tommy Kenville, then working on his third major fight after being transferred from the Garden's hockey division, "but it was my introduction to Dick Tiger. He just outgutted Torres. Torres at the time was I thought twice as talented a fighter as Tiger. Giving Dick Tiger his due, Torres was just bigger and stronger, and he was a much better puncher, but he just didn't –you hate to say it — he didn't have the heart that night. Tiger was never short of condition and was never short of desire. That night, he just had more heart and determination."

Safely ensconced in his dressing room, Tiger sat potentate-like on a chair that was placed on top of his green massage table indignant that his moment of triumph had been sullied. "In Nigeria," he argued, "people pay money to see a fight, not to throw bottles. Win or lose, they are not concerned. I don't know why such a disgraceful scene followed my victory. I won the fight and I'm sure all fair-minded spectators thought as I did. I did a good job in protecting my crown (and) Torres and his people had no fair reason to complain about the decision."

In Nigeria, however, events were taking an ominous drift. The time of reckoning was fast at hand and it would become apparent to him that he was going to be involved in a battle quite unlike the ones to which he was accustomed.

Eleven
REBEL WITH A CAUSE

Tiger returned to Aba content with victory but perturbed by the realisation that war was coming. The "line of no return" as Colonel Ojukwu put it, had long been crossed. Ten days after the win over Jose Torres, Ojukwu spoke before a throng of three hundred wildly applauding delegates of what was termed the Eastern Consultative Assembly and announced that the "East has no alternative but to make plans for a separate existence in the interest of self preservation."

It was the unmistakable prelude to secession. If this happened, a sizeable portion of Nigeria's vast crude oil reserves along with the attendant revenue would be lost. As a pre-emptive measure Colonel Gowon took to the airwaves to announce the abolition of the three regions and in their stead the creation of twelve states. The objective of this was he claimed to diffuse the old regional tensions (the vast Northern Region was divided into six states).

To the onlooking Igbos however, it appeared to be a slyly worked out exercise in ethnic gerrymandering, a 'punishment' in fact. They were affronted by the granting of a state which was landlocked and cut off from several outlying Igbo communities who would have minority status in two of the proposed states.

Gowon had represented his measures as offering the basis for the continued unity of Nigeria. The Igbos saw it differently, sussing a divisive motive; that is, one which played on the fears of minority groups of the dominance of Igbos in the Eastern Region and the continuation of Igbo hegemony within the envisaged breakaway republic.

At precisely 3.00 a.m. on May 30th, Colonel Ojukwu, sitting at his desk and attired in full military regalia, spoke through a battery of radio microphones to formally announce the secession of the Eastern Region and proclaimed the birth of the independent Republic of Biafra. He ended with the words "Long live the Republic of Biafra and may God protect all who live in her."

Then he journeyed a short distance to the parliamentary building to be sworn in as the head of state. Amid the clanking of champagne filled tumblers, the strains of 'Finlandia', Sibelius' homage to Finnish resistance to Russian domination, boomed as the national flag was raised. This tricolour montage consisted of 'red for the blood of the people, black for mourning and green for progress.' At its centre was a half risen sun symbolizing the emergent nation. The ceremonies included a gun salute.

As the first rays of sunlight flittered around Enugu, crowds appeared waving palm leaves chanting a serenade of collective defiance: "Nigeria is dead. We are Biafrans." The reaction from Lagos was predictable; the Federal government declared Ojukwu's announcement an act of "rebellion, which will be crushed." Four days later, all telecommunication and postal links with the eastern part of the country were severed.

Meanwhile pressure mounted on Tiger to come out publicly on the side of the new nation. The rallying cry of 'Igbo Kwenu,' an ancient invocation calling for solidarity among the Igbo people had been sounded incessantly during the crises, trumpeted by family heads, village elders and not least, by the Biafran's increasingly well oiled apparatus of propaganda. Figures, previously active in Nigerian politics, officers and men who had fled from the Nigerian Army, poets and playwrights, lawyers and labourers had been trotted out, one-by-one to pledge their unshakeable allegiance to Biafra. These press releases, radio and television broadcasts frequently ended with the solemnly expressed desire to fight for the cause.

In Dick Tiger, the rebels sought one of their biggest propaganda coups: a world champion boxer with the attendant profile would provide them with invaluable media exposure in the Western press and would serve as a focus of national pride and prestige. The charity bout held earlier on in the year provided an encouraging pointer to the chances of his accepting and the idea was broached to him. Making a public declaration, of course, would bring with it the potential of a Federal backlash.

But he ignored this, feeling himself to have no option other than to lend support to this cause. It was a question of pride and tribal loyalty; he hated the fact that his people had been put to death in frequently bestial fashion and he deplored the manner in which they had been in his words "shunted aside" from a position of national leadership. "Imagine after killing thirty thousand of us," he would later inform a visiting American correspondent, "Where did they want us to go?" As was the case with many of his fellow Igbos, he believed that the Nigerian government, now dominated by Northern Moslems, was bent on nothing less than their wholesale extermination. "If we don't fight back," he argued, "If we don't protect our rights, it will be –what's the word? –genocide. Like what they did to the Jews. They are out to kill us."

On June 15, Tiger, his mind firmly made up, arrived in Enugu to formally announce his backing of the creation of Biafra and to disavow his fealty to the Nigerian state. His opening words, echoing the chants being heard around the rebel republic were typically precise and to the point: "Nigeria is dead. I am a Biafran." He ended the press conference by making a plea to sports writers the world over not to continue to "associate my name with Nigeria." Plans to retire, he added, would be aborted so that "I may be able to put Biafra on the sporting map."

This defection, if it could be described as such, was not taken lightly by the federal military government and on one occasion at least, Radio Lagos, he heard had referred to him as a 'traitor.' It was an appellation that confounded him. It was he after all four years earlier who had announced after relieving Gene Fullmer of the world championship that his ambition was "to make good use of my title, not only for myself, but for my Nigerian nation." So great had been Tiger's national fervour that Jimmy August was heard to confide "he wants to win the title for Nigeria, like it was a Nobel Prize." Indeed, American writers would refer to the 'chamber of commerce' pitch he often used when describing his country and about how he appeared not merely to be a fighter but a 'pugilistic plenipotentiary' fighting for the glory of millions of his countrymen.

Although his brother Godwin recalls the "bitter" feelings that Tiger felt about the country's break up, Paddy Davies, during this period a young employee of the Biafran Propaganda Directorate, noted a pervading ambience of melancholia in Tiger. "I wouldn't say that he was depressed because of the connotation that word has," he says. "But he was very sad about the way things went." When, months later, an American journalist reminded him of the 'nation building' exercise which his homeland meeting with Fullmer became, all Tiger would utter was a wistful "I used to believe in Nigeria…" before his voice trailed off.

Dick Tiger, like Muhammad Ali, was a boxer who in the later part of the 1960s made a conscientious stand on a war, and as with Ali would bear huge sacrifices for his actions. Ironically, while Ali felt that he, an American black, had "no quarrel with them Viet Cong," and sought to by-pass what essentially was a colonial war, Tiger felt compelled to involve himself in a fratricidal conflict among ex-colonials, a conflict that would serve to destroy what a writer to the *New York Times* described as "the myth that all blacks are soul brothers."

A bout of sabre rattling and verbal jousting followed. In an interview, Colonel Ojukwu boasted "no power in this country or in Black Africa is capable of subduing us by force." But Gowon poured scorn on this and promised to mount a "Police action to penetrate the East Central State and capture Ojukwu and his rebel gang."

The battle commenced in earnest in the early hours of July 6 after shots were fired and returned on the border of the newly demarcated East-Central and Benue Plateau States. Skirmishes then developed around other border towns and the first Biafran areas fell. The Federal side quickly took the University town of Nsukka on July 15th, while the oil terminal on Bonny Island, on the Atlantic coast, was captured ten days later. The Federal side also tightened the knot by instituting a sea blockade using the ships of the Nigerian Navy. In early August, however, the Biafran Army, with the help of ethnic Igbo officers who had remained within the Federal Army structure of the neutral Mid-Western Region, overran this neighbouring region and came within 100 miles of the Federal capital. The offensive would, however, sputter and then stall.

In the midsts of this mayhem was Dick Tiger, anxious to leave Biafran territory in order to fulfil an obligation to face Roger Rouse, the mandated number one ranked challenger to his title. The 90-day limit that had been set by the W.B.C. after his title defence against Jose Torres would lapse in the middle of August, but Federal armies were now besieging the city of Port Harcourt, from where he intended to depart. It was around the early part of August that he encountered an about-to-be-evacuated U.S. Peace Corp worker headed back to New York. He scribbled a message for Jones saying only that he would embark for America when he could find a way out. The Federal government, wanting to appear humane and reasonable, offered him safe passage through Nigerian held territory, but he refused. His predicament came high on the agenda at the W.B.A's annual convention held later in August at Reno, Nevada. Addressing the delegates, the organisation's president, Robert Evans, announced that they would exercise forbearance in the circumstances. Tiger "through no fault of his, is isolated in Nigeria," he said and assured them "affidavits of every effort have been made to get him out."

To the dismay of many, however, Evans went on to announce that an 'Interim World Light Heavyweight Contest' would be staged between Rouse and another contender. While such contests were not unheard of in the sport –Ray Famechon and Percy Basset had fought it out the year after featherweight champion Sandy Saddler entered the service of the U.S. Army- the aim appeared less to be an attempt to establish a 'duration champion' (a la Jimmy Bivins who kept the heavyweight pedestal warmed up while Sergeant Joe Louis attended to his busy schedule of Army tours) as it was to serve as a first step at relieving Tiger of his title.

Desperate to leave Biafra, Tiger considered his options. The international borders of the old Eastern Region were not totally under Federal control because the Army was unable to seal off most of the roads and bush paths leading to Cameroon and he did use this route on at least one occasion after which rumours raged around Biafra about how he had been killed while making for the border. But the one which he would come to rely on the most, would be the foreign operated super constellations which headed 300 miles south of Biafran territory to the Portuguese controlled Island of Sao Tome, before going on to Lisbon. He spoke often of his pimpernel like "secret route," but never gave details, claiming that "when (I) leave Biafra, I just go straight on until they drop me. When I am in the air, I don't know anything except that I am going to New York."

His arrival in New York in the early part of October scuppered plans to stage the 'Interim contest.' He trained at the Garden while Jones entered into negotiations with Rouse's handlers. Soon it was announced that Mel Grebb's Silver State Sports Club in cooperation with the Garden, would stage the bout at Las Vegas's Convention Hall. He trained at the Fremont Hotel Gym until it came to his attention that Rouse would also be encamped there. He issued a protest and threatened to decamp to Los Angeles unless Rouse made other arrangements. But the Nevada State Athletic Commission duly informed him that they would acquiesce to any alternative training arrangements he wished to make for himself, so long as he turned up for the bout. Later, at the formal signing ceremony he insisted on being introduced as 'Dick Tiger from the Republic of Biafra,' stipulating further, that the Biafran national anthem be played during the introductions.

Training is an activity that places the severest of demands on both mental and physical resources and the backdrop of the war added to these burdens. He had received no word about Abigail's pregnancy since he had arrived in America. One report claimed that he was badly shaken and "did not train well" when it was confirmed that Enugu, Biafra's capital, had been captured.

The eve of the bout provided entertainment of sorts. He was

invited to the screening of a novel transaction: a computerised contest between Rouse and himself.

Arriving at the Clark County Courthouse in downtown Las Vegas, he noticed the formally attired audience and turned to gently berate Lew Burston for not telling him "to dress up."

What he saw when he settled down on his seat was a succession of electronic blips on a huge screen. A director of the Clark County Management Information Services had fed in approximately 2,700 items of information on he and Rouse into an IBM 3360 Modal computer that would now fashion out a conclusion. When the machine flashed 'ROUSE, WINNER BY DECISION,' Tiger affected a look of surprise. "Who lost?" he asked as he turned to the audience, then smiling, he told them, "Friday night, I'll win it back."

The next day, as he sat in his dressing room, contemplating the fight that was due in three hours, somebody knocked on the door to inform him that the Biafran Mission had sent word that Abigail had given birth to a seven-pound girl seven days previously. Gloria was his seventh child. "In this town Dick," Jones excitedly revealed to him, "three sevens is a jackpot in those one-armed bandits!"

The strategy he planned for Rouse, a balding thirty-two year old former drifter and rodeo rider, was simply to get under the over six-feet challenger, and pummel him to the midriff. But this was not at first possible. The challenger had taken the advise of trainer, Teddy Bentham's dressing room ministrations to "Get up close, BOP! BOP! BOP! Get outta there. In. Out. Stick and move."

In the third round, Rouse jabbed and then threw a combination that jolted Tiger who staggered backwards and looked to be about to land on the seat of his trunks before suddenly unbending his knees and bolting himself up. He stood upright, staring at the referee and began wiping the heels of his boots on the canvas. The deliberate movements were intended to suggest the slippery surface and not Rouse's power as the source of his near fall. The referee did not issue a standing count and he resumed to land a series of heavy blows around Rouse's reddening body. The last blow he threw before the round ended, a fierce left hook, driven into the pit of the stomach, lifted Rouse's leg off the canvas.

Tiger arrived at his corner bleeding from a cut above his left eye but he had the acumen of Freddie Brown, who had dealt with Rocky Marciano's many cuts, and the wound was quickly put under control. In the ninth, he stunned Rouse with a stiff left hook and followed with another that sent the challenger sprawling backwards onto the seat of his cardinal red satin trunks. Rouse grimly recovered his feet but was dropped again in the following round. Tiger battered him relentlessly and opened a gash on the bridge of his nose. By the eleventh, blood streamed relentlessly out of Rouse's mouth and nostrils, and when Tiger dropped him for the third time, the referee intervened and stopped the bout.

1968 began with a New Year's Day message to the Biafran populace from an Igbo loyalist to the Federal government. Dr. Ukpabi Asika, the designated civilian administrator of the East-Central State was appealing for their surrender. The rebel Igbos he said had "earned the admiration of the world" but advised them of the futility of the secession. "To continue such a fight is madness, not bravery. It is suicide, not courage. It is blindness, not wisdom."

His plea fell on many deaf ears, including Dick Tiger. A few weeks earlier, at an Army camp in Aba, he stood proudly, in an olive green uniform complete with lieutenant's pips and 'rising sun' shoulder patch, as he re-pledged his allegiance to the Biafran cause at the ceremony in which he received a direct commission into the Morale Corps of the Biafran Armed Forces. He said later that it was the duty of every able-bodied person to do something for the fatherland.

As Lt. Ihetu, he toured a range of military induction centres established at various urban and rural sites, where he devised fitness programmes. "Troop training, physical exercises, the obstacle course and running with the recruits," he would tell a reporter. The threat of strafing attacks on congregated troops meant that he did not stage any boxing demonstrations.

He divided his time between his military duties and attending to what remained of his businesses. On Sundays, he attended mass with Abigail at the St. Michael's Anglican Church. He moved his children to Amaigbo where he reasoned they would be safer from the bombing campaigns of the Federal Air Force. Like other Biafran children, the older ones became adept at taking cover when they heard the distinctive noises of approaching Illyushins and Delphin jets. Tiger worried often about the fighter craft, whereas the bombs appeared to fall slowly from the skies, the rapid fire coming from the jets were impossible to avoid.

He worried also about the unravelling of the early successes of the Biafran military. One-by-one, towns and cities in the northern sector had fallen and in desperation, the Army shortened its induction programmes from four weeks to a mere seven days. They had not called him to the warfront, but he expressed a willingness to do so if asked.

But even away from the fronts, he felt the terror of war. On December 21st, two Nigerian fighters bombed the heart of residential Aba, killing fifteen and destroying a number of houses on Cameroon Road, a few blocks from his home. One day as he sat at home listening to Biafran Radio, a bulletin flashed the news of a Federal mission over the nearby town of Ogui. Explosions, the broadcast informed its listeners had ripped apart the market place and that there were many casualties. Acting swiftly, Tiger jumped into his car and along with a handful of neighbours quickly arrived at the scene. Amid the shattered ruins that billowed pillars of hot black smoke and the stench of burning flesh which pervaded the air, he heard the cries of the maimed and the wailing of others who frantically searched for their loved ones. He joined in to help ferry the injured to hospital. Around 100 people died.

Tiger was enraged by what he had witnessed in Ogui and of other atrocities, including the destruction of a girls convent in Owerri. It was impossible for him to anaesthetize himself from what he perceived to be the moral consequences of the slaughter of his people and his attitude towards Federal Nigeria hardened. The Biafran authorities were not averse to exploiting these deep-rooted feelings, and would encourage him, inspite of his natural reticence, to play a more vocal role in their propaganda efforts. Such an opportunity arrived at the end of January. The Biafran government had engaged the services of a public relations veteran with connections to Hollywood, to organise a visit for a contingent of North American and European journalists –the perfect platform from which to state, forthrightly, his position on the conflict.

He journeyed to Port Harcourt, its defences bolstered in protection against the Federal Battalion encamped twenty five miles down the meandering creeks at Bonny Island. He was attired in his combat fatigues when he gave interviews to the *New York Times, Time* and *Newsweek*. He spoke plainly and passionately about the bombing raids, the confiscation of his property and the irony of being a patriot cum rebel.

Observing that "there does not seem to be a single Ibo man, woman or child who is prepared to give up the fight," *Time*'s John Barnes described Tiger's resolve as being "typical of the Ibo spirit." When Barnes asked him if he feared a call up to the front, he responded, clenched fist beating a steady pattern on his palm, "I'm never afraid in the ring, why should I be afraid to fight Nigerians to defend my own country?"

"I don't know what they want," he continued, affecting exasperation at the motives of the Federal side, "We all came back from the North (after the pogroms) because they wouldn't have us. And now they are fighting us in our own homeland."
Melancholic reflection replaced defiance when he spoke to the *New York Times*. "I know that this is a forgotten war as far as the world is concerned," he lamented to Lloyd Garrison. "Nobody really cares about Africa. Nobody in America understands."

The war aside, financial matters consumed his mind. The rewards of a lifetime's work threatened literally to go up in smoke. He had left Jones and Burston the task of negotiating the largest purse they could find for him. Bobby Diamond in England was instructed to do the same but although he was offered an undisclosed sum to fight the Italian, Piero del Papa in Italy, he refused to fight him on Italian soil.

In early February, he told journalists in Aba that he expected his next fight to be in Kilkenny, Ireland against the Commonwealth light heavyweight champion, Jim McCormack. The bout, to be promoted by Jack Solomons, was scheduled for April during the Kilkenny Beer Festival. He planned to leave in March as soon as he was able to get leave from his army duties. Events, however, surpassed him when on February 12th McCormack lost his title to the Australian Bobby Dunlop.

Meanwhile, Jones and Burston were under pressure to secure a match so that he did not run foul of the W.B.A. rules stipulating that champions were not to remain inactive for a period exceeding six months after a title defence. Burston had received a lucrative offer to fight Nino Benvenuti in New York but backed away because the Italian would be facing Emile Griffith in their rubber match scheduled for March.

Then came an irresistible deal. A $100,000 guarantee to face the dangerous Bob Foster. The background to how this came about is a story in itself. Foster's manager, Morris 'Mushey' Salow, had made an initial offer of $25,000 which Jones had rejected. Tiger, Jones insisted, would not step into the ring with Foster for anything less than $100,000. Salow returned to his base in Washington D.C. determined to raise the money. He called on Vince McMahon, a local promoter of boxing and wrestling shows. McMahon formed a syndicate of gamblers who went on to raise the money. In order, to recoup, their outlay, they wagered heavily on a Foster victory. Foster for his part stood to earn very little if anything. His training expenses would be taken care of but he could not earn a cent until the total receipts obtained from the box office and television exceeded $170,000.

Tiger arrived in New York on March 15th to begin his preparations at the gymnasium attached to the New Madison Square Garden. 'The House that Tex Built' was no more. This incarnation was a $43 million circular building, which was situated, further down Seventh Avenue. He was timetabled to train here on most week day afternoons. Free periods were spent watching television in his hotel room, from where he would write a great many letters. Occasionally he came up for air to indulge in spurts of window-shopping.

But his main pre-occupation outside having to prepare for the bout was with promoting the cause of Biafra. It is fairly certain that he liaised with the Propaganda Ministry, based at Ogbor Hill in Aba, before embarking for New York. The Biafrans, desperate for diplomatic recognition, which so far was yet to come from any country and concerned about improving awareness of their plight to the Western world, were keen to use the international profile of citizens like Tiger and Chinua Achebe in achieving this. Tiger himself carried no illusions as to the magnitude of this task: a poll conducted found that fewer than one in a thousand Americans were able to pinpoint the location of Eastern Nigeria on a map.

He had been in New York for only a few days when he arranged for Robert Lipsyte, a sports columnist with the *New York Times,* to visit him in order to discuss the troubles. Lipsyte arrived at the Colonial Hotel on the morning of March the 21st and observed in Tiger a man in apparent tumult.

Tiger sat himself on a straight back chair and opened his heart. "I used to be a happy man," he began, "but now, I have seen something I have never seen before. I read about killing in war but I had never seen such things. Now, I have seen massacres." He bolted from his chair and headed to a workstation that brimmed full of books, pamphlets and newspaper clippings. He scoured its contents and emerged with a collection of photographs, which he spread on his bed for Lipsyte to see. All depicted horrific images of the aftermath of Nigerian Air Force raids. One showed the bombed out remains of a hospital, another showed the severed hand of a little girl while a third one recorded the charred remains of a woman. "That is a woman," he said looking into Lipsyte's eyes, "No, it is not rags, it is a woman!"

That he considered himself to be irrevocably Biafran was all too apparent; pouring scorn on the Federal controlled media's insistence in referring to him as a representative of Nigeria. "The Nigerian radio says Dick Tiger of Nigeria will defend his light heavyweight championship against Bob Foster at Madison Square Garden on May 24th," he intoned. His words became slower and deliberate, reflecting the incredulity he felt at their effrontery, "Dick Tiger. Nigeria. They still claim me (but) they would kill me, they would kill us all. I am a Biafran."

As for the Federal rallying slogan that went, 'To Keep Nigeria One is the Task that Must Be Done,' he was derisive, asking "What will be left for them to rule if they keep killing our children?"

The rounds of interviews continued, seemingly unabated. To *Sport Illustrated*'s Robert Boyle, he extolled the virtues of his people. "Igbo people," he proudly claimed, "are not lazy people. Whatever we are doing, we put all our effort there. If we are studying, we study very hard. We like peace. We like to be jovial. We don't get angry quick. We play, we laugh, we are good business people and we respect (the) law." He was fond of telling people about the parallels between the Igbos and the Jews; that both were an industrious type of people who had absorbed the tragedy of pogroms, of the similarities between ancient Hebrew rites with Igbo customs. "Our opponents call the Igbos the Jews of Africa," he told Sam Toperoff. "It is meant as an insult. I interpret it as a high compliment."

The dressing room that he occupied at the Garden, like his hotel room, reflected his concerns. Visitors were confronted with a huge wall poster that proclaimed 'Days to Remember', days that is, like May 28 and July 29 1966. Jersey Jones was wary of his preoccupation with the conflict and of how he appeared to be devoting more time to discussing the conflict instead of talking up the impending bout with Foster. One day after he completed an interview, Jones stuck his head into his cubicle like room.

"Are you still talking about that Nigerian-Biafran mess? Why don't you talk about the fight?"

"Without Biafra, the championship title is no good to me. Without Biafra, my title is nothing."

"C'mon Dick, forget about Biafra. Bring your wife and kids over here and settle down."

"The United States is a very good country, a very nice country, but Biafra is my home. I was born in Biafra. I will die in Biafra."

Jones beat a silent retreat.

"Tiger is an old man and should retire instead of fighting me," Bob Foster was heard to say on more than a few occasions during the build up to the fight. The Lubbock born and Albuquerque bred man was used to being avoided. Willie Pestrano and Jose Torres, the light heavyweight champions before Tiger, had seen fit not to grant him a title shot. Three years earlier, Torres was sitting in the Garden offices of Teddy Brenner and listened as Brenner reeled off a list of prospective challengers to his title. Finally, Brenner asked Torres, "How about Bob Foster?" Torres brusquely replied, "I can't hear you."

Foster had always been feared. As an amateur, he recorded an amazing tally of 89 knockouts among his 94 victories, (he lost seven) and his stoppage ratio since turning professional in 1961 remained awesome. It also made for a career that so far had been overshadowed by bitter experience. Fighters regularly avoided him while promoters consistently underpaid him. The highest purse that he had ever received had been a less than princely $5,700 and the lowest, a measly $25, figures that presented him with the proper credentials to be made the centrepiece in a television documentary detailing the exploitative tendencies of the boxing industry. Frustrated that he was going nowhere with his career, he retired and went to work in a Washington D.C. bomb factory. But he decided to give the game another try, he claimed, after watching a 'lacklustre' defence by Torres. He went back into training and acquired Salow as his manager. Salow promised that he would get him a title shot within a year.

Foster was an awesome sight. A lanky, six-foot three with

devastating power in both fists, the physical advantages that he had over Tiger –seven and a half inches and eight inches in height and in reach- appeared overwhelming. Foster was also nine years younger. The statistics and the odds of twelve to five against, however, did not appear to ruffle Tiger. "He's tall, but Roger Rouse was tall," he explained as he pooh-poohed the physical differences. "It is hard for me to look up there, but, it will be hard for him to look for me down here." And as for the age factor, "People always talk about how old I am, but old or young it doesn't bother me. As long as I keep knocking these young boys out, I don't think that bad."

He betrayed no signs of trepidation when he came up close to Foster at the publicity shoots organised by the Garden. "He was never scared," says Tommy Kenville, "(but) he'd look at Foster once in a while, at the size of him." Others were struck by the pronounced differences in size when they sighted the stocky African and his elongated opponent. Harry Markson remarked that "they look like the old trylon and perisphere," while another quipped that "Face to face, they looked like Wilt Chamberlain and Flip Wilson."

The weighing-in ceremony was held on the morning of the fight. Foster confided to the onlooking pressmen about a recurring dream of his in which Tiger gets knocked out by "a straight right hand in the third." He also announced that he had already sent out invitations for his post-fight victory party. "If you want to see Tiger get knocked out," he warned, "just let him try to slug with me."

Tiger took it all in good humour but still found time to field questions from the journalists about the situation back home. Port Harcourt, the final link with the outside world, had fallen five days earlier and although Zambia had followed Gabon and Tanzania in according Biafra the diplomatic recognition it craved, Tiger appeared weary. "All I can do is hope for the best over there," he said to them, "No one seems to care for our struggle. Like in Vietnam, thousands are being killed and we want the world to know."

Now approaching the first anniversary of their declaration of secession, the Biafran nation was gripped in a frenzy over the bout. Millions of transistors would be tuned into frequencies carrying the fight and Biafran television was expected to broadcast it as soon as a tape could be flown in. The leaders sent him messages wishing him well. Ojukwu despatched a cable to him from his command quarters in Umuahia:

"Your second (sic) title defence offers me and the entire people of Biafra, another welcome opportunity to commend your outstanding qualities and your distinction as a torchbearer of our people." Major-General Phillip Effiong, the Chief of Staff of the Biafran Armed Forces also wired him, beseeching Tiger to "Please fight hard so as to bring back the boxing crown to Biafra which belongs to heroes."

Tiger acknowledged this saying, "I fight for the (Biafran people) as much as I do for my family and self. The money is real good but my people don't understand money, they only know that I am champion and that is why they care so much."

Deeply involved though he was in the events raging back home, Tiger unfailingly projected a sense of inner calm. Yet, concurrent happenings reflected a world enmeshed in a series of unsettling events. The Nigerian slaughterfest was being more than matched in the killing fields of Indochina. In April, Martin Luther King had been gunned down in the city of Memphis while Robert Kennedy would meet the same fate in early June. In the smouldering streets of the black inner cities there was talk of revolution while in France, President De Gaulle grappled with the stirring embers of a civil war, tormented by a student inspired revolt of the Parisian masses.

Tiger climbed into the ring that evening perhaps possessing wrote the *New York Times'* Dave Anderson, "the anxiety and desperation to supply the emotional stimulation needed to go through with the fight." Over 14,000 were present, paying for tickets that ranged from $5 to $25. Among them were Tiger's supporters; some carrying placards with the demand that BIAFRA MUST LIVE. Foster's name was announced first –to

211

scattered boos and muted applause. Then turning to the other corner, announcer Johnny Addie bellowed: HISOPPO-NET, FROM BUYAFFRA, WEARING BLUE TRUNKS, HE WEIGHS ONE HUNDRED, SIXTIE-EIGHT POUNDS, THEE LIGHT HEAA-VY WEIGHT KING DICK TIGER. The crowd roared its approval as Tiger, clad in an oversized green robe, strode forward to the centre of the ring to give three short bows.

Foster was nonplussed, remaining confident that victory for him was a virtual certainty. "I knew that I was going to beat him because he was too small for a light heavyweight," Foster says matter-of-factly more than thirty years later. "He was like five seven or five eight and I'm six three and a half. Fighters usually have butterflies before a match, (but) I didn't even have these because I knew I was going to knock him out."

Tiger sprang out at the sound of the opening bell, crouched low and with his hands held high. He feinted, employed the occasional lateral movement and rushed Foster in spurts. Foster, surprised that Tiger did not attempt to 'crowd' him and slug it out, stood off with a crouch of his own, and tried to establish his jab. "He was fighting on the defensive side," he recalls, "So my trainer said, 'Well you know we want to get rid of this guy and we're going to let him have to come to you." Tiger remained hunched, kept his chin down and guarded his face with his right glove. In contrast, Foster boxed loosely, throwing long jabs as he circled round Tiger. Tiger blocked many of these, parrying Foster's thrusts with his gloves and with the occasional side step. With a minute of the round left, Tiger bolted towards Foster and feet planted, swung lustily with a left hook and then with a right. But Foster coolly backed off and with almost effortless ease, resumed his stance.

Tiger searched Foster's eyes. But they gave nothing away. Foster resumed his jabbing motion and after a few probes threw a short, sneaky right hand upper cut which missed Tiger's head. Moments later, Tiger countered with a furious left that glanced off the top of Foster's head. Then Tiger stepped up the pace, the crowd roaring as he steamed into Foster with a left hook and right cross which sent Foster into the ropes. But Foster took the steam out of these blows by backing off and turning his slim frame off the ropes and calmly returning the proceedings to the centre of the ring.

The pattern of the first was largely continued in the second. Only now, Foster decided to bend his elongated frame to the extent that he appeared at times to be Tiger's height. Tiger stood off, waiting for Foster to come in. But Foster refused to rise to the bait and once again Tiger surged forward, launching a furious two-fisted attack. But again, Foster simply backed off before resuming the hunched stance. In the third, Foster began feinting to Tiger and to score with his jab. While they were lacking in power, Tiger's concentration began to be disrupted.

In the fourth, Tiger made another dashing surge at Foster but only succeeded in getting entangled in the thin man's grasp. Midway through the round he advanced towards Foster and absorbed a series of tremendous punches. "When he came to me," Foster recalls, "he was already low to the floor, so I just raised him up with a right upper cut and came across with a left-hook." Tiger was visibly stunned and before he could react, Foster stepped forward to land an identical combination. Tiger froze, paralysed by the assault and fell backwards onto the white canvas, his head hitting the surface with a sickening thud. The moment of impact, captured on camera show Tiger's visage, gnarled and contorted as sweat and saliva is sprayed in a thousand directions.

For a few seconds, he remained still. His left arm lay straight alongside his torso, while his right arm was half-raised, an abortive attempt at blocking the assault, frozen in time. With great effort, he struggled to get up. In the sightless, soundless throes of the enveloping 'black lights,' Tiger fought a losing battle with time. Reflecting later on these moments, he said, "I do not see anything. I do not hear anything. Everything is all quiet and it is dark." He had only managed to raise his back from the floor when referee Mark Conn signalled that he had been counted out.

His handlers rushed into the ring, placing a stool beside him. He was roused and the ring doctor gave him a quick examination before he walked, slowly and unaided, back to his corner. "Let's give Dick Tiger a nice hand folks," Johnny Addie requested, and the crowd obligated.

Arriving later in his dressing room, Tiger sighted a melange of fans, waiting for him. Some Africans, some Europeans, some Americans. Joey Giardello stood in one corner, a look of concern spread over his good-natured features. Joe Frazier's manager, Yancey Durham sat down, debating the question of which of Foster's punches had administered the coup de grace. On another side of the room, a young African did the same thing, only more physically, as he attempted to demonstrate Foster's exact arm movements.

Tiger's eyes briefly scanned the room. "Since I've been winning, I never had any of my fans stay in my dressing room so long. Now I'm a loser and everybody's here. I guess I'm a good man."

All perhaps were expecting a certain announcement and when this appeared to be delayed, Giardello walked over to him.

"Hey Dick, you alright?"

"Aahhh Jo-ee," he replied smiling. "Yes I'm fine."

"What you gonna do now?"

"Eat a big dinner. I am very hungry and thank God I can eat."

Head shaking, Giardello turned away, muttering, "Some guy."

Tiger then turned his attention to a young boy whose father had deposited him on his lap to take a picture. Extending his palm, he smiled at the lad saying, "You're a nice boy. Shake hands with a loser." A series of flash bulbs followed and Tiger gave the boy back to his father before returning to the crowd to quip, "It is the first time I was knocked out. Now I know how the other ones I knocked out felt."

The fight for him was of course fought in the backdrop of his campaign on behalf of Biafra, but he now assured his audience that this factor had not distracted him from his preparations. Nonetheless, at the very moment he spoke, men working on behalf of the Biafran Mission were handing out leaflets to the traffic of homeward fans, which accused the Nigerian Army of committing acts of genocide.

A few days after the fight, he flew to Lisbon to oversee the purchase of what he would later tell Robert Lipsyte was a "tremendous quantity" of non-perishable foods. There were large stocks of tinned meat and powdered milk for Biafrans in need as well as for his immediate family and the households of his brothers. The items were then loaded onto an aeroplane that had been chartered by the Biafran government. He had also reached an important decision: To bring his immediate family out of Biafra. Only a few weeks earlier, he had strenuously advocated the policy that Biafra would fight to the last man. "They can't make me run away from my country," he had said, "It's better that I die there than to carry my children and start running." But the gravity of the situation was not lost on him and the instinct to protect his family won over the bravura. It was agreed that the best way he could help the cause was to keep on fighting and naturally, he did not want to leave them behind. Before leaving, he found an apartment in the heart of the city, not too far from the stadium owned by the legendary Sporting Lisbon Football Club.

Tiger arrived in Biafra and found himself in a cauldron. The effects of the Federal blockade were biting hard. Ojukwu's government had already announced the rationing of petrol and wholesale foods. Prices of goods were spiralling: A pound of salt had a going rate of $5, a tin of condensed milk cost $1.50, a bottle of beer retailed at $2.80, one aspirin sold for fourteen cents and bicycles could be purchased for a consideration approaching $300.

Tiger would not have failed to notice the first visible signs of famine that had began to appear in parts of the territory and he would continue to expend his own finances on food and medical supplies as his contribution to population relief. He would also become the sole distributor of Radio Communicators or 'Walkie-Talkies', which were dispersed to the relevant Biafran security and emergency personnel. A grateful Ojukwu later received him at his fortified headquarters were Tiger was pictured handing a symbolic walkie-talkie over to him.

In Amaigbo, he endured the teasing enquiries from his brothers who wondered aloud about how Foster could have knocked him out. "They were making fun of him," says Charles Ihetu, "you know, 'Why did you lose this fight?' and he would reply that he was thinking about his wife and about (the situation back home) and that he forgot to duck."

Later on in June, Abigail, the children, Rebecca, a nephew and Tiger's sister, gathered at Uli Airport and were bundled into an expansive, seatless transport plane. When darkness descended, they took to the skies, leaving behind an extended family and a nation attempting to survive a very uncertain future.

Twelve
OLD MAN OF BIAFRA

Tiger stayed in Portugal settling his family and licking his wounds. He arranged for the older children to attend a nearby English speaking, privately owned Roman Catholic School. His son Richard recalls his father's outward calm despite all the upheavals. Tiger was always relaxed and applied himself at a moderate pace.

Most felt that he could not return to the ring after such a devastating loss and expected him to announce his retirement. Bobby Diamond, in England, felt concerned enough to airmail him a message of advice; Tiger, the missive went, had brought glory to himself and his country but as he now approached his thirty-ninth birthday he was "too old to start again." Diamond received no reply.

Many considered the fight to be the biggest mistake of his career. "His managers were braver than my managers," remarks Joey Giardello. "He shouldn't have fought Bob Foster. Guys like Henry Hank were tough but Foster was too good a puncher and much taller – too big. I didn't think Dick should have done that." "Bob Foster was a freak of nature," asserts Ron Lipton. "If I had been Tiger, I would never have taken that fight. I just think that as a chess move – to retain your immortality- it would have been advisable for someone to say, 'Dick, lets keep the title with a couple more easy shots and then retire and keep your record in tact.' It was a devastating knockout. It would have been prudent at Dick's age, after all the wars he'd been in and the debilitating anguish he was suffering because of events back home, to have taken some less arduous fights. But he was so confident. He was still brimming with that champion's belief in himself."

To quit or not to quit is the eternally recurring dilemma that fixates many a career. The diminishing powers of speed and reflex were not enough to stop Muhammad Ali and Ray Leonard from embarking on their ego-fuelled but deluded decisions to try to recapture past glories. Neither did it stop Joe Louis, bedevilled by tax demands, or Ezzard Charles, bankrupted by poor business instincts from clambering up the ring steps to play out the sad closing chapters of their respective careers.

A few years back, a reporter had asked Tiger when he expected to be retired and he responded: "My money will tell me what to do." Money was the key to supporting his family and his cause and so for him, the question was not whether he should resume his career but when. Boxing was the only medium through which he could make substantial quantities, in his words, "the only way I can make a good living." He admitted that he could not "go on forever", but believed that he had retained enough of his skills to continue. He convinced himself that the loss to Foster had more to do with poor strategy than with "old age"; Foster, he joked, had caught him with a "lucky punch." An article, which Jones had written three years earlier when the careers of the over-forty-year-olds Willie Pep and Sugar Ray Robinson were garnering a lot of attention could have served as a justification of sorts for him to continue his career: "Arguably," Jones wrote, "a fighter of forty may lack the speed, ruggedness or endurance that he knew at say, twenty. His vision usually dims, coordination of mind and muscle have suffered from a long, strenuous career and the legs have lost their one time resiliency. Yet, what he may be missing in equipment, is often balanced by experience, a valuable asset in any ringster's equipment."

Starting over was something that Tiger was adept at: after the losses to Tommy West, all those years back in Nigeria and after dropping the decisions in those first contests in Liverpool and not least, after losing his middleweight title to Emile Griffith, he resurfaced to win the light heavyweight championship.

The Garden got in touch at the end of August to inform him that his next fight would be against a light heavyweight contender named Frankie De Paula, a rough and tumble fighter who carried enormous power in his fists. Born on American Independence Day in 1939, DePaula made his professional debut six years earlier, taking bouts for about a year before taking a two-year hiatus. To be specific, he had been gaoled and struggled to regain his boxing licence until he was able to resume his career in the latter part of 1966.

"He had a concussive punch," says Ron Lipton, who trained with him at Rubin Carter's camp, Ehsans in New Jersey. "Rubin would paralyse you but De Paula would knock you unconscious. He hit harder than a winter on welfare." Referring to his sparring experiences with both fighters, Lipton opines that Tiger "was faster, more refined and more professional in setting up and delivering the short right hand and the short and long sweeping left hook. He moved his head much better than Frankie who stood too straight up when he came in on you. But DePaula was more of a counter puncher and deceptively sneaky with his shots."

Lipton also noticed deep flaws in the man. "At times in the ring Frankie did not have great heart. All fighters are fearless to a degree but in a real violent fight you must have great heart. I saw him in many fights at the Rag Doll Nightclub in Union City. Many of his opponents went out like a light but Frankie did not train right for many of his fights. He would quit trying hard during the middle of a fight if he did not knock the other guy out right away. He seemed to lose interest and confidence. I got along with Frankie, he liked me and I liked him but he partied too much before and between fights: drinking, chasing ladies and dogging training quite a bit."

"Frankie did most of his training in the shithouse," recalled Al Braverman, his manager. "He was supposed to run around the park, but he'd duck into the mens room and throw water all over himself from the fountain. Then he'd comeback and say, 'Look Al, I'm sweating like a bull.' I'd say, 'Okay, how come this sweat is cold?' Then he'd holler, ' Who told you? Who ratted me out'?" De Paula also saddled himself with an entourage, "A cast of characters," as Tommy Kenville recalls. One called Wimpy 'The Shadow' Vicente, was hired by Braverman to trail his frequently errant charge. Another was his mascot, Mario the Midget, whom Kenville remembers needed to be lifted up to enable him to "piss in the urinals." Braverman's relationship with De Paula was critical because it appeared to many that Braverman was one of only a few people who could motivate him to fight, employing a blustering style that had him frequently berating his charge with the foulest language. "I had to give him a slap in the face every now and then, pull his hair or punch him on the inside of the thigh to get what I wanted out of him," said Braverman, "He feared what I would do to him in the corner more than the fight itself." Crude he may have been, and perennially out of condition even for his bigger fights, De Paula nonetheless won on more occasions than he lost and in the process bagged a large group of supporters who followed his fights around Jersey City. His supporters later fell into the welcoming arms of the Garden.

"Duke Stefano (of the Garden's publicity department) and I were almost responsible for Frankie De Paula," recalls Kenville. "We used to work small clubs in Jersey to earn a little extra bucks. We got him some good fights and Frankie had the most fantastic fight you could ever see in your life in the old Garden against Charlie 'The Devil' Green. Finally, the 'Devil', who could punch like a mule –and Frankie, could also punch like a mule- stops him. So the next morning, Duke and I were sitting in Duke's office figuring out what we're going to do with Frankie, where we can move him, bring him back after the loss, and Harry Markson, just like a message from heaven, walked in and said, 'I'd like to see more of that De Paula.' And then he walked out. So we manoeuvred him into the fight with Tiger."

But De Paula needed to be coming off a win before he could face Tiger. So Kenville scoured a copy of the *Ring Record Book* for 'safe opposition', eventually settling for 'Irish' Jimmy McDermott, an Oregon based butcher. De Paula's knock out smoothened the way for the contest with Tiger. Tiger took the bout on the understanding that a win would bring about the desired rematch with Bob Foster. According to Kenville, he did not appear to view De Paula as much of a danger.

"Tiger walks in with the Goddamn hat, the overcoat on and asks, 'Who is this Frankie De Paula?' And I say, 'Tough. Tough kid. Jersey City. Murderous puncher.' Tiger replies;

'Ooooh….puncher.' I say, 'Yes champ, dynamite puncher.' And he goes, 'Huh'. Like 'I'm Dick Tiger, I've been a professional for fifteen years and I've got to worry about some guy this publicity man tells me is a dynamite puncher'."

Tiger had to adjust once more to the position of negotiating as an ex-champion –he would not be receiving a guarantee. Teddy Brenner preferred it that way since, he reasoned, fighters would be more inclined to help the Garden's publicity department and participate in promotions when they knew that the value of their purses rode on the number of fans who turned up. The terms of contract gave Tiger and De Paula twenty-five per cent of the gate receipts, this parity a concession no doubt to the Italian-American's pulling power. Tiger was always a part of the pre-fight bartering. "He participated in the negotiations with Jersey Jones," says Kenville. "He would be in the office listening to what they were offering him. Oh, for sure he wasn't going to let Jones come back and say, 'Well they're going to offer you such and such an amount.' Once the negotiations were done, he'd spend most of his time in the gym."

In the gym, as on the negotiating table, adjustments had to be made. He found it hard to obtain good sparring partners at reasonable rates and saw fit to change his long held preference for afternoon sessions to evenings. His chief spar, Freddie Williams, now worked as a docker and Tiger waited for his shifts to finish. A strongly built light heavyweight, Williams would be useful, having fought De Paula twice, winning one and losing the other.

When Robert Lipsyte visited him in the gym, he waxed philosophical about the painful changes in his life. "If I had being a flashy fellow with fancy clothes and many women and big cars and night clubs every night, I would be in trouble. But I have never been a flashy fellow; I eat what there is to eat. I am a very happily married man. I had apartment buildings in Lagos and Port Harcourt and a movie (theatre) and now with all the shelling, I guess it is all gone. Everything I have saved. But I am not sorry. If I had been a flashy fellow when I had lots of money, what would I do with myself now?"

He spent a lot of time at the Biafran Mission, monitoring the inflow and outflow of information. The Federal side had taken Aba at the beginning of September and were in control of the majority of the cities of the old Eastern Region –a fact duly reported by American newspapers but which he stubbornly sought to debunk.

"In every city they are still fighting," he told Lipsyte. "The Biafran fights to the end, the Nigerian kills him anyway." His body appeared wracked with emotion as he continued on the theme of genocide. "Their plan is to kill every Biafran over two years old. Then all the children will pray to the sun and moon instead of God, and never know who their fathers were. That is why we fight to survive."

On October 25th the new Madison Square Garden recorded its highest attendance figures, 14, 201, about half of whom were De Paula followers. Tiger was favoured at eight to five. De Paula was younger and outweighed him considerably. Although his official weight was 174 1/2 pounds, Ron Lipton insists that De Paula appeared closer to 185. The fight started tentatively with both men sizing each other up but loosened up towards the end of the first. Tiger semi-crouched, sidestepping and feinting coolly observed his bulkier opponent who studied him through gloves held high up in front of his face. DePaula swayed from side to side, in urgent, almost jerky motions, waiting always to throw his left –a chopping jab, and to follow this with the movement that brought him his knockouts: a sudden in step followed by a dip and then an Ingemar Johanssen style chopping right. Tiger broke through first; piercing De Paula's guard and stunning him with solid two-handed combinations. But De Paula quickly regained his composure and soon began retaliating with windmill-like flurries. Tiger appeared to be in trouble before the bell sounded.

In the second round there was no question that he was in trouble. As Ron Lipton recounts: "Dick stalked him and ran into a left and a very short right to the jaw and when he went down, his legs went out and he landed very hard on the seat of his pants.

In point of fact, he actually went through the air –his entire body, feet, back and arms were completely lifted off the canvas and he landed on his shoulder blades and then on his ass. I was right on the ring apron and they actually had to grab me, I was screaming 'GET UP IHETU! GET UP!' His great warriors heart brought him to his feet but his legs and thigh muscles –the quadriceps, were trembling. I saw them undulating and trembling."

There was, also according to Lipton, something quite profound in the aftermath of De Paula's assault: "I saw Frankie knock him down and this is one of the strangest things I've ever seen in my life in the ring. It was almost like the picture of Dorian Gray ageing before your eyes. I have never in my life seen a physical phenomenon like this. The only thing akin to this experience was when Sonny Liston literally aged before the sportswriters at the hands of Cassius Clay. I saw him arise and I actually saw –I thought it was Vaseline, but it was grey in his temples. It was almost as if his hair had changed on the side of his head."

Tiger struggled with his composure as referee Arthur Mercante administered the mandatory eight count. His head had thudded onto the ring canvas and for a moment his neck had gone limp. It is possible that he had been knocked out cold up to the point when his head bounced off the canvas and snapped him back into consciousness. DePaula had caught him in the middle of the face with his patented left chopping jab and right cross chop. Had the blows landed lower, in the vicinity of his jaw, he may not have had the resources to get up. When Mercante waved to both men to continue the action, De Paula crowded him, swirling his arms in a bid to end it all. One blow penetrated Tiger's upraised hands and knocked him on to the lower strand of the ring ropes where he sat for the briefest of moments before propelling himself upright. Mercante did not rule this a knockdown.

The sound of the bell came as a relief to Tiger who appeared worn out. "He walked slowly to his corner," wrote the *Ring*'s George Girsch. "He was very tired and very old. He appeared to be at the end of the trail, a beaten ex-champion who had gone to the well once too often."

The verve and the drama of the contest generated large roars of approval from the audience in the Garden. And it got better. In the third, Tiger unleashed a furious barrage of punches, constantly pressuring and finally connecting to De Paula's jaw with a sweeping left and powerful right. De Paula slumped to the ground. He got up onto unsteady legs and had a vacant look on his face. When Mercante waved him on, Tiger sprang forward and unmercifully attacked De Paula: Jabbing to set up the hook that opened the way for his smashing right hand. Again, DePaula crumpled to the canvas. He got up eyes glazed and legs wobbling. When Mercante signalled the end of the eight count De Paula still had not recovered. Tiger now thrashed him around the ring hitting him at will, if De Paula went down again, Mercante would have been compelled to stop the bout on account of the three knockdown rule. A full minute of the beating elapsed with De Paula, eyes still glazed and virtually immobile, recoiling helplessly on the ropes. Voices now began to come from ringside, pleading for Mercante to stop the bout but he ignored them. "Frankie De Paula was a very, very tough guy and I know that he could withstand taking punishment," he recalls, "That's why I let it go on. (Besides), he had the whole house in his favour –everybody from Jersey City was there!"

Tiger made his way back to his corner, clearly fatigued from his efforts. De Paula had survived his best efforts. The punch-drunk duel took another twist the next round; Tiger stumbled to the ring canvas after De Paula caught him at the side of the head. Tiger got up and again received the mandatory eight count before he resumed the bout.

The best moments of the bout had now passed and the pace of the fight markedly slowed down. De Paula claimed that he damaged a knuckle in the flurry that led to Tiger's second knockdown. At the end of the eighth, he turned to his corner men and informed them that he did not stand a chance fighting Tiger one-handed. They ignored him and sent him out for the ninth.

The damaged knuckle story, however, does not bear the ring of truth according to Ron Lipton who suspected that De Paula's performance in the later part of the bout was the result of a "swallow job," De Paula, in otherwords, had simply lost heart when he discovered that he could not knock Tiger out. "It looked like Dick really took it out of him from the body." (DePaula is said to have appeared on the Ed Sullivan show later that evening with his right hand in a sling.) The early pace took its toll out of Tiger and De Paula and in the tenth and final round, both were so physically spent that they did not throw any punches in the closing half-minute.

Tiger won the bout, overwhelmingly according to the ringside judges. Mercante, however, scored the bout as even, although use of the supplementary scoring system handed Tiger the unanimous decision.

Backstage after the fight, Lipton squeezed past the multitude of bodies that filled the Garden's halls and corridors. Arriving at the front of Tiger's dressing room his path was blocked by a member of security. Suddenly, a voice, that of John Condon, called out.

"If you know him, what is his last name?"

"Ihetu," Lipton shot back.

Condon gave the signal and Lipton was immediately ushered in.

Tiger, as was his custom after fights, was sitting down on his rubbing table. Looking a few years older, cheekbone slightly swollen. He appeared still shaken. Spreading his arms widely, Lipton approached and gently hugged him; carefully avoiding contact with his hands. A boxing rule of thumb is not to touch the hands of a fighter just out of the ring or about to go into the ring. "Champ," he said, looking into Tiger's eyes, "you are the only Tiger with the heart of a lion."

Tiger roared a deep belly laugh.

Then, just as quickly as he had entered, Lipton left.

The fight, quite simply, had been exhilarating, an unforgettable piece of gladiatorial theatre for those who witnessed it. Tiger himself regarded the fight so highly, that he hung four large framed photographs in his living room, each capturing the knockdowns in the fight. *Ring* magazine selected it as 1968's 'Fight of the Year.'

"It was a sensational fight. Unbelievable," enthuses Tommy Kenville. "He wins the fight and I'm sitting ringside trying to make sure that everybody is getting their story in because the electricity department were trying to pull the plugs out, and Tiger comes out of his dressing room and comes down the stairs with Chickie Ferrara behind him and he stops and says to me, 'You were right (about his punching power), he knocked me down.' And I said, ' He knocked you down TWICE.' And all he said was 'Ooooh'."

Tiger was the victor, he had overcome the problems De Paula had set him and won fairly convincingly. Yet to several observers, his performance had borne the hallmarks of a fighter matured well beyond his peak fighting capabilities. One of his best attributes had been his ability to absorb the effects of the hardest punches. Within the last two years, however, he had been floored by Emile Griffith, a welterweight not known for his punching power, knocked out by Bob Foster and twice knocked down by De Paula, in the estimation of many, little more than a glorified barroom brawler. To writers such as Girsch, the Dick Tiger of old was simply gone: "His spirit is willing, but the flesh is getting weaker. He's just plain vulnerable, spelled O-L-D. It would be a terrible thing if he fought once too often and got himself badly hurt."

With De Paula out of the way, Tiger next reminded the Garden powers that be about the rematch with Foster, implicitly promised since the match had proceeded under the assumption that it was an unofficial elimination contest for the light heavyweight championship. But all that Teddy Brenner would offer him was a rematch with De Paula, to take place at the beginning of 1969. The Garden brain trust shared Brenner's opinion that another Tiger-Foster match would fail to draw on account of Tiger's devastating loss.

Tiger was disgusted and refused outright. It all harked back to the days when Brenner promised him a crack at the middleweight title, only to be greeted with a post-match "Sorry Dick, but..." line. As Larry Merchant puts it, "The fight theoretically was to be an elimination fight, the winner to fight Bob Foster for the light heavyweight title. What they didn't tell us was that the winner would get eliminated."

To add salt into his wounds, the Garden, anticipating the financial rewards of attracting De Paula's merry band of supporters, soon announced that they would match Tiger's vanquished foe with Foster. The fight took place in January 1969 and Foster made short work of De Paula, stopping him in the first round. Brenner would later admit that it was a fight that he regretted making.

The Biafran war, meanwhile, was fulfilling Nnamdi Azikiwe's prophesy that the "experience of the Democratic Republic of the Congo will be childs play, if ever, it comes our turn to play such a tragic role." Its whole territory had been encircled since the time Tiger had evacuated his family to Portugal. Each incursion made by the Federal side was followed by large retreats by civilians, gripped by fear of being massacred. The ensuing overpopulation of its decreasing polity as well as the destruction of farmland enabled conditions to spiral to new depths. In August 1968, the International Committee of the Red Cross estimated that 61,000 people were dying each day. Biafra was now a sorrowful and terrifying montage of fleshed stripped and swollen bellied toddlers suffering the effects of kwashiorkor, the protein deficiency disease.

The war was long lost and many neutral observers questioned the rationale of prolonging it. The starving herds, it appeared, were being held hostage to a hopeless cause. Yet, if Tiger harboured any doubts about the direction of the Biafran leadership in its apparent strategy of exploiting its sick and starving multitudes in a chess game of political survival, he kept them firmly to himself and continued to act steadfastly in the service of the cause. During his stays in New York, he remained a regular visitor to the Biafran Mission and, on occasion, donned his native attire when attending fundraising gatherings in aid of

Biafra Relief. His efforts did not go unnoticed. Sam Toperoff, who still worked as a university professor recalls discussions about the genocide he had with Tiger. This information he imparted to his students who then went on to raise "a small amount of money for the aid campaign."

"He was instrumental in a way," remembers Larry Merchant "in informing journalists like myself and ordinary people about the fight of the Biafrans. About the division in the Nigerian society. They were like the Jews; hardworking and intellectual –a sort of ruling class, as I understood it. People in America identified with the Biafrans. A lot of people would not have known the difference between what these kind of wars were about, Tiger did, and was able to communicate that."

Jack Solomons got in touch with Tiger soon after the De Paula fight and informed him of his willingness to stage an over-the-weight contest with Nino Benvenuti, the middleweight champion. Benvenuti had emerged victorious from a three match series with Emile Griffith and had been bemoaning the lack of money spinning fights in the division. He hoped to meet Bob Foster in a marketable interdivisional clash of world champions. But first, he needed to 'test the waters' with a light heavyweight performer. Tiger appeared to fit the bill and Solomons envisaged that the bout would take place either in London or be co-promoted in Italy.

A match with Benvenuti appealed to Tiger, but he informed Solomons that he felt obligated to the Madison Square Garden organisation and so the bout was then co-opted on to the Garden roster and scheduled for May 26 1969.

Nino Benvenuti was a tall and classy fighter who had come away from the Rome Olympics with a gold medal. A panel of experts had in fact chosen him over the young Cassius Clay as having been the best boxer of the games. Born in Trieste, the son of a well to do fisherman who plied his trade on the blue waters of the Adriatic, off the Dalmatian coast, Benvenuti grew into a precocious, hyperactive little boy. Always self assured and supremely confident, he was eleven when he announced matter-of–a-fact to his ex-pugilist father his preferred profession. "Papa," he said, "I want to be a fighter."

His amateur career was outstanding culminating in Olympian achievement. He immediately turned professional, winning the world light middleweight title from Sandro Mazzinghi in 1965. After losing it the following year to Ki-Soo Kim, he moved up to the middleweights and won the title from Emile Griffith in April 1967. Although he lost the return bout, he regained the championship in the rubber match.

He trained at Grossingers, an environment that was no match for his Italian training patch, which was situated in a building on Bologna's 'Street of Poets.' There he sweated under chapel type ceilings, in rooms with walls covered by Monets and Utrillos and elegantly stained windows that combined with chanti coloured drapes.

Boxing pundits wondered about the effect Benvenuti's activities outside the game were having on his career. At home he was politically active, sitting as an elected counsellor on the Trieste City Council. He also dabbled in the insurance industry. But it was his new found passion for movie making that raised eyebrows, especially when his bout with Tiger had to be pushed back because of shooting commitments on the set of a cowboy movie. When in America, few noticed him making the fighter's obligatory six-mile daily jog around the nearby Catskill Mountain roads.

Then there was the matter of Tiger's whereabouts. Jerry Izenburg, a sports columnist would later write a charming piece on the uncertainties of the comings and goings of Tiger during this period. The fight contracts would be signed by mail or by telegram, after which Chickie Ferrera would begin, constantly, to drop by at Tommy Kenville's office, opening the lower draw of Kenville's filing cabinet only to find it empty. Both men would chat for a while and then Ferrera would leave. Then the day would come; Ferrara would slide open the drawer to reveal a large, dirty shopping bag stuffed with gym shoes, a protective cup and worn out trunks and would step back to exclaim: "He's here!"

The real story was a tad mundane. When Tiger arrived to train for the Benvenuti fight, he discovered that his usual training den, the New Garden Gymnasium, "a real schlock place" according to Kenville, had been closed. He went up to Kenville's office armed with a large shopping bag containing his training gear and asked Kenville to keep it for him. Kenville accepted and put the bag in an empty draw but wasted little time in summoning Chickie Ferrera, who moved the intruding articles to Gleason's Gym.

Situated on Westchester Avenue in New York's Bronx Borough, on the second floor of a building adjoining a post office, Gleason's was already one of the immortal names of New York City gyms. Tiger did not only change gymnasiums; the hotel he normally resided at was undergoing repairs. He stayed "with friends" somewhere in Brooklyn and everyday made the hour-long journey via subway to the Bronx. Taxis were never an option. Tiger was one of the few patrons to have a room to himself. Al Vialiardi, who had a long association with the gym, remembers Tiger as being a "very quiet guy" who would come up to do his work, take his shower and then leave. There was, however, one noisy incident Tommy Kenville remembers:

"One time, Bobby O'Brien couldn't fight the fifth or sixth round of a sparring session at Gleason's Gym. Bobby got pounded for four rounds. He's just a young big, tall white kid and Paddy Flood, who managed him, said: 'That's it!' and called it off. But Dick didn't want to pay him for the day. (But) Chickie Ferrera said, 'you can't do that'!"

Tiger trained as the betting underdog but he pushed himself hard. When he entered the ring for what was a sixteenth appearance at the Garden, few failed to notice the contours of the hard and sinewy physique, which he had "trained to perfection. Trained to the very edge of overdoing." There were, of course those, who expected this to be his last hoorah, the *San Francisco Chronicle*'s correspondent reporting that the Italian fighter was expected to win and so "send the sturdy Biafran a step nearer retirement."

Fourteen thousand three hundred and five spectators produced receipts of $147,431 at the Garden box office. For Benvenuti, Tiger professed to have no fight plan, except, that is, to get beneath the Italian's long jab and throw punches to the body. There was, however, a certain method behind the way he stooped low and stayed out of reach from Benvenuti's pole-straight left jab, before rushing forward to land combination punches to the Italian's body. Benvenuti was constantly off-balanced. Before the end of the inaugural round, he threw an overhand right, which glanced off the top of Tiger's head. He grimaced as he pulled it back; the big knuckle on his index finger had been broken.

From this point, Benvenuti appeared to lose heart. While Tiger dug crevasses into the sides of his abdomen, he began, increasingly, to turn to the referee, Tony Peres to complain that Tiger's shots were straying below his trunk belt. Peres ignored him and by the seventh, the shouts of 'NEENO, NEENO,' dominant in the early rounds, began to be swallowed by chants of 'TIGER, TIGER.'

Tiger was awarded a unanimous decision, inflicting on Benvenuti only the third loss of his career. Benvenuti left the ring, shaking his head, as he held up his bare right hand to indicate that he was injured, but it did not impress his supporters, many of who cast him wary glances. Others muttered 'Scuses, 'scuses.'

They hailed Tiger when he left the ring. He, by comparison, seemed so unspoilt, so down-to-earth and so giving to the fans. Wrote Dave Anderson in the next morning's *New York Times*, "Tiger isn't a movie actor. He doesn't sip wine. He isn't particularly handsome. But at the age of 39, he is a gladiator, perhaps the purest remaining and despite Benvenuti's injury, he was too tough, too strong and too willing for Benvenuti."

Tiger made the next morning's papers for something else. As he navigated his way back to his dressing room, a man blocked his path and thrust a document into his hand. It was a marshal

231

from the District Attorney's office who then informed him that his presence was required the following morning before a New York City Grand Jury.

The man behind it all was Frank Hogan. Manhattan's District Attorney had for the past two months been conducting a secret investigation into underworld connections to the boxing industry. This was the latest of several enquiries which Hogan, an avowed opponent of organised crimes infiltration of the sport, had carried out since the late 1950s. He had in the past declaimed Frankie Carbo and Frank 'Blinky' Parlemo, the latter whom he referred to as being the 'leader' of boxing's mobsters, as the schemers behind the scams, fight rigs and all round corrupting of the game. Hogan's work is seen as hugely influential in the setting up of the Kefauver Senate Hearings into boxing's criminal links.

The gaoling of Parlemo and Carbo however did not figure to Hogan to have solved the problem. Boxing people were nevertheless perplexed about his latest adventure. Especially since he and his assistant, Alfred J. Smith, who headed the Rackets Bureau, responded vaguely to the initial entreaties of the press. What however became deducible was the Tiger-Benvenuti bout was ostensibly under suspicion because of the reports that bookmakers had stopped taking bets after odds, which favoured Benvenuti by seven to five had subsequently shot up to twelve to five. But this in itself did not make anyone the wiser because little money had been staked on Tiger, the upset winner.

On the afternoon of Wednesday, May 28th, Tiger, dressed in a dark suit and tie walked up the steps leading to the New York Criminal Courts Building to wait his turn to take the stand. He, like the also subpoenaed Benvenuti, had already spent part of the morning at Hogan's office, being peppered with questions. The Italian arrived with his arm in a sling and had his right brow padded. "Funny," Tiger noted to reporters, "I didn't notice that last night."

At about two O' Clock, he was ushered into the courtroom. He held up a copy of the bible as he solemnly swore to 'tell the truth and nothing but the truth' then took a seat. His eyes searched around the room before the questions, numerous and fairly innocuous, began: 'How old are you?,' 'How long have you being fighting?' and the like. It was all rather cordial and he shot back his replies with equal brevity. The inevitable question of whether he had ever been approached and propositioned about fixing the outcome of any bout was met with the inevitable reply: "No."

He emerged an hour later to be greeted by the phalanx of press laying in wait. "They asked me questions, and I answered them," he stated blandly, "they were nice people." When a reporter asked him point blank, whether the fight had been fixed, Tiger shot back: "Ask Nino. All I know is I fought as hard as I could. I am a fighter."

He was not resummond. A few days later, Hogan admitted what most already believed, that the fight was not under suspicion. The general feeling among most observers was that he had acted overzealously and needlessly by involving both Tiger and Benvenuti. Writing in the *Ring*, Nat Loubet asked "What was all the shooting about when the District Attorney's Office served subpoenas on Tiger and Benvenuti and gave boxing some bad publicity in a matter that did not concern Dick or Nino in the slightest degree?"

Such was his reputation for integrity and trustworthiness that another sportswriter felt compelled to comment that Hogan's decision to summon a reputable character like Tiger had made a mockery of the proceedings. It was his reputation for integrity, which had dampened reports of a pre-planned fight against Bob Foster.

"The image that he had in the public was that he was a good man as well as a good fighter," recalls Larry Merchant. "And this was even before the war. There was a very positive image. Of course, there was interest in him early because he had tribal markings, etcetera; but the image of him was as a good man."

The image of his erstwhile foe, Frankie De Paula, was not nearly as pristine. De Paula had, along with Tiger and Benvenuti, been subpoenaed by Hogan. He had been scheduled to fight Don

Fullmer on the underbill, but was suspended by the N.Y.S.A.C. only a few days before the bout after his arrest by F.B.I. agents investigating the theft of $80,000 worth of electrolyte copper in New Jersey. Although he was acquitted along with his manager Gary Garafola at the subsequent trial, tragedy followed. DePaula had been having an affair with a woman who also happened to be the mistress of a local gangster. Stubborn as ever, he ignored several warnings to 'lay off' her. It was a warm summers evening in Jersey City when DePaula arrived at the woman's apartment. A note was stuck on the front door informing him that the doorbell was broken and instructing him to use the back entrance. In order to do this, DePaula needed to pass through a back alley. It was in this alley that a figure approached him from behind and when at close range shot him twice in the back with a .45 calibre gun. Instinctively, De Paula twisted round and grabbed his assailant. In the ensuing struggle, he managed somehow to break the attacker's jaw, before crumpling to the ground. Gravely injured, he was taken to the Jersey City Medical Centre where he lay immobilized by the onset of paralysis. An account of his stay in hospital relates a pitiful tale of a patient covered in bedsores, the result of neglect. His once Adonis-like physique was reduced to an emaciated 120 pounds. DePaula's end came from pneumonia, the result of an attending nurse forgetting to shut a window at night. He died on September 14 1970, four months after the shooting.

The Garden now offered Tiger the opportunity to challenge Benvenuti for the middleweight title, "If," Teddy Brenner stressed to a crowd of reporters, "he wants to make the weight." He had weighed in at 166 pounds and Brenner felt that he was capable of shedding a further six pounds to make the middleweight limit. This Tiger felt he could not do. He turned down the offer and announced that he was no longer interested in fighting for that title.

The fight with Benvenuti, like his bout with Frankie De Paula, had been billed as a light heavyweight 'elimination bout.' But again, victory did not bring the desired rematch with Foster.

Foster's backers had fallen short of their breakeven point by $21,000 and while he was willing to grant Tiger a match, he set his terms. "I had to guarantee $100,000 to induce Dick to fight me," he explained to *Ring* magazine, "now, I am in the commanding position. If Tiger wants the chance to regain his title, he will have to make sure that I get $100,000 for my end. That would only be fair."

Offers did come his way, like the one wired from a California manager guaranteeing him $25,000 to face a fighter called Jimmy Lestor. In London, Bobby Diamond had begun to negotiate a Commonwealth light heavyweight title bout with Bobby Dunlop, the Australian holder and also contemplating a European tour that would take place later in 1969. All, however, he gave short shrift. These were pretty testing times for him. But if people were expecting him to fade away, they were wrong. As his fortieth birthday loomed, he candidly explained to the *Ring*'s Billy Williams why he was intent on prolonging his career.

"The war between Nigeria and my native Biafra has been very costly to me. Most of my investments there have been wiped out, and I still have a large family to take care of –a mother, sister, wife and seven Tiger 'cubs'- and I need every cent that I can get my hands on. It's also a very big expense when I fight in New York. The Garden pays for my transportation, but it costs me plenty to bring the family out of Biafra and park them in an apartment in Lisbon while I'm in America. I'll continue to fight as a light heavyweight and hope and trust that I'll be able to keep going until the Nigerian-Biafran mess is cleared up and I can salvage something out of the wreckage of my investments there."

He felt driven and motivated by a hunger, not of the sort that had compelled him to persevere in his early years of struggle, but one nevertheless with its own brand of force and energy. The impulse of youthful enthusiasm was no longer there –once he could never refrain from fighting his shadow or mirrored image, yet, he had a purpose and a focus which his experience and dedicated sense of professionalism would, he believed, see him through.

The perils of fighting into what in boxing terms is a rather advanced age were not lost on him. But he felt reassured by the temperate lifestyle, which he had always followed; never smoking and rarely touching alcohol. He drew inspiration from the methusahlaen career of his hero, Archie Moore who retired when only just short of his fiftieth birthday as well as from old timers like Harry Grebb and Jack Dillon, who he read had 'specialised' in overcoming heavier opposition.

Tiger had always struck most Americans who knew him, as being a shy introvert whose living circumstances conveyed a certain monkish asceticism. Certainly the strains caused by the ongoing war did not make him any more amenable to conducting lengthy social intercourse with boxing people.

"He was a very private person," recalls Tommy Kenville. "I think that probably sums him up. He lived in a hotel room all by himself. No entourage. No women around –or that we knew of! He was away from his family, he was losing all the things he'd probably bled for in the ring, especially in Liverpool and places like that, and I guess that this kind of constricted his outward personality –if he ever had one."

"He was not much of a talker," remembered Les Matthews of the *New York Amsterdam News*, "(but) he was a good listener. Once in a while, he would talk seriously about his country and the world in general and his desire to return to his family." Emile Griffith recalls, "He was a quiet person, didn't tell me anything. He would tell you that his wife and family were okay when he last saw them." Of the war that still raged, Griffith surmises: "Sometimes he seemed glad to be away from it all."

Quiet and diffident, Tiger was keen to live an anonymous existence, a quest that he was not always able to accomplish, as Tommy Kenville relates:

"One time he was cooking something in his room. I don't know what it was, perhaps some kind of native dish or vegetables. But somebody later said that it smelt like burning socks. Somebody called the manager of the hotel and he called John Condon. He said, 'Mr. Condon, we're getting complaints here and people are going to call the board of health because they think that some kind of ritual is going on in there.' And Condon says, 'That god dammed, fucking Tiger'."

Thirteen
TWILIGHT: 'AS LONG AS THERE'S MONEY'

The Ihetu family lived a strange, cloistered existence at their Lisbon apartment. They spoke virtually no Portuguese and knew few people. Tiger, himself, grew tired of the endless commuting between New York and Lisbon. He made arrangements with the immigration authorities in America to have them resettled and in July 1969, they relocated to a house, which he rented in the Cambria Heights district of Queens County. Abigail arrived heavily pregnant and gave birth the following month to their eighth and final child, a son, whom they named George. His children were enrolled at a local school but he kept his family's presence a close guarded secret for the remainder of their sojourn. Those making queries about them were informed that they still resided in war torn Biafra.

In October, the Garden matched him with Andy Kendall, an Oregon-based light heavyweight contender who had been stopped in a title contest against Bob Foster the previous May. Born Andrew Howard Pierce, but later taking the surname of his foster parents, Kendall was a strong but methodical boxer possessing an infinite capacity to take punishment – a fact that was not confined to his excursions in the squared ring. Two years previously, he had been shot and left for dead by his irate father-in-law. He was moments from being locked and stored in a local mortuary when a vigilant coroner, noting signs of life, ordered the detour of his near corpse to the local hospital.

Tiger accepted a relatively paltry $15,000 to face Kendall. Although fully a decade older, he came into the fight the firm betting favourite. He was also a favourite of the fight fans, many of who recognised and stopped him as he walked around Manhattan. "They always want to know how old I am, I tell them thirty-two or thirty-three and they believe me," he joked. Describing him as "the warrior currently most admired by New

York aficionados," Dave Anderson's fight preview in the *New York Times* noted that "at the age of 40, the Biafran has developed a sentimental attraction for those who appreciate the violent majesty of a true gladiator...but in his recent role as an ex-champion, his mystique has increased." Teddy Brenner appeared to agree. "The thing about Dick Tiger," he commented, "is that he has an honest heart and willing hands. If he gets beat, it's only because the other guy was a better fighter that night. He usually gives away height and weight and age, but, he never gives away heart."

He staggered Kendall several times during the early rounds and in the third, appeared to be on the verge of stopping the Oregoan. That did not happen, but Tiger's control of the fight was complete enough for him to indulge the Garden audience with a Muhammad Ali like quickstep shuffle.

The bout went the ten round limit and the judges scored it unanimously in his favour. Although it had been a comfortable win, the degenerative signs of ring agedness were there for all to see. The *New York Times* summed up the contest as having been a "dreary duel that seemed to symbolize the decline of the light heavyweight division," adding that "although the quiet gathering of 6,083 spectators...appreciated Tiger's victory, his age was more impressive than his skill."

While Tiger was capable of beating the likes of Kendall and Frankie De Paula, feats that confirmed his number one ranked contender status to Foster's title, it appeared to many that the gap between the champion and the rest of the division was so wide as to being unbridgeable. "With Foster as the champion, we've been thinking about starting our own title, an American title," Kendall's manager had joked before the bout. "This guy's in a class by himself and there's no interests in fights and mismatches." Kendall himself summed up the predicament that he felt Tiger to be in: "Who else is he going to fight? He's sure not going to beat Foster anymore. Nobody is going to beat Foster in quite a while."

For his part, Tiger's post fight comment revealed the abiding concern: "Anybody, anywhere. As long as there's money."

Biafra, for him, continued to be a personal obsession and as 1969 drew to a close, the rebel republic, now merely a rump strip of land, teetered towards total collapse. At the start of the conflict, Biafra had controlled 30,000 square miles of territory in which close to 14 million resided. This now had been reduced to a tenth. An estimated 1,000 deaths due to starvation were occurring daily while a further untold amount were perishing from other illnesses.

Tiger, like many of his kinsmen, had remained perplexed and disheartened by the lack of recognition for the struggle. He could not understand why his people, Christian and progressive, had failed to receive the backing from more Western countries, especially from the United States, which had maintained through the administrations of Lyndon Johnson and Richard Nixon, a studious neutrality. It is possible that the adoption by the Biafran leadership of certain principles in the village of Ahiarra, the 'Ahiarra Declaration,' may have had a negative effect in this regard and may in fact have sounded the death knell to the possibility of American recognition. The declaration, occurring on June 1st 1969, decided that a sovereign Biafran state would be underpinned by the principle of communal property ownership. Even though the new egalitarian order would encourage 'private enterprise,' the image of Ojukwu, the head of the newly styled 'People's Army' captioned in a Fidel Castro like pose, cigar in one hand and rifle strapped to shoulder bore strong communist overtones. It was a turn of policy that Charles Ihetu is convinced his property owning father would not have approved of.

"(My father) was a man who worked hard to gain whatever he had and I would think that when he heard that declaration; that of all the houses he had he would only own one, that of all the businesses he ran he would only run one, it must have made him think of what he was getting himself into."

Tiger would nonetheless outwardly continue staunchly supporting the cause. While he had of course criticized the 'lack of understanding' that he felt Americans had for the problems of

Africa, his disgust was reserved for the role that the British government had played throughout the conflict in supporting Federal Nigeria. The alleged hand which certain expatriate Britons had in stirring up the unrest that led to the pogroms of 1966 as well as the British role in the about turn in the decision of the North's plan to secede after the counter-coup of July that year had been a staple of Biafran propaganda. The anti-British stance was reflected by Tiger himself through an act that found its inspiration from an unlikely quarter: John Lennon's return of his M.B.E. medal on November the 25th. One of the reasons cited by Lennon referred to the support that the British government was giving to its Nigerian counterpart in its prosecution of the civil war.

His own M.B.E. medal, handed to him six years earlier with much pomp and ceremony had travelled with him. He took the medal, now a faded silver; its pink ribbon grimy, out of its locket and resolved to give it up.

It was a sunny but bitingly cold Friday afternoon when Tiger, wearing the perennial furlined white overcoat and black homborg hat, walked up the steps of a Manhattan Post Office. Accompanying him was a Biafran friend.

"If they ask me how much it's worth, what should I say?" he asked.

"We should try to pawn it and find out," shrugged the friend.

"I'll say a million dollars," Tiger replied laughing. "I'll say fifty or a hundred (dollars) so that it gets there."

He stood in line, and handed his package over the counter. The clerk looked at the object disapprovingly and shaking his head told him, "No good, you've got scotch tape on it. Go round the corner, they'll give you some brown paper."

Another clerk handed over a long strip of gummed brown paper and a wet sponge in a dish. He took it to a writing desk and carefully tore the brown paper into smaller strips. He re-taped the package and again, stood in line.

He came before the same clerk who had ordered the re-wrap and handed it over. The clerk observed the package for a few moments before looking up.

241

"Okay," he snapped, "What's in it?"

"A medal," replied Tiger.

"What's it worth?"

Shrugging, Tiger replied: ""I don't know, fifty, one hundred dollars."

"No value," the clerk said to himself. He weighed and registered it.

"Do you want it airmailed?"

"Yes"

"One-sixty"

Tiger brought out two dollar bills. He received his change and walked out of the building then turning to his companion shook his hand.

"If you look at Africa now," he told Robert Lipsyte, "there is fighting and trouble in every country that was once under the British government. They were forced to give the countries independence but they gave it with the left hand and are now trying to take it back with the right hand."

Worse of course could have been said about his erstwhile Portuguese hosts, who while supporting Biafra, had continued to remain unyielding to international demands to give independence to their African colonies. Then suddenly becoming self-conscious at his comments, he told Lipsyte, "I am not a politician. I don't want people to say, 'Ahh, there's a dumb fighter who does not speak good English talking'."

Inside the package which soon would be making its way to the Ambassador's office at the British Embassy in Washington D.C. was the following typed message:

I am hereby returning the O.B.E. (sic) **because every time I look at it, I think of millions of men, women and children who died and are still dying in Biafra because of the arms and ammunition the British government is sending to Nigeria and its continued moral support of this genocidal war against the people of Biafra.**

Signed
Dick Tiger Ihetu.

In the days following the onset of the new year, the potholed roads and muddy paths of the Biafran heartland teemed with swarms of refugees trekking away from advancing Federal troops. On the flanks lay the weak and the aged, the hungry and the pregnant. In the fortified bunker now serving as his cabinet headquarters, Ojukwu searched the faces of colleagues, some with tears streaming down their faces and called on the few remaining diehards to admit that the war was lost. Two days later, he made a final broadcast on Radio Biafra, announcing his imminent flight to an unknown destination to, as he put it, "explore possibilities for peace." On January 12, the voice of Phillip Effiong, commander of Biafra's bedraggled forces, emerged over the airwaves to announce an unconditional truce. A week later, the process of capitulation was completed in Lagos, where before General Gowon and the Supreme Military Council, he declared, "we are loyal Nigerian citizens and accept that the Republic of Biafra ceases to exist." Two and a half years of war had sown a bitter harvest of death: There had been 100,000 military casualties and harrowingly, two million civilian lives, most of them starved Biafrans, had perished.

On the night of Biafra's surrender, Gowon broadcasted to the nation on television and radio to issue a solemn guarantee of a general amnesty to those whom he claimed had been "misled into rebellion." This was not unexpected. As the war had drawn inexorably closer to a Federal victory, he began laying the foundations of a policy of reconciliation with promises of amnesty and repeated stresses that the war was not being prosecuted against the Igbos but against what was conveniently termed "Ojukwu and his clique." With the ending of the war, he now decreed that Versailles-type reparations would not be demanded from the Igbos and that no medals would be awarded to Federal soldiers and civilians for their war time conduct. There would he said be "no Nuremberg trials here" and he went on to popularise the policy with the comment cum slogan that the war had produced "No victor and no vanquished."

Tiger listened and read the bulletins from home. His mood

243

remained far from grateful. "Nothing matters anymore," was the initial assessment proffered in an early interview. There was for him the inevitable feeling of disappointment, a crushing of the soul and spirit. At the same time, he yearned to return to his homeland and anxiously pondered on the fate of family and friends. What he wondered was the state of his houses and the properties that he heard had been 'requisitioned.' Despite the positive nature of Gowon's promises, he wondered if he would truly be allowed back home, for there was, he suspected, a price which would be paid for the efforts he had made on behalf of the rebellion.

There was a change in him. The contagiously cheerful smile was mostly gone, replaced by a blankness, an almost somnambulant quality. The defeat of Biafra, the diminution of his purses, worry over his extended family and investments as well as his exile were all contributing factors. In February, Desmond Hackett, a sportswriter for the London *Daily Express* happened upon his solitary figure ambling down an avenue in Manhattan's concrete jungle. Both men exchanged pleasantries but it was, claimed Hackett, the "first and only time I had seen Tiger downcast."

And for good reason. The acute shortage of money held by the newly instituted East-Central State reflected the generally penurious state of the population. Money which he had sent to the families of his brothers during the war years and which had been converted into the Biafran currency, was now virtually worthless. A government decree issued in April 1970 allowed exchanges of the rebel currency at a flat rate of £20 per individual. It was partly, because of the need to be able to send valuable foreign currency to his family that he resolved to take his career into a third decade.

He now managed himself, the contract with Jones having since expired. In the spring, the Garden came up with an opponent, his old foe, Emile Griffith in a fight billed as an elimination contest for the middleweight championship, which was still held by Nino Benvenuti. In the 1960s, he and Griffith had been two of the Garden's biggest draws, but at the beginning of the new decade, both careers were waning. After losing his middleweight championship series with Benvenuti, Griffith had in October 1969 made an unsuccessful challenge to Jose Napoles' welterweight title. Perhaps fearing both ex-champions would attract only a miniscule audience, the bout was initially scheduled to take place within the 4,000 seater Felt Forum but this was changed to the main arena.

It was around this time that the Independent Television (I.T.V.) channel in England, contacted him to express interest in making a documentary feature on his early fight experiences in England. But his scheduled visit was postponed when he stumbled, fell and wrenched a shoulder muscle during a training jog. The project was later cancelled.

He received a visit from Dave Anderson on the eve of the fight. The *New York Times* columnist found him in melancholic mood; full of longings, regrets and proclaiming himself to be " a nobody, just another fighter."

"I deserve to fight Foster again," he told Anderson, "but he won't listen to me. He does all the talking now."

When Anderson asked him about Biafra, he bore a look of resignation: "Now it's all Nigeria again. Now that the war is over, I am from Nigeria again. After this fight, I hope to go home again to see my family. Things are so hard there."

He continued to deny the presence of his immediate family in America: "No, they are still back there. I wish some of them would surprise me. I live in an apartment in Brooklyn on Alabama Avenue and I haven't seen my family since last August, but any time I fight, I send my money home to them."

Of Anderson's enquiry on how many more years of prize fighting he had in him, he replied, "I'm thirty-nine (sic). I'm a fighter. I didn't go to college. I have no other job."

On the morning of the fight, his usually calm and affable demeanour was broken. Bernard Forbes, the cousin and camp companion of Emile Griffith, a loud, brash and frequently excitable person, decided to use the occasion of the weigh-in to

245

continually direct taunts at him, saying that he was "old" and "past it." He predicted that Tiger would be knocked out and sent into retirement. Once he might have ignored it, but with the strains that currently burdened him, he cracked. Apoplectic with rage, he approached Forbes and issued a tirade:

"Do you want to take me on?" he asked angrily. "I am a real African, what are you? I have been a world champion, a captain in an army, who are you?"

Forbes fell silent.

"Bernard sort of tried to put the 'whammy' on Tiger and Tiger put him right in his place," recalls Victor Zimet, who witnessed the altercation. "I'm sure that Emile didn't appreciate Bernard opening his mouth because nobody asked him to. Emile didn't need that kind of assistance."

His rage apparently exhausted, Tiger turned away as Griffith, who had walked over to calm him muttered, "Easy baby, easy."

Later on in the day as they stood facing each other in the ring, few would have failed to notice the signs of agedness in both men. But although Griffith's bald patch made him appear the older of the two, it quickly became apparent that he had retained more of his skills. Tiger, slow and ponderous, seemed incapable of keeping up with Griffith's clockwise rotations and found it difficult to set his punches. The first punch he managed to throw did not happen until the bell was sounding to end the first round.

Griffith continued to move, peppering Tiger's face with rapier fast left jabs, occasionally coming off his toes to exchange punches. In these, Griffith's speed ensured he dominated. Anger and frustration mounted in Tiger as he followed Griffith's retreating footsteps, calling on him to "stand and fight." The verbal exchanges became so frequent, that the referee, Peter Diele, stepped in to warn both men. Griffith was winning the psychological battle and began punctuating his flurries with clowning antics, first by dropping his guard and then by executing taunting, mincing steps. He rubbed it in by performing a feet shuffle. In the eighth round, Tiger replied by dropping his guard to mimic his tormentor. The crowd cheered his every attack, but still, Griffith's jabs continued piercing his guard.

As both waited for the din to signal the start of the final round, Griffith, sensing no doubt, the ill feeling that he was causing in his friend, called out: "C'mon Tiger, lets make a good fight. I'm beating you but we're still good friends." But this was hardly an effective apology. His cocky yelling and attempts at intimidation both surprised and upset Tiger who later confided to Ron Lipton that he thought it beneath Griffith to have reduced himself to this level given all the years they had known each other. "I saw hurt in his eyes," relates Lipton. "Emile's conduct embarrassed him."

The unanimous verdict that the judges granted Griffith surprised no one. Tiger's performance had been brave but sorely lacking in the essentials of foot and hand speed. The *New York Times* concluded that he "never once flashed the form that had enabled him in his nineteen years in the ring to gain the middleweight and light heavyweight championships." "Tiger apologised to reporters afterwards for being beaten," wrote the match reporter for *Boxing News*, "but they knew like the disappointed fans that Dick had simply grown old in a young mans trade. If Tiger does decide to retire as seems likely, he can look back with pride on his career. If he keeps boxing, however, the going will get tougher and the returns will get smaller."

Those looking on all presumed his career to be at an end. But it appeared that Tiger did not when he announced that he would "keep fighting on."

In London, Bobby Diamond had been aware of Tiger's need to replenish his drained finances. Before fighting Griffith, Tiger had received word from him about a fight tour of South Africa to take place in September. The idea was for him to fight three local (black) fighters in Orlando, Alexandra and Cape Town. Diamond also relayed news of a $5,000 offer from a German promoter to meet a middleweight, Horst Benedens in Berlin. Neither offer, however, interested him and Diamond's cables were left unanswered. There was no chance, Tiger later told a reporter, that he would have considered fighting in the then apartheid state.

He reportedly spent a lot of time after this bout trawling around New York City gymnasiums and making frequent visits to the Garden offices of Harry Markson, in both cases, desperately trying to engineer the 'right' bout. Teddy Brenner had offered to "use" him if he was interested but when he was offered a small purse to face an erstwhile sparring partner, Tiger turned it down, saying that he had "too much pride." He added for the benefit of the press the comment that "I will shine shoes first." He was simply not interested in seeing out his career in a series of low purse, deadend contests at venues like Sunnyside Gardens and the Felt Forum. The offers did come, but he remained steadfast in his refusal to fight those opponents, who as he put it, "wish to use my name as a ladder." He found promoters more interested in staging heavyweight contests than those involving fighters from lower weight categories. This was partly true, in the sense that relatively little money could be made at the light heavyweight division even at the best of times, but with the dominance of the behemoth like Foster, these really were the worst of times. He may have had a ray of hope when in November 1970; Foster was stripped of the W.B.A. version of the title for "consistently failing to defend his title against top rated contenders." However, the W.B.A. ignored him when it came to nominating the fighters who would succeed Foster.

By now, the Roberto Durans and the Ken Buchanans of this world had assumed the mantle previously worn by the Tigers and Griffiths on the Madison Square Garden roster and Tiger, who against all the odds had succeeded in prolonging his career, now had to face the stark truth: He was yesterday's man.

"After that last fight with Griffith, he just kind of faded," says Tommy Kenville, "you'd see him around once in a while but your mind would say 'Dick Tiger. Gee, I guess he's still trying to hang on.' But this is like twenty odd years after he turned pro and the hardest thing to explain to a fighter is that they don't go on forever. What's funny about boxing is that someone like Tiger, who's been an integral part of the sport and to see starts to fade, other people come to take his place and you're tied up to them. You try to be kind and gentle and behave well and show a little class but you can't have time for people who now are gone. It's a tough thing."

Tiger continued to train regularly after the Griffith fight, but the cost of hiring sparring partners and the cumulated booking fees for the time used in the gym became an intolerable burden. He found himself a job doing security work at Manhattan's Natural History Museum for which he received the weekly remuneration of $96.

In time, the press discovered this. It made for good reading: The familiar tale of the former boxing champion and his descent into penury. The sort of down-on-your-luck yarn which had famously blighted the post-fight careers of the likes of Beau Jack, the shoeshine boy who earned four million dollars but returned to shoe shining after his boxing career and Randy Turpin the former middleweight champion who in less than one year after finishing his professional career, was earning five dollars a day for a ten hour shift in the breakersyard owned by the man who had managed him.

Of course many who were aware of the war and of the presumed expropriation of his properties were unsurprised. Some observers like Tommy Kenville were convinced that he had been "milked by the Biafrans."

Tiger read the piece written by Larry Merchant in his *New York Post* column and cut it out. It survived in the Ihetu household for many years. But the commonly held perception that his father ended his career impoverished and working in the men's room of a city museum is one that does not rest well with Joseph Ihetu.

"Everybody seems to write that my father (ended up) broke," he says, "when he took a job that paid him an amount, which was nowhere near the income he received as a champion, people assumed that he was down and out. But (the fact is) he liked to stay busy –rather than stay at home, he had to do something. He was never broke."

249

An Igboman, a saying goes, will not tell you what he has. It is only when he has nothing that he tells his neighbours and what Tiger had told acquaintances in New York was that he had "lost a lot" not the lot. Working in a menial position perhaps did not bring with it, the sense of degradation others might have felt it brought him. He had after all absorbed the tenents of a belief system and culture which while promising the inevitability of the rewards that come from hard work, was also tempered by the humbling philosophy that in this world, no 'condition is permanent.' "I was a big shot (in Nigeria before the war)," he told enquiring voices, "that's how life is, it goes up and down."

Ron Lipton, by now a part time police officer, continued to visit him, coming over from West Orange, New Jersey to "hang around" all day in Manhattan. They talked and would often lunch together. He felt deeply for his friend and former employer.

"The strangest thing was to see him there. There was a terrible pathos there that he had to wear the mantle of something less than he was and it made me very sad. He was very introspective and taciturn and he wouldn't discuss it. He'd say a lot of personal things but I could see that there was a great sadness on him. There was something gone from his eyes. I would make him laugh and he would be polite but I couldn't get him to open up to me much. He would always ask me how *I'm* doing! But I couldn't say how are you doing because I know he wasn't doing well."

Still Lipton often worked to bolster Tiger's spirits.

"I would tell him how in all of boxing history there was never a fighter like him and I would tell him why. It made him smile and that made me feel like a million bucks, as he would nod his head humbly and reach out and squeeze my shoulder as if to say thank you for thinking of me like that now."

While Tiger worked his shifts at the Museum, he never gave up hope of landing a 'big time' fight. Still refusing the small promotion offers that continued to be dangled before him, he diligently maintained a fitness rota that included a thrice-weekly jog around the nearby Central Park reservoir. But Bobby

Diamond, who was aware of this, felt that Tiger was refusing to face reality: "The days of the $50,000 purses are over for Dick," he told *Boxing News* in June of 1971. "If he wishes to continue boxing, it will have to be for smaller amounts."

And then, his health took a turn for the worse. Painful spasms, located on the right side of his abdomen, at first occasional, now began to occur with more frequency and with increased intensity. He suffered from other maladies including consuming bouts of weakness and pains in his stomach. In the past, he routinely ignored the pains but in early July, a sudden crises caused him such trauma, that he doubled up in pain and almost collapsed to the ground.

He was admitted to the Polyclinic Hospital, a large establishment located on 50th Street, right opposite the location of the old Madison Square Garden. The doctor who attended to him, one Donald Gordon, proceeded to conduct a battery of tests, the results of which he found to be "very suspicious." Gordon then called in Harry Klieman, a neurologist, who had performed many of Tiger's pre-fight medicals in the capacity of Chief Physician to the N.Y.S.A.C. After running further tests and conducting observations, both men came to the unmistakable conclusion that Tiger had developed a hepatoma of the liver. Tumours of the liver are forms of primary cancer, one which is centered in the liver and has not spread there from another part of the body. It was a condition which Gordon, more used to detecting liver cirrhosis, had never dealt with, but one which he immediately recognised as being "not uncommon in Africans."

Even today, the survival rates for this form of cancer remain abysmally low, the symptoms of the ailment tending to reveal itself only at a late stage. He and Klieman could see that Tiger's cancer was simply too advanced to attempt any form of surgery. Moreover, hepatomas are not readily susceptible to either radiation or chemotherapy treatments. "There was no hope," Klieman would say later and he and Gordon performed the delicate task of informing Tiger of the grim news that he was going to have to endure a very painful demise.

It appears from the brief statements which both doctors issued to the international news agencies, after his death that he was almost certainly chronically infected by the hepatitis B Virus, a symtomless condition which contemporary medical opinion recognises plays a major role in neutralising the body's 'tumour suppressor genes,' that is, nature's in-built defence against the growth of tumours. When they are 'disarmed', the result is the formation of cancerous cells.

There may also be a dietary angle to Tiger's ailment; that is, through the toxins produced by the aspergillis fungus that thrives in hot, humid conditions and is observable as a white layer in stored rice and grains. Aflatoxin, a natural carcinogen, is associated with the formation of tumours. Still another contributing factor to his illness may lie in the paint-mixing job found for him by his manager Tony Vairo. For a period over twelve months, Tiger continually imbibed the factory's pungent fumes. Research in the 1970s postulated a causal link between certain cancers and the persistent exposure to chemicals. Others, like Ron Lipton, however, have their own opinions on the source of his illness. "I believe an inner sadness actually caused that cancer. I think that one of the worst things that came out of the pandora's box was grief and it laid the warrior low."

Now that death was to be his lot, Tiger became resolved to die among his people. Since the ending of the civil war, Tiger, his family recall, had increasingly become homesick and longed to go home. But he had remained in exile, very conscious of the fact that his efforts on behalf of the Biafran cause had been construed as overt and hostile political acts by many of those now holding the reins of power. There were those who would not easily forget the toxicity of his comments and the vehement denunciations during the war years. Over in Nigeria, the political situation was calm. General Gowon, whom many Igbos during the war years, had ascribed to as having 'genocidal tendencies,' had continued, skilfully, to chart a course of national reconciliation. Savage retribution in the form of mass killings or in the selective extermination of the Igbo intelligentsia, had failed to materialise and Igbos were beginning to be reabsorbed into the national body politic; traders began returning to the North, civil servants and portions of the Biafran military were in instances given their old jobs (although their ranks remained at the pre-war level.) But if his people were being 'forgiven' and a charge of treason did not await him, what did Tiger have to fear?

"The ones who were forgiven," relates Charles Ihetu, "were those who did things inside Nigeria. But my father brought an awareness of the Biafran cause to people outside Nigeria, that is, to the Western world and to a lot of people in the Nigerian military this was unforgivable. Because of him, the awareness of how people were dying of hunger and other things came to the forefront. During the civil war, the Biafran national anthem was played in place of the Nigerian one before he boxed. He would have been easily forgiven if he had merely been a military commander simply following orders."

Tiger now sent a missive to the Nigerian authorities stating his intention of returning but also requesting an assurance that Gowon's amnesty applied to him and that no reprisals would be made against him once he landed on Nigerian soil. The embassy replied that he had nothing to fear. This, however, was not enough for him. He called for a meeting with a government representative at which a foreign party would witness the assurances. The person he called on was Larry Merchant of the *New York Post*. They met up in mid-town Manhattan and strolled over to the offices of the Nigerian consulate where Edwin Ogeve-Ogbu, the Nigerian Ambassador to the United Nations made a formal undertaking that he would not be subjected to harassment or imprisonment.

"He called me and asked if I would accompany him to the Nigerian consulate office in Manhattan," recalls Merchant, "he just wanted me to be witness and the fellow there (Consular official) understood why I was there and agreed that the government would permit him to return, and in effect, permit safe passage. Tiger felt that that was enough, that I had borne witness (and) that he would be given safe passage."

Merchant remembers Tiger's demeanour during the

253

conference, which lasted for fifteen to twenty minutes as being "stoic and respectful." He did not grovel: "He wasn't in a posture of beseeching anything. In other words, he didn't have to kneel to get this. He was there as Dick Tiger who was a formidable person and presence, and although he was respectful, he was not (Kow-towing)." Like most others, Merchant was unaware that Tiger was dying.

He arrived at Lagos Airport on Sunday, July 18th accompanied by Richard Junior, Victoria and Grace, the oldest of the brood. Abigail and the rest of the litter would soon follow. Wearing a dark suit and carrying a slim brief case, he smiled at awaiting reporters, saying, "It's nice to be back home." As one whose name was surely on the government's list of 'prominent rebels,' he was not surprised at being waylaid by a posse of waiting security agents. They ushered him into a room located in the airport's V.I.P. section while his children were kept in an adjoining area. For about two hours, they bandied questions about his wartime activities and asked him about his future intentions. They also embarked on a thorough search of his possessions and a number of documents including his passport were seized.

When his ordeal ended, he settled himself and the children in suites at the plush Federal Palace Hotel. The following day, he granted an interview to the *Daily Time*'s Charles Igoh and for the first time announced his retirement from boxing. "Boxing," he said "has been good to me, but I think that I've been good for boxing." He planned to look over his properties and was hopeful of setting down to a coaching job. The article made no mention of his detention.

While in Lagos, he began making enquiries about his properties. During the war years, government authorised 'caretakers' had occupied many of the properties owned by Igbos who had fled. After the Federal victory, Gowon had issued a notification that such properties be restored to their original owners and so Tiger was able to reclaim the plot of land in Surulere that had been uncompleted at the time of the outbreak of the troubles (Abigail would supervise its completion in the coming years). As for the property in Ikoyi, there was little he could do to reverse the sale and its loss remained a cause of profound regret for Tiger.

After a two-week stay in Lagos, he left for Aba. For the last time in his life, Tiger played the role of the prodigal son returned home. In the days that followed, family, friends and the curious deluged his Cameroon Road residence. "There were celebrations, but it was not a carnival atmosphere," recalls his son Richard. "People were glad that he had come back. Many had heard it as a rumour."

His holdings had remained intact, save for the apartment that suffered minor damage. He turned his attentions also, to the properties he had owned in Port Harcourt. The issues here were always going to be less than straightforward. Port Harcourt had, right from its beginnings in the early part of the 20th century, attracted many migrant Igbos who to the chagrin of the natives, went on to dominate the city's business and administrative life. The indigenes of Nigeria's delta region, of which Port Harcourt was a part, had not at all been enthusiastic about joining the largely Igbo rebellion against the Federation and had been rewarded with the creation of the Rivers State, for which Port Harcourt served as capital. The fact that a number of these communities suffered at the hands of Biafran regiments exacerbated anti-Igbo feelings. Wartime pronouncements of Gowon and Federal propaganda actively encouraged the take over of Igbo-owned properties, on the basis that they had been 'abandoned.' "The Igbos are welcome to live among us," commented Alfred Diete-Spiff, the young naval officer whom Gowon had appointed in 1967 to serve as the military governor of the state. But his addendum spoke brutally of the resentments that lingered: "As long as they don't try to take over again."

It was in the light of this background that Tiger was fortunate enough to be able to re-assert his ownership over the cinema and an apartment block. As for the two remaining properties the

Ihetu family, inspite of the best efforts of his widow, have like many Igbo pre-war owners, been unable to regain control.

While he busily sorted out his financial affairs, he had to contend with the painful tremors caused by the festering cancer. Morphine had its limits and he was reported to have sought the assistance of local herbalists whom Tiger, one Nigerian paper would posthumously report, informed that he was suffering from a rare "mystery illness" for which he had undergone "several unsuccessful treatments overseas." Inevitably, a number of his friends and acquaintances got wind that all was not well with his health. But his replies gave little away. Some like Abraham Ordia, the chairman of the National Sports Commission was of the impression that Tiger himself did not know the precise nature of his illness. Ordia, who planned for Tiger to play a major role in the events surrounding the October visit of Muhammad Ali, presumed it to be "some sort of kidney ailment."

His illness remained unspoken in his household; a cultural facet of many Africans is to refrain from talking about death, particularly in regard to children. His son Richard recalls that his father did not specifically apprise his older children about his impending death.

Tiger apparently did not resign himself to dying. According to his family, information came to hand about a radical, highly experimental course of treatment. What the nature of such treatment was to be is not certain but he told Abigail of his willingness to undergo it and decided to apply for the return of his passport. His request was refused.

In September, he met with Jerry Enyeazu, the Commissioner for Sport of the East Central State and was appointed the state's Chief Boxing Coach. A national newspaper would later, perhaps, erroneously describe his circumstances before the appointment as being "pathetic and unenviable." Whatever the truth, the meeting was not likely to have been instigated by Tiger, according to Charles Ihetu.

"One thing I do know is that my father was a very proud man and he wouldn't believe in begging or asking for anything. Same with my mother. My mother did not believe in going to any body." His brother, Richard concurs with this, arguing that given the precedent already set by Hogan Bassey's coaching appointment, his father's own appointment was considered to be a matter of course. Many, at home and abroad, who continued to be unaware of his illness, expected he and Bassey to lead Nigeria's contingent of amateur boxers to the Munich Olympic games due the following year. The 'dream teaming' of course never took place. Although he remained active for as long as he possibly could, the illness visibly took his toll and his once magnificently muscular frame was reduced to a frail leanness. After he suffered an extreme deterioration of his condition, he was admitted to Aba's St. Anthony's Hospital where in the early hours of the morning of December 14, 1971, Richard Ihetu breathed this last.

257

Fourteen
HE NEVER GAVE
HIS HEART AWAY

His body was laid in state at the mansion in Aba. Outside, everyday queues of mourners filled Cameroon Road, patiently waiting their turns to file past his coffin, and pay their respects.

On Sunday the 20th, the funeral service was held in Amaigbo. Cars, buses and mopeds choked the expressway which led out of Aba, and the cortege travelled at a snails pace. In Amaigbo itself, a crowd, estimated at 15,000, thronged the hot and dusty roads that led from the local Anglican Church to the place of burial. Every vantage point from buildings to tree branches to the roofs of vehicles was taken as they struggled to glimpse the coffin.

The service was presided over by the Reverend John Kilpatrick who eulogised him as a man of many qualities: decent, courageous and devoted. Listening were Abigail, the children and the Ihetu clan. Hogan Bassey and around 600 athletes from around the country were present. Also present were a number of government officials of the East-Central and Mid-Western States but it was not apparent that the few who worked for the Federal Government had turned up in anything other than a personal capacity. Indeed, the Ihetu family do not recall any official message of condolence being received from General Gowon or any member of the Supreme Military Council.

After they committed him to his place of rest, a salvo of twenty-one shots of canon, thundered in the skies. The day ended with a welter of activities: memorials and boxing exhibitions.

News of his death brought a series of encomiums, which affirmed the high regard that he was held in, both as a man and a fighter. Dr. Kingsley Mbadiwe a prominent Igbo politician spoke for the Nigerian nation and for others further afield when he said: "We admired him because he mastered his profession with precise efficiency. We adored him because his simple and unadulterated manner evoked sympathy and admiration."

His obituary in the London *Times* concluded that he "will be remembered as one of the most consistent modern world champions in boxing and a warm human being," while Graham Houston of *Boxing News* wrote that "Tiger was a great fighter by any standards" and deserved to be "remembered as one of the ring immortals." In England, the country which served as the staging post for his subsequent success in America and where he had maintained an enduring popularity, a great many tributes, poignant and heartfelt, came from fans, fighters, managers and promoters, among them Terry Downes, Bobby Neill, Henry Cooper, Jack Solomons, Harry Levene, Mike Barratt, Bobby Diamond, Mickey Duff and Tony Vairo.

Across the Atlantic, touching essay length tributes came from his former championship foes, Jose Torres and Gene Fullmer. Wrote Torres: "I was not ashamed to lose my title to him, for he was a good champion and a great man." His sentiments were echoed by Fullmer who recorded: "He gave me some of the worst moments in the ring, but if you have to lose, it's a pleasure to lose your championship to a great fighter, sportsman and gentleman." "He was one of our great modern champions," said Harry Markson, "win or lose, he never failed to give his best. But outside the ring, he was a gentleman and that was important, we were fond of him." Obituaries written by Dave Anderson for the *New York Times* and by Jerry Izenburg and Milton Gross for syndicated coverage were respectful and filled with charming anecdote on the man and fighter.

His untimely passing appeared to boxing aficionados to be the latest in a grim instalment in the demise of a host of men who held the world middleweight title: Stanley Ketchel, the 'Michigan Assassin', murdered by the infuriated husband of his lover; in the 1920s both Harry Grebb and Tiger Flowers lost their lives on the operating table within months of each other; Marcel Cerdan, perhaps the greatest middleweight to come out of Europe, killed in a plane crash in the Azores before he had the chance to reclaim the title he had lost to Jake La Motta and Randolph Turpin, beset by financial worries, ended his own life by pumping a bullet into his head.

The early death of Tiger, like that of many young, famous individuals would be followed by insinuations that his death did not occur naturally but instead, was the result of an elaborate conspiracy play fashioned by the enemies of Biafra. The story went as follows: During a post fight medical examination, Tiger received an injection that unbeknownst to him contained a 'poison' put in place by the British with the connivance of the Nigerian government. The poison, it was claimed, immediately induced pains in his liver. On a stop over in France, Tiger is said to have consulted a physician who is said to have informed him of "the date on which he would die." With this knowledge in hand, when Tiger returned home, he informed the elders in his community of his impending death and before the event, dressed up in flowing traditional robes to tour around Aba one final time, waving to the gathered crowds from his car.

They still remember Tiger today, but the memories are dimming, much to the extent that the greatest fighter ever produced by Nigeria is barely known by a generation of his countrymen. Apart from the few boxing tournaments that have borne his name and a smattering of standard newspaper articles occurring once in blue moon, a sense of national amnesia has continued to subsist. And this in a country not unfamiliar with the raising of monuments and the naming of universities and airports in favour of departed 'big men.' It is a state of affairs, which has not gone unnoticed by friends.

"I actually thought that he would become the Jack Dempsey of Nigeria," says Maurice Foran, "the way Jack Dempsey was thought of in America, I thought that he would probably be idolised as such, but, some how or another he didn't seem to get it."

While the Nigerian establishment has paid homage to Africa's greatest fighter through posthumous honours via the National Sports Commission and election to the Nigerian Boxing

Hall of Fame, there has being an absence of larger forms of recognition. It would not be overstating the case that the reason for this is inextricably linked to Tiger's involvement in the Biafran saga, for when in the middle 1980s, one of his daughters mounted a quiet campaign to have a redeveloped wing of the National Sports Stadium named in his honour, she was told by a high placed official that while he had every sympathy for her, many still remembered his role at the height of the civil war and that it would not be a "politically positive act" to proceed with such a bestowal.

For many, the abiding memories of Dick Tiger are those of the die-hard apostle of secession; the avowed enemy of the Nigerian state. For too long, this has obscured from view the heady days when he bore the mantle as Nigeria's beloved sporting son. From Nigerian hero to Biafran hero to a kind of purgatory, Tiger died with his image in limbo, in part perhaps, because he did not live long enough to 'atone' for his transgression against the Nigerian state.

Criticism, however, does not extend solely to the Nigerian establishment, which for the majority of the years following the civil war has been accused of persistently marginalizing the Igbo people. Some responsibility for this lack of recognition should perhaps be borne by those to whom Tiger's name became a highly prized asset in the propaganda war that was played out during the civil conflict.

"He was a pawn for the Biafrans and later on, he acknowledged that he had been used," says his son Charles. "Selfish people, when embarked on what they deem to be a noble cause, step over people and use people without realising what they are doing. All of these people he was aligned with for that cause, none have spoken out for him or his family. None! None have acknowledged, publicly at least, the merits of trying to ascertain the accomplishments that he made when he was paving the way for Nigeria."

To Charles Ihetu, his father was a sportsman, not a politician and ought not to have maintained the high profile that he did during the rebellion. He may have played things 'safer' and supported his people without putting himself, so to speak, in the 'firing line. Some did. Nnamdi Azikiwe, contrived to keep the door open to the Federalists and his newspaper business in Lagos continued during the period he spent serving as an advisor to the secessionist government. Before the war ended, he returned to Nigeria expressing his disillusionment with the policies of the Biafran leadership. The irony for Charles Ihetu is that his father's dogged adherence to the Biafran cause has been deleterious to his rightful place in Nigerian history.

"They managed to use him as a stooge and I believe that when you use somebody as a stooge, you've got to pay that person. But in his case, he was paying to be used as a stooge. He lost all round. I believe that he lost his name. If not for the civil war, he would be revered in Nigeria."

But if Tiger's legacy in his own country remains a somewhat troubling one, it is on more secure footing in boxing. As a fighter, he will occupy a special place by demonstrating for posterity that Africa can produce great fighters and hugely popular ones at that.

"One of the few foreign fighters to have made a better impression in America," noted the *Ring*'s Ted Carroll. "Fight fans and journalists loved him," says Sam Toperoff, "first because he was indeed a Tiger: stately, noble and ferocious. Secondly, he was bright and articulate –the very example of the Greek ideal of sound body and sound mind."

For Jonathan Carroll, like Toperoff, a one time English language professor and now a distinguished novelist, Tiger projected values that transcended his role as a pugilist. "Tiger," he says, "was my favourite fighter, probably of all. Compared to today's show offs, small talents and loudmouths, he was the picture of competence and decorum. A man who with all the grace in the world did his job beautifully, but made no loud noise about it. In other words, the consummate professional. It didn't matter that he was a boxer- he was simply very good at what he did and an example both in and out of the ring to us all."

"I don't recall another incident where another foreign fighter

262

sort of 'planted his flag' in America and said, 'Here I am'," is the way Larry Merchant puts it. "Tiger made his residence in America, he fought his fights in America so people identified with him. They understood him (and) were connected to him –not necessarily in an emotional sense but he was a very respected fighter who figured prominently in the last days of serious fighting in Madison Square Garden."

There were, in fact, those who did 'connect' to Tiger in an emotional sense, among them, Jonathan Carroll, then a gangly, star struck teenager. Many years later, on his internet Web site, he told of how he "used to sneak down to Madison Square Garden every time Tiger fought, just to bask in his magnificence."

"After one of his fight's," he related, " I waited for him at the entrance to the arena. When he came out, I was absolutely stunned to see him five feet away. He looked at this dumbfounded tall kid and started laughing a great deep, toothy laugh. Then he said in this thick accent, 'You want my autograph or you want to stare me to death?' I didn't know what to do. It's hard suddenly being in the presence of your hero."

Here was a fighter, foreign and black who stirred Garden audiences regardless of ethnicity. Tiger had a fan base, a sort of constituency among fight aficionados, which guaranteed him support when he came up against well supported Irish Americans, Italian Americans and Hispanic Americans. Recalling the bout Tiger fought with Joey Archer, Ron Lipton plaintively recalls the lack of racial antagonism among the fans as they rowdily chanted opposing choruses. "One thing is for sure," he says, "there was not one scintilla of black versus white in the air, as many of the white fans screamed for Tiger who was simply their kind of fighter and had earned that respect many times over in the Garden and elsewhere as a diehard warrior who came to rumble."

Fundamentally, the attraction to Tiger for boxing audiences was his skill and entertainment value as a fighter. "He was a well schooled boxer-puncher who advanced in a very measured way," Merchant recalls. "He would engage you but it was always on his terms. There's a fighter from Ghana who reminds me of him, Ike

Quartey. Not the same style, but the same type of demeanour. Very strong in advancing, almost in a territorial way. He would make his chances and then take his chances."

"The most frightening thing about Dick," remembers Ron Lipton, "was his focus. He had a deadpan look on his face. There was no hate in his eyes (but) it was as if you were being stalked by a jaguar. The only face I've seen like that was Joe Louis: The deadpan look of no hatred, no meanness but of a superior athlete that reached the epitome of what his body could do."

Dick Tiger was never a one-punch knockout artist, but the effects of the blows he wielded on opponents like Terry Downes were not easily forgotten. "In boxing," Downes explains, "someone can hit you and it's like a hammer: Very sharp. And another guy hits you and it's like hitting you with a sack of coal: Shakes all your body. That's what Dick was like, he hit you on your chin and it would hurt your ankles."

Joey Giardello, who completed no less than 50 rounds with him is in no doubt as to what he considers to be Tiger's fighting strengths: "His stamina was great. He was just a strong, strong guy and he could hurt you. He took a good punch. He wasn't a great puncher, I don't think that he could knock you out with one punch, but he could hurt you. Nobody wanted to fight him, Dick was tough –I fought him four times, so I know he was tough."

But tough though he may have been, Tiger struck some as being a rather predictable fighter. Not perhaps in the monotonously suggestive 'Don't-back-up-look-for-a-place-to-land-the-hook' mould described by sportswriter Jerry Izenburg, but predictable all the same. It was a lack of adaptability which Robert Lipsyte chose to refer to as Tiger's "tactical mediocrity" when many felt that he ought to have stopped the bloodied, beaten Giardello in their final confrontation in 1965. Harry Scott, a Liverpool bred middleweight, who sparred many rounds with Tiger as an amateur described Tiger as being "a very powerful man but not very clever" and actively sought a match with Tiger whom he was confident he would out-box. Certainly one major flaw observers attributed to him was a tendency to be out-manoeuvred by 'stylists,' those, that is, who pragmatically did not face him in tests of strength but rather fought him from a distance. As Freddie Steele, a middleweight champion from the 1930s once remarked, "A good trombone man will beat Tiger," a fighter, in other words who could slide into range to pick him up with jabs, and then, just as quickly slide out.

The defeats he suffered against the likes of Joey Giardello, Emile Griffith and Joey Archer seemingly bore this out. Yet, here, it is useful to mention the ethos that he maintained throughout his career: fights, particularly those of the championship variety should only be won by men who stood their ground and fought. It was a point of principle and he was disdainful of those who fought in retreat. It appeared to him to be a virtual manifestation of unmanliness. He never failed to register his exasperation and aggrievement when decisions went against him in this manner: "I am a fighter, not a dancer," he lamented to Robert Lipsyte after being relieved of his middleweight title by Giardello. "Aaah, these days you get a title by running away." Other times, his engaging humour came out, as when bemoaning the tactics of Don Fullmer (whom he did beat), he proceeded to complain that he had trained for a fight and not a "marathon."

These losses appeared to baffle him. He had, after all, arrived in America predisposed to believing that while English judges tended to place almost equal weight on the defensive skills displayed by boxers as their offence, their American counterparts were apt to be impressed more by fighters consistent in their display of aggression: "I thought in New York they didn't give fights to runners," he once complained, "I thought wrong, didn't I?"

He never failed to complain. His pride and his stubbornness ensured that. But although many recall the plaintiveness and lack of vulgarity in his protests, Tiger did not strike Gil Clancy as being particularly graceful in defeat. "I thought that after both fights with (Emile Griffith), he never gracefully accepted defeat. Especially the second one which wasn't a close fight –and he still thought he won the fight!"

Where then is his position in the pantheon of middleweight greats? Reg Gutteridge, the veteran fight commentator for Britain's Independent Television Sports Network got to know Tiger very well having covered most of his English fights and some in America. "Dick Tiger, with Azumah Nelson," he says, "was no doubt the best African fighter. He wasn't that scientific; he was more of an action type fighter (possessing) great durability among other things. I think that he would have given Hagler hell –that's an even money fight. (Sugar) Ray Leonard the same. (Carlos) Monzon would have beaten him, he was just a better fighter."

"Monzon was a superior talent," proffers the veteran referee Arthur Mercante. "He had such a long reach, that he was virtually impossible reach. He would jab you and then retreat. He stood straight up and was a good banger. I wouldn't classify him with Monzon and Hagler, he was a little bit below them, but he was a good competitor, very serious, well conditioned and didn't abuse himself."

"I never considered him a great fighter," says Tommy Kenville, "that is, not in the context of a Robinson, Pep or Ali –he was not that great a fighter, but he was a terrific, very good fighter. I would put him in the top ten. I don't think he could have beaten (Tony) Zale –Zale punched too well. I don't know about Graziano. I doubt he could have beaten Monzon –I think Monzon was too big for him; he was awfully tall and had an enormous reach. I don't think he could have beaten Robinson, although Robinson wasn't as good a middleweight as he was a welterweight. Hagler? He would be too strong for Tiger."

"I don't think so. No," says Ron Lipton. "You know why? They want to think that because he's contemporary. But they don't make men like Richard Ihetu anymore. I saw Marvin Hagler fight Bennie Briscoe and he ran from Bennie. Marvin was a technician and he was a good leftie (but) Dick would hunt him down and blast him out. Tiger had the most formidable style, I don't care about Stanley Ketchel and all the legendary middleweights, no one at 160 pounds could survive Dick Tiger in a head on fight. If you came to war with him, his strength, endurance, durability, crunching left hook to the head or body thrown short or long and his short right hand and body and head work would always take away a man's desire to be there."

"In the modern era, by which I mean the last forty to fifty years, only the absolute elite in the middleweight division would rank above Tiger," opines Larry Merchant. "I'm not sure if he was as good as Jake La Motta or as good as Tony Zale, (but) you could say that he was an outstanding fighter, period. He won the middleweight and light heavyweight titles and few fighters have done that."

"I think of him everyday," admits Ron Lipton. "I practice for hours on the heavy bag in my kitchen with Dick Tiger imitations. Now and then in self-defence, I get into a fight because I can't get the fighter out of me and everything that I learned from him and Carter –but more Tiger- keeps me young. But what he means to me the most, is that he was living proof to anyone that knows about boxing and fighting: You don't have to be a thug or criminal to be the toughest lion in the jungle. He was so well spoken, gentlemanly, humble, sweet and meant no one any harm. He was the strongest middleweight -and the most brave that ever lived."

For many others Dick Tiger was and remains a person who impressed not only as a fighter but also as a man. As Ted Carroll eulogised soon after his death, Tiger "was that rare individual whose abilities in his chosen profession matched his abilities as a man."

CHRONOLOGY

1929

14 August····· Dick Tiger born as Richard Ihetu in the village of Amaigbo, Eastern Region of the British Protectorate of Nigeria.

1943····· Leaves for Aba Township.

1949····· The Nigerian Boxing Board of Control is formed with Douglas Collister as its chairman.

Tiger begins his amateur career.

1950

January····· The inaugural Collister Belt Tournament is held at the Glover Memorial Hall in Lagos.

Formation of the British Empire Championships Committee in London.

1951

April····· Roy Ankrah of the Gold Coast (later Ghana) wins the British Empire Featherweight title.

December····· Hogan 'Kid' Bassey leaves Nigeria for England.

1952····· Tiger has his 'first' professional bout.

September····· The imposition of an increased levy on entertainment events in Britain leads to a recession in the boxing industry.

| December | Tiger loses to Tommy West in Aba but afterwards is invited to fight at the Collister Belt Tournament. |

1953

| January | Decisions Blackie Power, the Nigerian middleweight champion, in a non-title contest. |

| May | Retires in the seventh round of a middleweight title contest with Tommy West. |

1954

| January | Loses to Tommy West for the third time. |

| March | Tommy West dies. |

1955

| October | Tiger sails for Liverpool to be managed by Peter Banasko. |

| November | Hogan Bassey acquires the British Empire Featherweight title by knocking out Billy 'Spider' Kelly in Belfast. |

| December | Tiger's first fight in Britain ends in a points loss to Alan Dean. |

1956

| March | A quartet of successive losses is completed when George Roe decisions him. |

| | The British Parliament repeals the entertainment 'Double Tax'. |

1957

March — Tiger joins Liverpool manager Tony Vairo's stable of fighters.

May — Stops Terry Downes in seven rounds in London.

June — Hogan Bassey wins the world featherweight title in Paris by stopping Cherif Hama.

1958

27 March — Tiger wins the British Empire middleweight title by knocking out Patrick McAteer at Liverpool Stadium.

June — Loses to the highly ranked American contender, 'Spider' Webb.

1959

June — Makes his American debut by drawing with Rory Calhoun at New York's Madison Square Garden.

1960

1 October — Nigeria gains her independence from Britain.

1962

23 October — Tiger defeats Gene Fullmer to win the N.B.A. world middleweight title. (Later he is accorded universal recognition when Paul Pender is stripped of the alternate title.)

1963

July	Awarded the M.B.E. medal in the British honours list.
August	Knocks out Gene Fullmer in Ibadan, Nigeria. The fight is the first world title fight to be staged in Black Africa.
December	Loses his title to Joey Giardello in Atlantic City's first world championship bout.

1964

September	His bout with Don Fullmer at the Cleveland Arena is the last of the weekly televised fights run for twenty years by the Madison Square Garden organisation in association with the Gillette Corporation.

1965

October	Regains the world middleweight title from Giardello and becomes the oldest active world champion.

1966

January	An army mutiny orchestrated by officers drawn largely from the Igbo ethnic group brings the first Republic to an end. Major General Aguiyi-Ironsi assumes the leadership of a military government.
April	Tiger loses his title, controversially, to Emile Griffith.
May	Pogroms directed mainly at the Igbo community in Northern Nigeria.

July	A second mutiny, this time effected by officers of Northern origin topples the military government. Ironsi and many soldiers of Igbo origin are slain.
August	Lt. Colonel Gowon emerges as the supreme military figure. But his ascension is disputed by Lt. Colonel Ojukwu, the military Governor of the Igbo dominated Eastern Region.
Late September / Early October	Igbo communities in Northern Nigeria are subjected to further pogroms.
16 December	At Madison Square Garden, Tiger defeats Jose Torres to become only the second fighter in 63 years to win the world light heavyweight title in addition to middleweight laurels.
1967 February	Boxes a non-title bout in the city of Port Harcourt to raise money for Eastern refugees fleeing from the North and other parts of Nigeria.
April	The *Eastern Outlook* newspaper, owned by the Eastern government, urges all Igbos to return from all parts of Nigeria.
May	Tiger retains his title against Jose Torres
	Lt. Colonel Ojukwu announces the secession of the Eastern Region from the Nigerian Federation and proclaims the existence of the Republic of Biafra.

15 June	Dick Tiger publicly declares his allegiance to the Biafran state and renounces all associations with Nigeria.
6 July	The first shots are fired in what turns into a full-scale civil conflict.
December	Tiger receives a commission into the Biafran Army as a second lieutenant in its Morale Corps.

1968
May	Loses his world light heavyweight title to Bob Foster, the only time he is knocked out in his career.

1969
May	Outpoints the world middleweight champion, Nino Benvenuti, in a non-title bout.
	Is subpoenaed to appear before a New York City grand jury investigating links between organised crime and boxing. Makes a brief appearance but is not recalled.
December	Returns his M.B.E. medal, by post, to the British Embassy in Washington D.C.

1970
January	Biafra capitulates, ending the 30 month long Nigerian Civil War.
July	Loses to Emile Griffith in what turns out

to be his final professional bout in Madison Square Garden.

1971

19 July   Announces his retirement from the ring.

September   Is appointed the Chief Boxing Coach for the East Central State of Nigeria.

14 December   Dies of cancer in Aba and six days later is buried in Amaigbo.

RECORD OF DICK TIGER

(Richard Ihetu)

Born: August 14 1929, Amaigbo, Orlu, Nigeria
Managers: A.K. Gikonou (Nigeria), Peter Banasko, Tony
Vairo (England) and Wilfred 'Jersey' Jones (U.S.A.)

Tale of the tape

Height:	5ft 8in	Thigh:	23in
Weight:	158 to 168pds	Calf:	15in
Reach:	71in	Biceps:	15in
Chest (Normal):	42in	Forearm:	12in
Chest (Expanded):	44in	Fist:	11in
Waist:	32in	Wrist:	7in
Neck:	17in	Ankle:	10in

1952

-- ---	Simon Eme	W(KO)2	Rex Cinema Hall, Aba
-- ---	Lion Ring	W(TKO)6	-
-- ---	Robert Nwanne	W(KO)2	-
-- ---	Peter Okpara	W(KO)8	-
-- ---	Simon Eme	W(Pts)8	-
-- ---	John Ama	W(KO)2	-
-- ---	Koko Kid	W(Pts)8	Port Harcourt?
-- ---	Easy Dynamite	W(KO)3	Port Harcourt
13 Dec	Tommy West	L(Pts)10	Rex Cinema Hall, Aba

1953

30 Jan	Blackie Power	W(Pts)6	Glover Memorial Hall, Lagos
20 May	Tommy West	L(TKO-Rtd)7	African Tennis Club, Lagos
	(Nigerian Middleweight Championship)		

1954

29 Jan	Tommy West	L(Pts)6	Glover Memorial Hall, Lagos
12 Jun	Mighty Joe	W(Pts)6	Rex Cinema Hall, Aba
18 Jul	Super Human Power	W(Pts)8	Rex Cinema Hall, Aba

1955

31 Jan	Raheem Fagbemi	W(Pts)6	Glover Memorial Hall, Lagos
31 Aug	Bolaji Johnson	W(Pts)6	Glover Memorial Hall, Lagos
08 Dec	Alan Dean	L(Pts)6	Liverpool Stadium

1956

27 Jan	Gerry McNally	L(Pts)8	Blackpool Tower Circus
01 Mar	Jimmy Lynas	L(Pts)8	Blackpool Tower Circus
22 Mar	George Roe	L(Pts)8	Liverpool Stadium
03 May	Dennis Rowley	W(KO)1	Liverpool Stadium
10 May	Alan Dean	W(Pts)8	Liverpool Stadium
28 May	Wally Scott	W(TKO-rsf)4	Engineers Club, West Hartlepool
02 July	Jimmy Lynas	W(Pts)8	Engineers Club, West Hartlepool
18 Oct	Alan Dean	L(Pts)6	Liverpool Stadium
09 Nov	Alan Dean	W(Pts)8	Blackpool Tower Circus

1957

29 Apr	Johnny Read	W(TKO-rsf)2	National Sporting Club, London
14 May	Terry Downes	W(TKO-rtd)7	Shoreditch Town Hall, London
04 Jun	Marlon Dori	W(TKO-rtd)7	Harringey Arena, London
15 Jul	Willie Armstrong	L(Pts)8	Engineers Club, West Hartlepool
25 Jul	Alan Dean	WPts)8	Liverpool Stadium
09 Sep	Phil Edwards	W(Pts)10	Sophia Gardens Pavilion, Cardiff
21 Oct	Jean-Claude Poisson	W(Pts)10	Sophia Gardens Pavilion, Cardiff
11 Nov	Pat McAteer	Drew 10	Sophia Gardens Pavilion, Cardiff
28 Nov	Freddie De Largy	W(TKO-rsf)6	Birmingham Indoor Stadium

1958

13 Jan	Jean Ruellet	W(Pts)8	City Hall, Hull
03 Feb	Jimmy Lynas	W(TKO-rsf)8	Manchester Trade Hall
25 Feb	Johnny Read	W(TKO-rsf)6	Harringey, London
27 Mar	Pat McAteer	W(KO)9	Liverpool Stadium
	(British Empire Middleweight Championship)		
01 May	Billy Ellaway	W(TKO-rsf)2	Liverpool Stadium
24 Jun	Spider Webb	L(Pts)10	Empress Hall, London
14 Oct	Yolande Pompey	W(Pts)10	Wembley Pool, London

1959

21 Jan	Jimmy Asani	EXH 4	Ibadan Football Stadium
24 Jan	Joe Quadri	EXH 6	Ambassador Hotel, Lagos
19 Mar	Randy Sandy	L(Pts)10	Liverpool Stadium
12 May	Randy Sandy	W(Pts)	Wembley Pool, London
05 Jun	Rory Calhoun	DREW 10	Madison Square Garden, New York
17 Jul	Rory Calhoun	L(Pts)10	War Memorial Auditorium, Syracuse
02 Sep	Gene Armstrong	W(Pts)10	Convention Hall, Camden New Jersey
30 Sep	Joey Giardello	W(Pts)10	Chicago Stadium
04 Nov	Joey Giardello	L(Pts)10	Cleveland Arena
30 Dec	Holley Mims	W(Pts)10	Chicago Stadium

1960

24 Feb	Gene Armstrong	W(Pts)10	Chicago Stadium
01 Apr	Victor Zalazar	W(Pts)10	Boston Arena
22 Jun	Wilf Greaves	L(Pts)15	Exhibition Gardens, Edmonton
	(British Empire Middleweight Championship)		
30 Nov	Wilf Greaves	W(TKO-rsf)9	Exhibition Gardens, Edmonton
	(British Empire Middleweight Championship)		

1961

18 Feb	Gene Armstrong	W(TKO-rsf)9	Madison Square Garden, New York
15 Apr	Spider Webb	W(TKO-rsf)6	St. Nicholas Arena, New York
15 May	Hank Casey	W(Pts)10	Municipal Auditorium, New Orleans
16 Dec	Billy Pickett	W(Pts)10	Madison Square Garden, New York

1962

20 Jan	Flo Fernandez	W(TKO-rsf)6	Convention Hall, Miami Beach
31 Mar	Henry Hank	W(Pts)10	Madison Square Garden, New York
23 Oct	Gene Fullmer	W(Pts)15	Candlestick Park, San Francisco
	(N.B.A. World Middleweight Championship)		

1963

23 Feb	Gene Fullmer	DREW 15	Convention Hall, Las Vegas
	(World Middleweight Championship)		
10 Aug	Gene Fullmer	W(TKO-rsf)8	Liberty Stadium, Ibadan
	(World Middleweight Championship)		
07 Dec	Joey Giardello	L(Pts)15	Convention Hall, Atlantic City
	(World Middleweight Championship)		

1964

31 Jul	Jose Gonzalez	W(TKO-rsf)6	Madison Square Garden, New York
11 Sep	Don Fullmer	W(Pts)10	Cleveland Arena
16 Oct	Joey Archer	L(Pts)10	Madison Square Garden, New York

1965

12 Mar	Juan Rivero	W(TKO-rsf)6	Madison Square Garden, New York
20 May	Rubin Carter	W(Pts)10	Madison Square Garden, New York
21 Oct	Joey Giardello	W(pts)15	Madison Square Garden, New York
	(World Middleweight Championship)		

1966

01 Jan	Abraham Tonica	EXH 3	Ahmadu Bello Stadium, Kaduna
01 Jan	Sandy Luke	EXH 3	Ahmadu Bello Stadium, Kaduna
18 Feb	Peter Mueller	W(KO)3	Westernfallen Hall, Dortmund
25 Apr	Emile Griffith	L(Pts)15	Madison Square Garden, New York
	(World Middleweight Championship)		
16 Dec	Jose Torres	W(Pts)15	Madison Square Garden, New York
	(World Light Heavyweight Championship)		

1967

05 Feb	Abraham Tonica	W(TKO-rsf)5	Mile One Park, Port Harcourt
16 May	Jose Torres	W(Pts)15	Madison Square Garden, New York
	(World Light Heavyweight Championship)		

279

| 17 Nov | Roger Rouse | W (TKO-rsf)12 | Convention Centre, Las Vegas |
| | (World Light Heavyweight Championship) | | |

1968

| 24 May | Bob Foster | L(KO)4 | Madison Square Garden, New York |
| | (World Light Heavyweight Championship) | | |

| 25 Oct | Frankie De Paula | W(Pts)10 | Madison Square Garden, New York |

1969

| 26 May | Nino Benvenuti | W(Pts)10 | Madison Square Garden, New York |
| 14 Nov | Andy Kendall | W(Pts)10 | Madison Square Garden, New York |

1970

| 15 Jul | Emile Griffith | L(Pts)10 | Madison Square Garden, New York |

1971

19 Jul   Announced retirement.

Overall: Fought 81 Won 59 Lost 19 Drew 3

Compiled by Adeyinka Makinde

ACCOLADES

SPORTING AWARDS

Ring Magazine Fighter of the Year 1962 and 1965
Edward J. Neill Award for Fighter of the Year 1963 and 1966
Norwich Union Trophy for Nigerian Sportsman of the Year 1961, 1962, 1963, 1965 and 1966

CIVIL MEDAL

Member of the Civil Division of the Most Excellent Order of the British Empire (M.B.E.) 1963
(Returned in December 1969 in protest against British Government support for the Federal Republic of Nigeria during its war against the secessionist state of Biafra.)

HALL OF FAME

Elected to the Ring Magazine Hall of Fame in 1975
Elected to the Nigerian Boxing Hall of Fame in 1987
Elected to the World Boxing Hall of Fame in 1987
Elected to the International Boxing Hall of Fame in 1991

SOURCES CONSULTED

BOOKS

My Bleedin' Business An Autobiography – **Terry Downes** (Robson Books) 1989

A Neutral Corner – **A.J.** Liebling (North Press) 1990

In this Corner – **Peter Heller** (Robson Books) 1972

Bassey on Boxing – **Hogan Bassey** 1963

Twenty and Out: A Life in Boxing –**Mickey Duff** (Harper Collins) 1999

One Hundred Greatest Boxers – **Burt Randolph Sugar** (Bonanza Books) 1984

A Pictorial History of Boxing - **Nat Fleisher and Sam Andre** (Hamlyn Books) 1988

Ringmasters – **Dave Anderson** (Robson Books) 1991

Boxing Babylon: Behind the Shadowy World of the Prize Ring - **Nigel Collins** (Carol Publishing Group) 1990

Encyclopaedia of Boxing – **Maurice Golesworthy** (Robert Hale)

The Nigerian Civil War – **John De St.Jorre** (Hodder & Stoughton) 1972

The Biafra Story: The Making of an African Legend — **Frederick Forsyth** (Pen & Sword Books) 2002

Colonialism in Africa 1870 – 1960 Volume Three Profiles of Change: African Society and Colonial Rule – Edited by **Victor Turner** (Cambridge University Press) 1971

A History of Nigeria – **Elizabeth Eziachi** (Longman) 1983

Modern Africa: A Social and Political History – **Basil Davidson**

Liver Cancer – Edited by **Kumo Okada** and **Edward Tabor** (Churchill Livingstone) 1997

Comprehensive Textbook of Oncology – **Stacey Nerenstone** and other's (Williams and Wilkins) 1991

Oncology – Edited by **David Horwich** (Chapman and Hall) 1995

NEWSPAPERS

Nigeria
Daily Times, Sunday Times, Daily Express, West African Pilot, Eastern Outlook/ Nigerian Outlook, Daily Telegraph

Britain
Liverpool Echo, Daily Mirror, Times, Observer

Ghana
Ghanaian Times

North America
New York Times, New York-Journal American, San Francisco Chronicle, Edmonton Journal, Los Angeles Times, Chicago Tribune, Washington Post, Washington Evening Journal, New York Amsterdam News, International Herald Tribune, New Orleans Times-Picayune, Time and Newsweek.

SPORTS JOURNALS

Britain
Boxing News

America
The Ring, Boxing Illustrated and Sports Illustrated.

FILM

'Profile of Dick Tiger.' Directed by **Charles Shutt**. Hearst-Metrotone Corporation. (1962)

INDEX

285